warrior odyssey

the travels of a martial artist through asia

antonio graceffo

T0149815

BLACK BELT | valencia, ca
B·O·O·K·S

Note from author: Some names and details in this book have been changed to protect the identities of various people. I have played with chronology in a few places, for the sake of narrative structure. Readers should also be aware that standardized spelling is not available for many Asian terms. Thus, the spellings seen here may be exclusive to this book.

Black Belt Books, Valencia CA 91355
Copyright © 2010 Cruz Bay Publishing, Inc
First Printing 2010
All Rights Reserved
Printed in the United States of America

Library of Congress Number: 2010908031
ISBN-10: 0-89750-190-X
ISBN-13: 978-0-89750-190-3

This book is published by Black Belt Books, a special division of Cruz Bay Publishing, Inc.
Edited by Sarah Dzida, Wendy Levine and Cassandra Harris
Cover and graphic design by Nathan Wong
Backcover and additional design by John Bodine

For information about permission to reproduce selection from this book,
write Black Belt Books, 24900 Anza Dr. Unit E Valencia, CA. 91355

For information about bulk purchases, please contact (800) 423-2874 ext. 1633

warrior odyssey
the travels of a
martial artist through asia

contents

dedication

"All men dream: but not equally. Those who dream by night in the dusty recesses of their minds wake in the day to find that it was vanity; but the dreamers of the day are dangerous men, for they may act their dreams with open eyes, to make it possible. This I did."

—Excerpt from *Seven Pillars of Wisdom* by T.E. Lawrence

This book is dedicated to seekers of knowledge, those who thirst after knowledge about other cultures, and those who can't sleep because they know there is another bend in the road that they have yet to travel.

prologue

MANILA, THE CAPITAL OF THE PHILIPPINES, is a crazy, loud and smelly city full of some of the nicest and most unfortunate people in the world. Nothing, not even New York, prepares you for the overwhelming feeling of walking down those blazing hot, circus-like streets.

That day, I pushed through the city's street vendors, tricycle cabs and jeepneys to get to a hybrid *yaw-yan* training center to see how the Filipinos practiced their kickboxing. I had a busy schedule that day because after my class at the center, I was to teach paramedics self-defense. In Manila, paramedics get calls to some of the worst neighborhoods, at night and when the perpetrators are still around. The official policy is that paramedics shouldn't even get out of the ambulance if the scene doesn't look safe. That's why the course I was planning to teach them was a practical fighting program I had developed for the Shan State rebel army when I was in the war zone in Burma.

Then, like a bolt of lighting, I suddenly realized how far I had come from my home in Brooklyn. I had just passed my 40th birthday, and here I was in Asia, studying martial arts, living and traveling for nearly seven years. Since my arrival, I had visited 10 Asian countries, learned four Asian languages and studied countless arts with a variety of masters, some good and some bad. Several of the arts I had the privilege of studying were unknown even to the locals. For example, many Filipinos were unaware of *kuntaw*, which is the most ancient of Philippine arts, and those who did know of it were shocked to hear that I had studied it. Other arts I had studied, like Cambodian *bokator* or Shan *lai tai,* were completely unknown outside of their native countries.

In fact, these arts are so obscure that I wouldn't be surprised if I were one of the few Westerners privileged to see and practice these arts. In the case of bokator, I'm honored to say that a former U.S. soldier named Sgt. Derek Morris and I were the first Westerners to ever make rank in bokator. In the case of Shan lai tai, I was lucky to escape with my knowledge and photos of the art because its native practitioners are being killed off by Burmese government forces— but more on that later.

The last several years have been a wild, exciting, funny and sometimes awful ride. When I began my journey, I arrived in Taiwan as an angry and aggressive New Yorker with a chip on his shoulder. I was a 5'8" boxer with some limited *muay* Thai and grappling skills who weighed 198 pounds and had something to prove to myself and anyone else who got near me. If all you want to do is fight, who I was back then was a pretty good place to start. But now, I can see the value behind a martial art, and I can certainly see the value of the masters who have dedicated their lives to that art. Don't get me wrong—I'm still aggressive and arrogant, but I also hope that I'm closer to being human than I was when I first came over to Asia.

But it was a long path from New York to Taiwan to Manila, and it begins in my childhood.

My whole life, I had dreamed of traveling to China and studying at the Shaolin Temple. My family came from New York, but we moved to Tennessee, where I started martial arts at the age of 11 and studied boxing and kickboxing, or as my innovative teacher H. David Collins called it American kung fu.

Martial arts helped me out a lot because as a child I was an outcast. First, I was diagnosed as learning disabled, or dyslexic, at an early age. A lot of skills that were simple for other boys were impossible for me. I had no hand-eye coordination. I couldn't catch and throw a ball. To this day, I'm terrified when a ball is thrown at me. I didn't learn to ride a bicycle until I was 16 and I didn't learn to drive a car until I was 20. (As a native New Yorker, even now I've never developed a taste for driving.) I couldn't do geometry or trigonometry because I had no spatial reasoning ability. The way this translated into my little-boy life was that I couldn't build models or play with construction toys like erector sets. Cars and mechanics were never of any interest to me because I lacked the intellectual skills necessary to operate them. It was also the reason I couldn't play baseball or football; I couldn't understand the rules or calculate the scores because my brain did not process information the same way that other brains did. I couldn't even tell which team was which because my eyes visually process things differently. I couldn't tell which way the ball was supposed to move—up or down the court. I could just as easily kick it into my own goal as the opponent's goal. And frankly, I just didn't care.

Second, I was branded a "Yankee" when my family moved from New York to Tennessee. It was a different world where I was also picked on because my family was one of only two Italian families in town, and we were Catholic. I got beat up and bullied a lot at school.

By the time I was 11, I could take a punch like no one's business. There was a TV show with Lee Majors called *The Fall Guy* (1981-1986), and I couldn't believe Majors got paid to let guys beat him up. I was getting beat up for free. That show gave me my destiny. My dream was to find a way to get paid for getting beat up. I was planning to be the champion of the world in withstanding a beating as well as coming back at 'em with a smart insult.

Eventually, our family friend Carmine arranged for me to start taking kung fu lessons with H. David Collins. His son, Chris, was also studying kung fu.

Both Carmine and my dad had grown up in tough Italian

neighborhoods back East. Carmine had even boxed in the Navy. Like all immigrant families, they wanted their sons to graduate university, take the step to become white-collar Americans and live the American dream. But they were both men who couldn't shake the experiences of their youth that taught them that being a man meant standing up for yourself and that fighting was acceptable for solving certain situations. The reason martial arts appealed to both fathers was that they saw it as a clean, gentlemanly way to fight. As fans of Sean Connery's James Bond, they interpreted martial arts as a refined form of self-defense that was different from the brutish violence they had seen as kids.

Until Chris and I learned enough martial arts to fight fair and square, they encouraged us to use any method at our disposal to win a street fight.

For example, there was this bully in a class that Chris and I had together, and he had beaten Chris up every day since the beginning of school. When he sent Chris home with shattered glasses, Carmine said enough was enough. He told Chris what the plan would be for the next day and Chris agreed to it.

Class started at 8:00 a.m. At 8:10 a.m., Chris's older brother Mike arrived at the principal's office. He told the secretary, "I am here to pick up my brother."

"Is he ill?" the secretary asked.

"No," Mike said. "He is about to get sent home for fighting."

I was in class. Roll had been taken, but there was no sign of Chris. I didn't realize this was all part of his dad's plan. Carmine told him to hide in the bathroom till 8:15. At exactly 8:16, Chris came running into the classroom and punched that bully right in the nose. The kid never saw it coming. He was sitting in his chair pretending to listen to the biology teacher.

Blam! Chris knocked that bumpkin right out of his chair. Unfortunately, the kid was still a huge farm boy who had been held back a few years. He proceeded to beat the crap out of Chris as he had done every day. But this time, the bully was bleeding and crying.

Chris was taken to the principal's office where Mike was waiting to take him home. That night Carmine told us, "That kid is never going to mess with Chris again."

It was true. By all rights, the bully had won the fight, but Chris had shown the bully how tough and scary he could be. Chris never got picked on again.

With me, it was a little less heroic.

There was a bully on the bus—actually there were several. My father said to me, "In this family, we ain't that big. When one of these smart aleck American kids starts giving you grief … wait 'til he isn't looking. Then hit him. And when you do, use a pipe or a hammer or something."

The next day, I went to school on the bus with a pipe up the sleeve of my jacket. *The Wild, Wild West* (1965-1969) was my other favorite show at the time, and I loved hidden weapons. The bully smacked me around on the bus, tore up my homework and did a dance on my lunch. I said nothing. When he turned to walk away, I smashed him in the back of the head with the pipe.

It was pretty much the same result as what happened to Chris. I got beat up, but that kid was terrified to even look at me again.

What I remember about those experiences is that, even though Chris and I didn't know how to fight, we had the courage to stand up for ourselves—physically, spiritually and intellectually. And when I talk about courage, I don't mean that we need it to fight. Courage has absolutely nothing to do with being able to fight. In fact, it's almost the opposite. It doesn't take courage to stand up for what you believe is right or if you know you can win. Instead, it takes courage to stand up and fight when you know you might lose. Chris and I knew there would be consequences to our actions, and we were willing to accept them.

It was because of those experiences, too, that Carmine and my dad signed Chris and me up for martial arts. They hoped that we wouldn't need to fight like animals. They wanted us to learn to avoid fighting except when necessary, and if we had to fight, we would do it skillfully, quickly and efficiently. Like H. David Collins, my dad stressed that many fights I would face would never require fists.

Carmine once told me, "When you're a kid, you think you are smarter than your parents. When you turn 30, you suddenly believe your parents got smart." And it was true. As an adult looking back at my life, my dad was right. Most of the fights I have had and most obstacles that I have had to overcome weren't solved by fighting with my fists. But learning to fight with my fists taught me how to fight with my brains, my spirit and everything I had at my disposal. Life may not be a fistfight, but it is a struggle, and you will have to fight to achieve any goal.

The martial arts gives people many skills, like uncovering your own bravery and courage. I saw a lot of people come and go from H. David Collins' school. They didn't quit, but instead, they got what they needed from the arts. Then, they went on to have great success in business or academics. If you asked them what made them lead successful lives, they would often say how great Collins was at helping them reach their full potential. And he was, but the important thing to remember is that the potential for goodness was in them already. A truly successful martial artist is someone who can take the lessons learned in the ring and apply them outside of it.

When I started training with H. David Collins I knew absolutely nothing about martial arts. At first, martial arts came just as hard for me as other sports. There were three principle bullies—brothers—who lived down the hill from my family, and they were at least half the reason I started martial arts. When I walked into the martial arts school, who was there to greet me but the three evil brothers! They beat me every day even worse than before to try to get me to quit martial arts school.

But I hung in there.

Eventually, my American kung fu improved. I had another showdown with another bully, but I made sure to draw a crowd this time. I went up to people in school saying, "Whoever wants to watch Ricky beat me up after school tomorrow, come to the park."

By this time, I had been training for about three or four years. I knew I would win, but I wanted it to be the last street fight I ever had. I figured the more people who witnessed it the better.

In the end, it worked out exactly as I had hoped. Ricky came at me overconfidently. I kicked. I boxed. I moved. When it was done, he had hit me only once with a big, looping roundhouse punch to the back of the head. But I had hit him a ton. His face was all bloody and one eye was swollen shut. He missed several days of school. When he came back, he told everyone, except me, that he was going to get me.

He never did.

As for the three brothers who terrorized me at kung fu and at home, H. David Collins eventually kicked them out of the school. All three of them wound up getting arrested before the age of 18. None of them graduated high school, and two of them would eventually be wanted for murder. Oddly enough, I owe a lot to kids like these three brothers and Ricky because they served as a cautionary tale for my own life: If you follow the narrower path of a good life without drugs or excessive alcohol, good things will come to you. Of course, I made my fair share of bad decisions that I had to pay a price for, but thankfully and unlike those bullies, I never did anything so terrible that I couldn't recover from it.

I went from being a youth who was preoccupied with fighting to the military and then to universities in Europe, but that's all part of another book. This one is about martial arts and how my childhood dream of getting beat up and fighting for a living became a reality.

I boxed in the military and continued fighting and training. When I was in my mid-20s, I moved to Germany where I spent four years studying applied linguistics and working as a translator and teacher. I went from Europe to Costa Rica, then moved back to my birthplace, New York City, where I worked in investment banking for four years. For the first time since returning to the United States, I had money to buy UFC videos, pay for training and start fighting—but with a different motivation this time. I decided to try and get into professional fighting and to eventually pursue MMA competitions. In the day, I worked in my office. In the evening, I trained. At night, I still had my childhood dream of studying martial arts in Asia, especially at the Shaolin Temple.

Then 9/11 happened, and it changed everything for me. After

that horrific day, I realized how short life really is. I decided to quit my career and follow my dreams. You can be an investment banker when you are 90, but the window of availability for hard physical training is narrow. So I decided to leave New York and head to China for training. Knowing that I would need to learn Chinese first, I used the Internet to find a teaching job in Taiwan. I went from decision to action in a short blink, and at the end of October, I landed in Taipei.

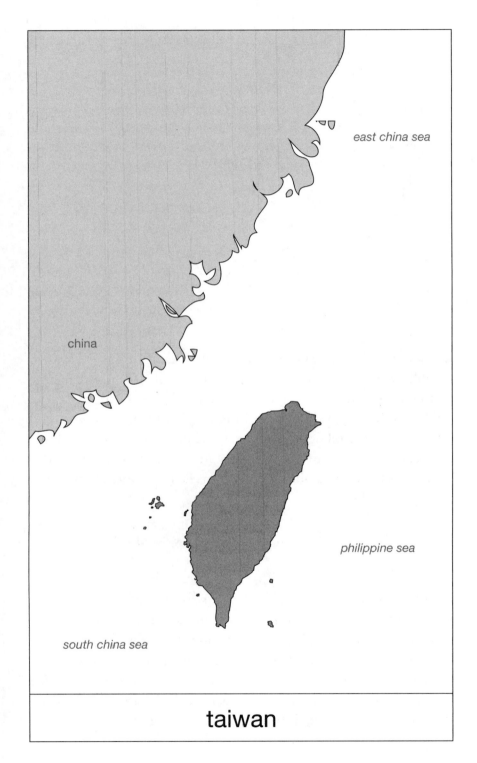

east china sea

china

philippine sea

south china sea

taiwan

chapter 1

My FIRST TEACHING ASSIGNMENT on the island of Taiwan was in the village of Do Lio, where I hoped to learn the Chinese language and kung fu before moving to the Mainland. My dream in Taiwan was to study kung fu from a real master. Shortly after arriving and settling in at the bilingual elementary school where I was teaching, I asked my job agent Joshua—like many Taiwanese, he used a Western name when dealing with foreign clients— where I could find a kung fu teacher.

"China," he said.

"But we are in Taiwan. Surely they have kung fu here, too," I insisted.

"China Shaolin Temple. That's the place to learn kung fu."

I was a little disheartened by Joshua's reply. I had given up a very well-paying job in New York to come to Taiwan to study kung fu, and he was basically telling me that wouldn't be possible.

The next day at the bilingual school, the principal told me that I was responsible for an after-school sports program for the kids. When I explained to them that I couldn't play basketball, baseball or football, they said, "That's no problem. You can teach kung fu to the children."

I had gone to Taiwan to learn kung fu, and instead, I now had a job teaching kung fu. To me, it would have made more sense to have a Taiwanese master pass his skills on to younger students, but Taiwanese parents would never have agreed to that. With the Taiwanese economic miracle, the Taiwanese had rushed to embrace the West and all things modern and American. This meant that they had lost touch with their traditional culture. Every minute a Taiwanese youth spent in horse stance was a minute he could be studying math. But having a real American teach martial arts to the kids in English was OK. So I decided that if they asked an American to teach martial arts, they were going to learn American martial arts. I wore a muscle shirt, boxing shorts and carried a whistle. I even made the kids call me "coach."

Every morning, the school driver, who had taken the unlikely Western name of Hans, picked me up at my apartment. As we drove, we would see the elderly in every park and open field we passed doing *tai chi* or *chi gong*. Hans once told me that chi gong is a type of kung fu. Or at least that's what I think he was telling me. His English was painful to listen to.

"There are two types of kung fu," he (I think) said. "There is tai chi, which is related to chi gong. This is a type of exercise form which is healthy for the body. It is not for fighting."
"What is the other kind of kung fu?" I asked.

"It is for fighting only. You can toughen your body so, even if someone hits you with a knife, you will not get hurt."

"What is this kind of kung fu called?"

"Just kung fu," said Hans, and we drove on.

I would tell everyone I met that I wanted to learn kung fu in the hopes that they would help me find a teacher. The interesting thing was that they would always ask, "You mean Chinese kung fu?" And I would always think to myself, What other kind of kung fu is there? What I figured out later was that Chinese people use the word kung fu to refer to martial arts in general. Instead of karate, for example, they would say Japanese kung fu. Thai boxing was Thailand kung fu. Western boxing was often referred to as American kung fu.

My roommate, a Canadian called Teacher Joe by his students, knew how much I wanted to learn kung fu. So he took me to meet the owner of a local pub. "He knows everyone," said Teacher Joe. "He could help you find a kung fu teacher."

Ajan, the pub owner, looked exactly like one of those smuggler/mafia guys from a Vietnam-war movie. Like the guys running the Russian roulette games in the *The Deer Hunter* (1978) or buying and selling weapons in *Air America* (1990), he wore Western clothes, had a cheesy mustache and had long, stringy hair. Ajan's bartender, on the other hand, was this gorgeous girl, whom I silently vowed to try and marry.

Teacher Joe told Ajan that I wanted to learn kung fu. He immediately replied, "I teach you." This, of course, was after I had drunk about a liter of beer. I still drank in those days, but later in my quest, I would abandon alcohol and late nights completely.

Ajan walked around the bar and motioned for me to stand next to him. He immediately started taking me through some tai chi exercises. I thought: Doesn't anyone in this country practice real kung fu?

"Not tai chi," I said. "Not chi gong. I want to learn classic kung fu."

Ajan thought a moment and then said, "OK, I teach." He began showing me some basic moves. It was all stuff I already knew but just a little more authentic. Then Ajan said, "I teach you to block."

He showed me a block and a counter. Again, it was stuff I already knew. He started throwing punches at me that I blocked and countered, then blocked and countered with the same hand. I realized that I was doing stuff H. David Collins had taught me 23 years ago. I guess practice doesn't necessarily make things perfect, but it does make them permanent. I don't know if I could do those techniques any other way.

Ajan threw another punch at me, but I slapped his fist down and caught him in the jaw with the back of the fist I had used to block, pulling it just before I would have hit his jaw. H. David Collins had called this block and counter "the ever-returning fist" because you could practice it with a partner for hours. Strike, block, strike, block, etc., with your hands moving in circles forever.

Ajan laughed at my counter and said. "You are very fast."

"You are a good teacher," I said.

Ajan and I continued sparring. He stepped in to attack me at close range, and I immediately did the short, inside kicks to the shins that are indicative of kung fu. The kick, often called a shovel kick, is done with the inside of the foot and can be used from a range of as little as nine inches. Most karate or *taekwondo* practitioners would be helpless if their opponent got in that close. In fact, Bruce Lee said that it's unrealistic to believe that two guys would kick each until one gives up. We squared off several more times, and each mini-bout ended with Ajan bowing out. I didn't understand at the time, but I was matching fighting against art. Ajan just wanted to share his knowledge with me, but I was competing. By deferring to my skill, Ajan was actually deescalating a potential conflict. At the time, I didn't realize how much I had to learn about living in Asia.

Next, Ajan wanted to hit me in the stomach to see if I had *chi*. Everyone technically has chi, but Ajan wanted to see if I was capable of using and controlling it. I said, "Go ahead."

He hit me lightly. I said, "Harder."

He hit me again, a little harder. I said, "Harder."

Ajan kept hitting me harder and harder, but he never reached the point that I couldn't take it. This is a favorite trick of mine, which isn't so much a trick as years of working on my abs. It always manages to impress others.

I let him hit me about 50 times in the stomach. Then I said, "My turn. But I will only hit you once."

There is no way someone can say "no" at this point because they would look like a jerk. I dropped low and hit Ajan with an uppercut in the solar plexus. It wasn't that hard but it was hard enough. Two hours and ten beers later he was still rubbing his belly. "Hurt," he said in the broken English that many non-native speakers know and use.

In writing this now, I'm reminded what a jerk I was when I

first came to Asia because I felt like a kid in a candy store. I wanted everything. I was in Taiwan, but I wanted to be in Thailand, Japan and China. I wanted to be doing kickboxing, chi gong, samurai stuff … anything and everything! Nowadays, I probably meet guys like Ajan on a daily basis, but I don't hit them and they rarely wind up as characters in my diary. But back then, I was so excited to be in this new world that I was almost spastic in my attempt to participate in it through martial arts and what I believed it to be.

I hope that people like Ajan forgave me, and I hope that other foreigners learn from my mistakes when they come over. Otherwise, I recommend you go straight to Thailand where you can get all the fighting out of your system before attempting to learn art in a peaceful country like Taiwan.

Anyway, back to our story, I knew it was time to go home when Ajan went into his yard and came back with some bricks. "You break with hand," he said.

"I'm from Brooklyn," I said. "If I want those bricks broken, I'll pay somebody 10 bucks to sneak up behind them with a baseball bat." Teacher Joe and I thanked him and left. Ajan promised to help me find a teacher, like every other Taiwanese. I never knew if any of them were serious.

For example, a mother of one of my students stopped by the classroom to ask about her child, but actually, I think she just wanted to find out more about me. When I said that I wasn't married, she said that she had many single female cousins and would be on the lookout for a girl for me. I told her that learning kung fu was higher on my priority list, so she also promised to find me a kung fu instructor. She also said that she wanted me to teach kung fu to her son in the spring. If I got one kung fu lesson from everyone who promised to find me an instructor, I'd be a master by now.

Everyone from my school principal to my coworkers to the local bar patrons—in short, everyone I talked to in Taiwan—told me that there was kung fu in Taiwan and promised to help find me a teacher. And yet, I still hadn't seen it.

Finally, after nearly two months of searching, the influential Mrs.

Lee, who was the owner of the elementary school where I taught, arranged for me to go to the small village of Ciro to meet a kung fu master who was a second-generation disciple of the famous Masters of Ciro. According to legend, seven Shaolin masters at the end of the 19th century were driven from the Mainland and resettled in Ciro, which is located on the southwest coast of Taiwan.

Mrs. Lee's assistant, I-Ching, was sent to brief me on my upcoming meeting. Apparently, it was a big Sino-political situation, which meant that if I gave a bad showing, Mrs. Lee would lose face. "The master said for you to come see him," I-Ching explained. "He wants you to demonstrate your kung fu. If he is impressed, he will teach you."

But what could I show a master? I had never learned a significant kung fu form with H. David Collins. What I had learned was a very minimalistic combat-effective fighting style that didn't include breaking bricks or other flashy moves.

All the years that I trained, it was only with fighting the good fight in mind. Should I ask the master to put on boxing gloves? Like Ajan, should I tell him to hit me and see how well I take the blow?

In the days leading up to the meeting, it seemed the whole village of Do Lio got involved or had an opinion. Everywhere I went, people wished me luck on my upcoming fight with the master. At one point I was called out of class to meet a congressman, Mr. Hong, who said, "Tomorrow you meet the master, so you must prepare." Talk about pressure. I had waited my whole life to meet a real Chinese kung fu master, and now that I was so close, I had to impress him somehow.

"Do you believe you can beat him?" I-Ching asked.

"Beat him!" I said. "I don't even want to fight him. I just want to study kung fu with him."

"Yes, but usually he want to see what you can do, so he want to fight you."

This is not how I wanted to meet this or any other master. I asked I-Ching to straighten things out for me. Later, she told me everything would be fine, but I wasn't so sure. In the hallway, staff members, who I didn't know continued to give me knowing little looks and wish me luck.

Hans the school driver drove me out to meet the master. We were accompanied by Mrs. Hans, Anita, the cousin of Congressman Hong, as well as Mr. Liau, who was a school board official and a local political figure.

I didn't know what was expected of me. I didn't know if they wanted me to fight the master. I was very nervous about the entire meeting.

On the ride over, Hans said, "Tell me about your training in the United States, so I can tell the master when we meet him."

"I don't want to tell him anything. I want to start as a brand new student and just learn from him," I said.

We rolled to a halt and Mrs. Hans said something to Anita in Chinese to ask me. Anita asked, "So, you are going to fight the master?"

"NO!" I said. "I don't want to fight the master. I mean, unless he wants me to."

"Should I tell him you fight him?" she asked, trying to be helpful.

"No, thank you," I said. She nearly, literally, killed me with her kindness. On the one hand, I was grateful that she was instrumental in helping me find and communicate with a master. But on the other hand, she was still trying to instigate a fight.

We met the master at his home. Because kung fu masters are rarely wealthy, his house reminded me of Master Yoda's cave in *Star Wars Episode V: The Empire Strikes Back* (1980). He even had a pot of stew on a little hotplate. His house was a converted restaurant. I say "converted" only because his bed probably wasn't sitting in the middle of the room when it was a restaurant. The huge, stainless steel sinks, ovens and stoves took up most of his living space. Otherwise, the house was bare. The master's only extravagance was a 400-year-old VCR, probably from the original Shaolin Temple, or so it seemed to me. On a metal folding table in the corner, there was an unimpressive collection of kung fu weapons.

I had no idea what to expect from a Chinese kung fu master. H. David Collins, my martial arts teacher back home, was the highest-ranking martial arts person I had ever known. He was not only Caucasian but from Tennessee, too. The only preconceived notions I had about what a kung fu master would be like in the Republic of China were from the 1970s TV show *Kung Fu* with David Carradine. I expected the master to be really old and look like Master Po. I even half-expected him to be blind. Instead, what I got was a guy in his mid-fifties, with a huge belly sticking over his belt. Instead of a robe, he was wearing a polyester pants suit, a white T-shirt and sandals. He bore a striking resemblance to the alcoholic character, Cousin Eddie, played by Randy Quaid in the *National Lampoon's Vacation* films.

The master took me over to the table and, through Hans, asked me if I knew how to use any of the weapons. I admitted that I had dabbled with every single one of them. There were *nunchaku*, *sai*, short Chinese swords, a *bo* staff, and a type of spear.

But once again, rather than teaching us impressive demonstration forms, H. David Collins had taught us how to fight with these weapons. We even used to spar with bo staffs and training swords—something I have never seen in Asia except in *arnis* in the Philippines and *kendo* in Japan and Korea.

"I will tell him," Hans said.

"Don't tell him!" I said for the hundredth time, afraid that I would have to fight. "Just let me learn with no pressure."

Hans didn't seem to understand or didn't like what I had said, but he went along with it by not telling the master. The master set the weapons aside and asked us to sit at the table and drink tea with him, which we did for about two hours while the women patiently waited in the car.

While we drank tea, the master said something to Hans, and Hans translated it for me. That is, to the extent that Hans could translate anything.

"The master said he wants to show you the fist now."

I thought, "OK, this is it. I've got to fight this guy." I stood up, took off my watch and began removing my shoes. The master motioned for me to stop. I thought that he wanted to fight with shoes on.

"No," said Hans. He clarified, "He *show* you the fist."

I still don't know what he meant by "show me the fist," but the master began to go through a kung fu *kata*.

There is no convenient Chinese word for kata. The most common Chinese word is *chuen*, which literally means "fist" but can also mean "style;" it also means a kung fu form similar to a kata in karate. Because it can get confusing, I will use the more familiar Japanese one instead. A kata is a choreographed, fixed set of martial arts techniques that you must memorize and perform exactly as taught. Kata can be short with as few as five distinct techniques—say, two kicks, two punches and a spin—which are then repeated several times to give the kata length. Other kata are very involved, with 50 or more distinct movements. Some are very hard to perform physically because they include leaps and techniques where you throw your body at the ground and spring back to your feet. Kata are the main means of studying kung fu. In the old days, a master may have spent his entire life perfecting a single kata or learning just three or four over a period of 50 years.

As a Westerner, I had always thought of kata as a very slow series of movements, which are the basis for most martial arts. I thought they served to teach discipline and classical techniques, as well as to weed out students who weren't serious about practice because kata are generally tedious and boring. In my own martial arts classes, I had learned kata as something you did as art and for show, but for real fighting, I was to use boxing and kickboxing techniques. This was the first kung fu kata I had ever seen, and it was anything but boring.

The movements were fast, fluid and strong. I could both see and feel the change in the master's mental and physical state. I had always had the attitude that you learn kata because you have to learn kata. Then, you can forget them and begin to learn the real stuff, but this Chinese kata *was* the real stuff. I had seen kata movements like Snake Hands, and Finger Spears, and various other kung fu techniques growing up, but I had never actually used them for fighting, opting instead to box with a closed fist. This master could definitely have used these techniques for fighting.

He went through the moves, with purpose, and every move made sense. If you were to take a freeze-frame photograph of each position he passed through, you would see absolutely perfect alignment of his body, which optimized his muscular strength, weight and natural skeletal structure. In the same way that a boxing punch is perfect for focusing the entire mass and energy of a heavyweight fighter on the first two knuckles of his punch, the master's every move focused every ounce of his body on the technique at hand. That kind of physical perfection could only be achieved through years and years of repetition and practice.

The master's stance was so low that his butt was about eight inches off the ground. There is no way you can knock a man down who is that low. You also can't punch him. You can kick him, but he only has to move his arms or legs a few inches to block the blow. A taekwondo guy would have been defenseless against this master.

I could also feel the chi flowing through him. When he had finished the kata, he was soaked in sweat, and his muscles were completely pumped up. He was probably 20 pounds lighter than me, but I suspected that he was much stronger.

"You like?" he asked.

"Yes," I said. "I like it very much."

"OK. Do you want to train tonight?"

Hans left me with the master, who took me to the home of another kung fu instructor and third-generation disciple from the masters of Ciro named Master Wu, whose wife had prepared a huge meal for us. When we had eaten, we went into the backyard, where 20 or so boys, ranging from early teens to early 20s, had gathered for training. I didn't know if they ever did sparring, but the only guys who seemed solid and strong enough to fight me were the two masters.

They didn't do any exercises or running. They just went right into these beautiful kung fu kata. After the empty-hand kata, they all picked up their weapons and began practicing. Several of them used a traditional Chinese spear, which is a five-foot staff with an 18-inch sword blade at the end. Others looked like Roman gladiators, armed with shields and tridents. Before each weapon kata, Master Wu brought me the weapon, so I could feel the weight.

He did a kata with a 12-foot pole. I know what you're thinking: I wouldn't do that kata with a 12-foot pole. But Master Wu did. Then he brought me the pole and wanted me to take it by one end, with both hands on my chest, and hold it straight out in front of me. I did it, but it took all of my strength.

The kung fu kata—empty hand and weapon-based—were designed to be done in pairs, with one person striking while the other was defending. The first boy would lower his body all the way to the ground, then come up and kick. The other would block and strike. The sequence looked like a kung fu movie where two combatants were evenly matched and threw hundreds of techniques at each other in rapid-fire succession, but this time each opponent is able to block all of the strikes.

While the other master drank tea, Master Wu took me aside and we began working on my kata. Much of what Master Wu showed me was reminiscent of what I had learned from H. David Collins. There were no kicks above the waist. You never stood more than eight inches away from the opponent. Every technique formed some type of circle. There were grappling techniques, whereby you grabbed your opponent, and then dropped all the way to the ground, pulling him down on top of you. Then you would spring up and kick him, as he was coming down into the kick. They were all techniques I had learned before, but now I understood them. The kata I had learned in America were very basic; they contained moves, which were limited to demonstrations. The moves we used in fighting were completely separate and different. But here in Taiwan, the kata contained moves that were used for fighting. It was a beautiful experience.

Between kata, Master Wu and I would sit with the other master and drink tea. Even the kung fu guys in this country aren't health conscious, so during the breaks, they all smoked cigarettes. In fact, while the master was adjusting me, he had a cigarette in his mouth.

Master Wu pulled up his sleeve and showed me his forearms. They were three times as thick as mine. He then began hitting himself as hard as he could in the stomach. His fat, protruding belly was hard as a rock. He then grabbed my arm, and it felt as if his fingers were like iron wire tearing into my flesh. He held out a forearm and began pounding it with his opposite fist. His arm didn't bruise or give. This forearm demonstration is actually a necessary exercise in many kung fu styles. And instructors often use it as a way of determining whether newcomers can take the heat. Over the next several years, I would have many masters banging me with their forearms. I would often go home with purple bruises on my arms while the masters were left unscathed.

After another tea break, we went back to kata. Master Wu squatted low and thrust his hands straight out in front of him with his palms face down, mummy style. Next, he very methodically clenched his fists while rotating them in an upward direction. All of his muscles pumped and bulged as he completed forming his fists.

Next, Master Wu retracted his arms, lightning fast, landing in a horse stance. All my life, I had thought that the purpose of making a fist was for punching. Watching Master Wu, I realized that he wasn't making a fist at all. He was tearing into the flesh of an opponent. And when he shot his hands back to his sides, he would be ripping the opponent's flesh wide open. I had felt his grip, and I knew I didn't want to be the victim of such an attack.

He had me do the exercise so many times that I thought I would die. Then Mr. Liau, an official from the elementary school in Do Lio, turned up in his car to take me home. Hans, Anita and I-Ching had already left. As we were leaving, Mr. Liau told me that Master Wu wanted me to come back.

"Tell him I'll be back tomorrow night," I said.

I asked Mr. Liau how much I should give the master. He said, "No. They train the boys for free. They don't want any money from you."

The next night, Master Wu rolled up his sleeves and extended both arms in front of him.

"You do chops on my arms," he said.

I began hitting his arms for all I was worth, but he didn't even flinch. Finally he said, "OK, enough. You strong."

I thought, "You're the one who is strong. I couldn't take a beating like that." Compared to the beating I took from pub owners like Ajan, when I asked them to hit me, there was no way I could withstand hits from a master like Wu.

Master Wu continued the lesson by showing me how to correctly throw a chop. In the style I had learned growing up, a chop belonged to the sets of movements we did in kata. I never learned that it was possible to use them in a fight, so my technique was not very good. I squatted down into a kung fu stance and began throwing hundreds of chops in the same way I would practice throwing air punches in a boxing gym. Master Wu was impressed. He was unused to seeing chops practiced with the immediate intensity that is characteristic of many Westerners. In Asia, people tend to work with less intensity but for long hours with fewer breaks. So in my mind, throwing 3,000 chops a day for 6 weeks was the best way to train. In the Asian mind, doing 300 a day for the rest of your life is the way to go, but because I was new to Asia, I kept thinking, "How else would you practice throwing chops?"

That day, training with the master, I got my speed up on chops and could throw them about as fast as I could throw punches. When I am in shape, I throw about 130 jabs and about 80 right hands in a 3-minute round. At kung fu training, they didn't have a round timer, so I am not certain how fast I was throwing, but it was pretty darn fast. For the first time, I began to wonder if chops would be effective weapons in real fighting. One advantage to a chop was that you wouldn't damage your hand or risk breaking a knuckle. I also imagined that it would be impossible for me to stop Master Wu in his low stance, coming at me, throwing low, leg-breaking kicks, and grabbing at me with flesh-tearing claws.

On the other hand, none of Master Wu's students was nearly as impressive as he was. If he trained them only once a week, while they continued to smoke, could they ever reach his level of perfection? Why had he become so fat and lazy?

Some neighbors came by to see a foreigner practice kung fu, and one of them spoke English. "Master Wu say you very strong."

"He's very strong," I said.

"He say you not want rest. You train too much."

Sitting on his stool, Master Wu was looking more like a happy

Buddha than Bruce Lee. He had sweated through his shirt, and it clung to his fat belly, which continued to hang over his belt. Most of his regular kung fu students had gone. The few who remained had been sitting, smoking and drinking tea for the last half hour or so. Now I realized what the neighbor had been saying to me about being strong. It wasn't a compliment so much as a criticism. I was screwing up the master's day by training with intensity

For several weeks, I trained during the weekdays with Master Wu, until one morning, Mr. Hans came to me. Hans said, "Master Wu said that he normally only trains people on Saturdays, so could you please come for training on Saturdays?"

Because I travelled on weekends, I had managed to become acquainted with a kung fu team in the large city of Kaohsiung and had been training with them on the weekends. "I can't train with him on Saturdays because I am in Kaohsiung training," I answered. "But anyway, who trains only once a week? I need to train every day."

"OK, I will tell him," Hans said.

However, the next day Mr. Hans told me that the master was emphatic about only teaching students once a week. And so, even though I wanted to continue training with Master Wu, I believed I was a much better fit with instructor Wang *jiao-lien* and his team in the city of Kaohsiung, not only because they practiced every day and competed in international competitions but also because they were more modern in their practice. I still sometimes wonder if I missed out on something amazing by not choosing to follow the disciples of the seven masters of Ciro.

The short story of how I met Wang jiao-lien and the Kaohsiung team starts out like this: One weekend, I went to visit Kaohsiung, Taiwan's second largest city. Friday night, I went dancing and met a girl. Saturday morning, I found kung fu in a park. And Sunday, I cancelled my trip to mainland China. For the next three months, I would take the train from Do Lio to Kaohsiung every Friday, spend the weekend at the school training and living, then return on Sunday.

The long story will obviously take a few more pages. In Kaohsiung, my first stop on Saturday was at a park where there were many Buddhist temples and a monastery. The taxi dropped me off at the foot of a steep stone staircase, which led upward for what looked like a third of a mile. It may just have seemed that way because of my hangover and because of the heat, but the people at the top of the stairs looked very small from where I was. There was an old man walking up the stairs backward. This type of exercise is part of chi gong and a type of inversion training. By working your muscles in a way that they are not normally worked, you receive great muscular and cardiovascular benefits. And consequently, blood flow occurs in parts of the muscles that are normally ignored.

Chi gong is both spiritual and physical training. It seeks to reset the balance between various forces in your body—what some people call yin and yang. Another benefit to walking backwards is to see the world in a different way. It is all so simple, and it makes perfect sense. This old man that I was watching must have been 90 years old, and yet he was walking slowly and methodically up those stairs backwards. The look on his face was one of single-minded determination. But, at the same time, it was a look of abandoned ambition. His face said, "I am going to make it to the top of these stairs, no matter what. But if I don't, that's OK, too."

I walked up the stairs frontward. This probably tells you a lot about who I am. At the top of the stairs, there was a long walkway made of highly polished black stones. The pathway was not just a mere conveyance but actually part of traditional Chinese medicine.

Practitioners believe that all major nerves in the body end in the feet. So, by manipulating the feet or by stimulating the various nerve endings, you can cure many illnesses. In China and in Japan, this type of therapy is also used to relieve stress in over-worked business people. Wanting to be one of the guys, I removed my hiking boots and began my Herculean journey across the polished stones.

The rocks are set at varying heights and angles, so each step stimulates a different set of nerve endings and causes a different set of sensations. Some steps felt very pleasant, like getting a foot massage. Some hurt horribly, with pressure shooting all the way up my spine. Some felt incredibly good, almost like having an orgasm. I have been told that if everything is in order in your body, there will be no sensation at all, certainly no pain.

The pain is caused by stored up tension in the body. In theory, if you were to walk across these stones every day, your body would eventually come into alignment. The flow of energy along the invisible paths through the body would become unblocked, stress would be reduced and there would be no pain. I must have had a lot of stored stress, because I only made it about 70 percent of the way before I had to step off the path. I bet that the old man could have break-danced on these rocks and not felt a thing. Was this the Eastern version of *The Princess and the Pea*? If so, I could never marry the prince.

There was another path that ran through the woods and down the mountain with stops at prayer sights and temples. Along the way, I passed some older couples doing their tai chi exercises. I love tai chi and think it is beautiful, but I would never have the patience to learn it.

Leaving the well-worn path, I stumbled onto some small hovels that were really just manmade caves in the natural stone with blankets strewn across their openings. They all had some type of primitive chimney protruding from the rock above. Were these quarters for monks? I wondered while I climbed to the top of a big rock and found a prayer mat laid out at the bottom of a tree. There was a flimsy blanket tied in the branches above to give some meager protection from rain and sun. It looked to me like a place where a monk could sit and meditate for days or even weeks at a time. What I knew of the monks, which wasn't much, was that they ate very little—just enough to sustain life. They slept little. They were unmarried and even had to reject their families. They were to love all living creatures equally. This meant that they could love their family, but only to the extent that they loved a moth.

At the base of another high staircase, I found a kung fu master training his students. He had them lined up in twos. They hopped up the steps on one leg then ran down and hopped up on the other leg. Next, they went up backward on their bellies, using only their arms to push themselves to the top. Then they partnered up and did the wheelbarrow walk to the top, one partner holding the legs of another. After switching off, they each took a partner on his shoulders to walk to the top. Next, they walked to the top while throwing a kick on each step. One kick, one step, one kick, one step. They would go all the way to the top, kicking with one leg. Then they would come down and go back up, kicking on the other leg.

Watching these kids train made Rocky look like a wimp for making such a big deal about running up the stairs of the Philadelphia Art Museum. First of all, he was running on his feet and not his hands. Second, he was only carrying his own body weight.

One of the guys had apparently injured his leg, so instead of running up and down with the others, he stood in front of a stone pillar and pounded it with the sides of his hands. I watched the training for about an hour, and he never relented. He just pounded away with his hands in a white-crane claw position.

One of the other students was doing push-ups on his knuckles on the hard stone. This type of training reminded me so much of training with my old teacher, H. David Collins. We never had weights or a Nautilus machine or anything from this century. We ran on a track and up and down stairs, carrying a partner. Or we ran as a team, carrying a big telephone pole. At other times, we ran carrying smaller versions of telephone poles, like I also did back in army basic training. We climbed rocks and ladders. We crawled. We practiced throwing punches while holding a brick in each hand. It was all in the name of becoming stronger, faster and more limber, so that we could master American kung fu.

I wished desperately that I could talk to this master. Finally, I got up my courage. I walked up to him and said, in Chinese, "I want kung fu." I couldn't remember the word for "study." He smiled and seemed as if he would be open to having me study with him, but we couldn't communicate. Using gestures, he somehow helped me understand that he had a school nearby. I pulled out pen and paper and asked him to write his phone number. (Actually, I showed him my phone and handed him a pen, and he figured out what I needed.) I would ask a Chinese friend to help me call him later and arrange my lessons.

Back at work in Do Lio, my co-worker I-Ching helped me call the kung fu master. He was apparently the trainer for the official kung fu team of the city of Kaohsiung. Not only did he say that I could train with the team, but he also said that he would pick me up at the station and I could live with the team all weekend.

"He said there is no fee for training," said I-Ching. "You just have to pay for your food."

This was a dream come true! I would be studying kung fu and living at a kung fu school in China—at least in the Republic of China. It was a lot like wanting to go to Disney World in Florida and going to the one in California instead. The wish and the experience couldn't compare, but either of them beat the hell out of a mall in New Jersey.

Friday night the kung fu teacher, Wang jiao-lien—jiao-lien was his instructor title like *sensei*—picked me up at the train. He took me to a Japanese restaurant with his family and paid for dinner. It was really funny because I wanted to ask him tons of questions and he wanted to ask me tons of questions, but he knew about 10 words of English and my Chinese still wasn't very good. He had an electronic pocket translator. We used this to make simple questions and answers to one another. But it was slow going. You inputted one word at a time, and when you gave it an English word, you got several choices in Chinese. Since I couldn't read Chinese, I didn't know what any of the choices were, so I couldn't tell him which of the words was the one I wanted. Another consequence of not being able to read Chinese is that I couldn't learn the new word that showed up on the screen because I didn't know how it was pronounced. The machine was just giving me a fish instead of teaching me to fish.

The one question Wang was able to ask me was if I had studied kung fu before. I said that I had studied boxing for 23 years. He was impressed but then told me that in kung fu it was necessary to kick.

I tried to tell him this is what I wanted to learn, but the words just weren't there.

After dinner, he took me over to the school to meet the team. All the other students were half my age. Teacher Joe had warned me of this before I went. "In Taiwan it's just not normal for adults to do anything. They're all married, eh."

These kids would come to the kung fu school and sleep there all weekend, every weekend. There were three dormitory rooms, each of which contained a huge piece of plywood with sleeping bags on it. Each room was big enough to sleep four foreigners or eight Taiwanese. They gave me one whole room to myself. The team slept in another room, and Wang jiao-lien had a private bedroom. Once he saw that I was settled in, he went home with his wife for a while, and I was left alone with the team.

They were really cool kids, but none of them spoke English. They didn't wear *gi* or traditional martial arts uniforms. They wore tracksuits. They seemed to be moving constantly—jumping, standing, playing—always in motion. Pong was the biggest and the oldest of the students, who ranged in age from 13 to 20. We weighed ourselves. I only outweighed him by 20 pounds. I outweighed Wang jiao-lien by more than 65 pounds.

Pong was like a comic-relief character in a Disney movie. He was the big, brawny, good-natured, mellow Little John-esque sidekick of the intelligent Robin Hood hero. Think Baloo the Bear, and that was Pong. When there was work to be done, Pong always disappeared, leaving the heavy lifting to the smaller boys. But when it came to food, Pong was your man.

We sat around a table where Pong made pot after pot of tea, and we talked and listened to music. In retrospect, I have no idea how I communicated with Wang jiao-lien and his team. But when I would go back to Do Lio on Sunday nights, I would keep Teacher Joe up for hours with my retellings of our conversations. Joe would always point out, "But you don't speak Chinese, dude." And I would say, "I know. But somehow we understand each other."

Making tea or coffee in this country is a very elaborate and social event. It takes a long time, and you are expected to talk and commune while the tea is being prepared. There is much ceremony involved. The difference between their tea and tea in America would be the difference between dinnertime on a farm and dinnertime at Top of the Sixes in New York City. They both serve to feed, but dinner in New York also serves to entertain. It is an event not to be hurried.

Pong heated water in a huge kettle. The kettle, which held about two gallons of water, was set on a hotplate on the living room table and we all sat around it. Next, he took some of the hot water and washed all the cups and the teapot, dumping the water into a catch basin at the bottom of the tea maker. Then, he filled the pot with tea leaves and poured water into it. While the tea was brewing, he continuously poured boiling water over the outside of the teapot to keep it hot. There was even a huge paintbrush to make sure that the hot water covered the whole teapot in a uniform manner. Next, he washed all the cups with boiling water again to get them hot. Then he poured the piping hot tea into the warmed cups. The cups were like sake cups, about the size of a double shot glass and without a handle. As soon as the cups were filled, he cleaned out the teapot and began the process all over again. We sat and drank tea like that for about two hours. It was a lot of fun, and I found it very endearing that these boys would spend a Friday night at tea. I couldn't picture American kids doing this. During the whole process of making tea, there was good-hearted conversation and a lot of giggling and laughing. For a minute I thought maybe the tea was laced with something, but it wasn't. It was just typical Taiwanese good cheer.

When one of the kids, Duan, opened his bag, I looked inside. There was one change of clothing, and all the rest was Taiwanese junk food. Like teenagers anywhere, Taiwanese teens just kept eating all the treats that Taiwanese kids love. They ate dried seaweed pieces, which I find frightening. They ate onion cookies. They had clove cookies, which are made from congealed oil of clove. And, of course, what Friday night would be complete without dried squid chips? Typical for Taiwan, every time they ate something, they offered me some. Even if the food hadn't been stomach turning, which it was,

I would have declined because I had eaten so much with their instructor and his family.

The guys on the team were a bunch of pranksters, so every session of tea drinking was always punctuated with kung fu antics. Since Wang jiao-lien had told the kids before he left that I had come to learn kung fu with them and had boxed for 23 years, it wasn't long before one was holding an air shield. They wanted to see what I could do with my hands. I pounded that shield for all I was worth and backed the kid up into a corner in the process. Although everyone was so nice, I was still a little nervous about what I had gotten myself into. I mean, here I was locked in a building in the middle of the night somewhere in the outskirts of Kaohsiung in a village called Nan Ze. I didn't know the address of where I was. I didn't know the names of most of the people in the room. I didn't know what was expected of me, and I didn't know what was going to come in the morning. For all I knew, they had brought me there to be a sparring dummy. Whatever the situation was, I wanted to demonstrate some skill and strength so as to lay down the law from the get-go. On the other hand, I was outnumbered six to one. Like I said, I was a little nervous.

They really liked my punching, and as soon as Wang jiao-lien came back, they made me do it again. He laughed and said, "Very good, very good." Then he told the kids that this was the result of 23 years of training. But then he turned to me, and with the help of his pocket translator, said, "Tomorrow morning, training. Because they are smaller, you and I shall perform."

I had no idea what he meant. Had I insulted him by showing off my punches in his school? Did he want to kick the shit out of me in front of everyone to prove his superiority? I didn't like the word "perform." But, as always, I went with my Taiwan instinct that says, "If you think someone is trying to pull a fast one on you, they are not." Or, "If you think someone is being too nice, they are just Taiwanese."

Wang jiao-lien showed me where I could take a shower before sleeping. It was an aluminium stall with three inches of smelly water on the floor. As with all showers in Taiwan, you were expected to change and dress in the shower stall, but there was no place to put your clothing while you washed. There was a shower stool, but it was filthy and wet. In the end, I put my shaving bag on the stool and laid my clean clothes on top of the bag. After washing, I dressed, hoping I wouldn't drop my training shorts in the water, as I only had one pair with me. The whole time, I was standing in smelly water. When I came out, I noticed two of the kids were missing. A few minutes later they walked in and handed me a bag from the local department store with a brand new pair of sandals inside—so I wouldn't have to get my feet wet and dirty.

I slept well that night and I woke up around six in the morning without an alarm, but with a belly still full of wasabi and fish broth. Everyone was still sleeping, so with all the stealth of a ninja assassin, I slinked across the training room. I stole a box of toilet paper and headed outside to the girl's restroom, which is generally the only restroom with a Western toilet. (The alternative is a traditional squat toilet, which takes some getting used to.)

Heading back down the stairs, I found a large group of old people doing tai chi in the open corridors of the school. One incredible thing about this country is that you are apparently permitted to do tai chi anywhere you want, even on private property—in front of a bank, a school or a hospital. It is so beautiful. I watched the old people going through their slow, balletic journey. They were doing the Sunrise Form, which H. David Collins had taught me when I was younger. The normally brittle bones and stiff joints of the aged become supple as they move through the form, which tells the story of the rising sun. First, the sun slowly comes up over the horizon until it peaks in the east. The body turns to face the rising sun. The palms are turned outward to absorb the heat energy, which radiates down upon the earth. Slowly, the sun begins its journey westward. Just as the sun reaches its zenith, at noon, the wind begins to blow. The wind brings the clouds. The clouds cover the sun and it begins to rain. Next, the rain makes the plants grow up to the rising sun. The leaves fall back down to the earth, and the sun sets. The whole journey takes about a half-hour to move through. Once the sun had "set," the old people got back on their bicycles and went on about their day. I headed back down to the gym to start mine.

Apparently, Wang jiao-lien hadn't stayed at his house and had slept at the school. So when the team woke up around 7:00 a.m., he was also stirring in his sleeping bag. He shouted for everyone to wake up. Training needed to begin.

First, we got in a circle and did stretches and warm-up exercises, typical of any martial arts school in the United States. When I met the team at the park, they were on a conditioning outing. Over the next year and a half that I trained with them, we would go on these outings from time to time. But on a daily basis, kicking was the bulk of their training. They would throw thousands and thousands of kicks every day. So after we warmed up, that's exactly what we did.

I started with a basic sidekick, which I did hundreds of times on each side. Wang jiao-lien spent over an hour with me, helping me to perfect the kick. The boys did their kicks and then began what I would call flying practice. They held multiple targets in the air, some 6 to 10 feet off the ground, and the boys had to jump up and kick all of them before coming back down to the ground. It was true magic. I had never learned these types of moves. My old *sifu* H. David Collins had said that they were showy and ineffectual in a fight. I agreed with him; these techniques were showy and ineffectual, but they were really cool—and I was getting to do them for the first time in my life.

Next, the boys erected a barrier about one and a half meters high and three meters long. They had to run and jump over the barrier, sail through the air, and hit a target three meters away. It was like the stunts you see in movies.

Then, they held a target up, and a boy had to jump in the air and kick it as many times as possible before falling back to earth. Some of the boys could go four kicks before touching ground, and they didn't use any special effects from *The Matrix* (1999).

Every time the students were asked to jump up and kick something, Pong disappeared or just plain refused to participate. I was wondering why he wasn't just kicked off the team—until we came to the strength portion of the training. Pong could throw a punch and crush an 18-inch stack of bricks. He could also break cinderblocks with his head.

Pong was also the boy I had seen the previous week doing push-ups on the hard stone surface with his knuckles. Wang jiao-lien told Pong to come over and show me his hands. His knuckles were huge and calcified. The skin was as thick as shoe leather. Since I am primarily a boxer, my hands have been pampered, wrapped and protected my whole martial arts career. My hands are big and strong, but the skin is soft from having been steamed inside of gloves for all those years. Wang jiao-lien held up one finger and said that Pong could break a brick by spearing it with a single digit. I was impressed. They showed me how to do push-ups on my knuckles.

"This will be easy," I thought. Boxers also do push-ups on their knuckles. I started banging out push-ups when Wang jiao-lien stopped me. Apparently, in kung fu you do push-ups only on the first two knuckles instead of on four like I had always done before. I was able to do only two before I collapsed.

These guys were also really into breaking wooden boards. Growing up, I had a prejudice drilled into my head against this type of training. "Boards don't fight back," I had been told. Also, "Just because you can break a board doesn't mean you can fight." Although both of those statements are true, I didn't know that I wanted to learn kung fu to be a better fighter. I didn't think that in learning to break a board I would lose my current abilities. I felt a little sad that after so many years of training I had no skill that I could demonstrate in front of people.

Eventually, Wang jiao-lien gave us a break. The school apparently had rest periods, meal periods and sleep periods built into the day because training took so long. Two of the boys were dispatched to McDonald's where they not only bought me breakfast but two cups of coffee. I guess they knew that foreigners liked hot coffee. Again, I tried to give money to Wang jiao-lien. Again, he refused. After we ate, Pong made more tea and we rested. We went back to work, and I learned two more kicks.

The second kick was one I had learned in Germany; I attended university there and practiced martial arts with a team mostly made up of Russians and Turks. It was a straight kick whereby you bring the front foot, board-rigid, straight up to the sky. The bottom of the foot passes just in front of your opponent's nose, and continues up over his head. Once over the head, the angle changes slightly, and you bring your foot down hard so that the heel smashes the bridge of the nose. It is both brutal and sneaky. When the kick goes by the first time, most people think that you have missed the blow. When the foot comes back down, your whole body weight is pulling the foot into the nose, smashing it. I practiced for a while, and Wang jiao-lien kept saying, "Very good."

Then he said, "I think you are ready to break wood."

"I don't think so," I laughed. Then, he said something in Chinese, and while I couldn't be certain, it sounded like, "Wait here. I'll go get some wood."

Sure enough, a few minutes later, two of the boys, Win and Ze, were holding up a board, and Wang jiao-lien was telling me to kick it. I had never kicked a board in my life. On top of that, I was barefoot. In Brooklyn, if you kick someone at all, it's because he is lying unconscious on the ground, you are wearing army boots, and ideally two of your friends are holding him down. Now these guys were asking me to hit this wood with my bare foot and break it.

I refused two more times, still thinking it was a joke. Not only was it serious, but I was going to lose face if I didn't do it. I took a deep breath and shot out my foot like a bullet, only half believing I could break the board. My foot passed the board on the way up and crashed down on the right side, just beside the fingers of the kid who was holding it. The shot was way off center but it split the board from end to end. Ze jerked his hand back, ghost white. I apologized to Ze, and Wang jiao-lien reiterated that I should hit it in the center. This time, I knew that I could do it. My foot shot up and ripped the board in half, right down the middle like it was supposed to. There were cheers and smiles all around. I was so happy. I couldn't believe that I had done it; after 23 years in martial arts, I had finally broken a board. I grabbed Wang jiao-lien and gave him a big bear hug. Immediately, I let go, thinking that this may not have been the right thing to do. He was still laughing, telling the others in Chinese how I had broken the board. He told one of the kids to get a pen, and we wrote my name, the date, and the name of the kick on the board. Wang jiao-lien hung it on the wall. Now, I was one of the guys.

We took a rest before eating lunch, which was fried chicken cutlet and a rice box from 7-11. After lunch, I sat and talked with Wang jiao-lien. While we had been training, he had been diligently writing me a note with the help of his pocket translator. It said, "I'm glad I meet you." I told him I felt the same way. Then it said, "First sleep. Then training: 14:00." This pleased me as I needed a nap. The next question was, "You stay?" Here I was torn. I really wanted to stay the rest of the weekend with them, but I had plans to go out with Karen, the girl I had met in Kaohsiung the previous weekend.

"15:00 I go Kaohsiung," I said. (Actually I said, "I go Kaohsiung," and wrote the time because I still didn't have my numbers memorized.)

"Where?" he asked with the pocket translator.

"Train station," I said. Karen was going to pick me up there.

"When come back?" he asked. He seemed really disappointed that I was leaving. I was wondering if he was glad to have another adult to talk to—that is, to the extent that we could talk."

"Friday," I said. Now this was problematic. I didn't know how to say next Friday, so I just said "Friday." The problem is that Friday in Chinese is like "five day," and Wang jiao-lien at first thought I meant that I would come back in five days on Wednesday or that I would come back at 5 p.m. that day. Once he realized what I meant, he said, "You take shower."

"Training 14:00," I said, meaning I could train for an hour and then go.

"Too short," he said.

After I had showered and changed clothes, he handed me another note. "First day training to relax. Not too stiff. Sleep." I thanked Wang jiao-lien, then lay down on the training mats with the rest of the team, and we all went to sleep. Wang jiao-lien didn't wake us at 2:00 in the afternoon as I had expected. He woke us up at 2:30 p.m. We had slept nearly two and a half hours. I felt good, but I could already feel the soreness setting in. As much as I wanted more training, I figured that six hours was enough for the first day.

I grabbed my gear, thanked Wang jiao-lien and headed for the door. He asked me how I would get to Kaohsiung station. I said, "With a taxi."

He said, "No, I drive."

He left the boys where they were and drove me all the way to the train station. The trip took about 25 minutes and was much farther than I originally thought. After I thanked him, he said, "You very good student."

"You very good teacher," I told him.

He laughed and then made a noise like a board breaking and kicked his foot. He pointed at me and shook his head.

"You break wood," he said.

I laughed. "Thank you," I said.

I wished that I could have said more or that I could have done more to repay him, but I couldn't. He got back in the car and headed back to the school where they would train until 9:00 at night and then repeat the process the next day.

I envied their lifestyle. And I looked forward to the following weekend when I would spend the whole weekend training with the Kaohsiung kung fu team.

About three months later, I quit my job in Do Lio and found a job at a private English school in Nan Ze. I moved my apartment to Kaohsiung, bought a motorcycle and was able to train with my team every day from about 10 a.m. until lunch time. Then I went to my school, ate lunch, took a nap and started teaching at 2:30 p.m. One of the nice things about Taiwan is that you are encouraged to nap at work. In New York, you would get fired for that.

When I had been in Taiwan for seven months, I began attending Chinese school in Kaohsiung in the early mornings before my kung fu practice. Every morning, on the way to Chinese school, I could see people doing martial arts in the park. One morning I decided to stop off and investigate. There were groups practicing tai chi, chi gong, kung fu, sword form, and *twe so* (pushing hands). Arguably, twe so is not a martial art in itself. It is actually a tai chi exercise. However, in Taiwan and many other places in Asia, twe so is a competitive sport, and not all of the competitors study tai chi.

Taiwan's most widely practiced martial art, by far, is tai chi. But today it is mostly practiced by older people. Taiwan's number two martial art is taekwondo, which is primarily practiced by boys through the age of 20. Compared to the Chinese tai chi and Korean taekwondo, twe so is an interesting martial art that is nearly unique to Taiwan in how it is practiced.

In twe so, two opponents stand more or less squared off to one another with one foot just slightly forward. The opponent's hands make contact with the other opponent's hands. When the referee or teacher says "go," the opponents start to make circles with their hands but never break the contact. They are in a meditative state, similar to moving through a tai chi form. They are feeling the changes in energy in their opponent as he moves and looking for weaknesses in the opponent's defense.

When one opponent senses an opening, he makes an explosive motion, either pulling his adversary forward or pushing him. The goal is to make one of his feet leave the ground. In Taiwanese competitions for twe so—they have regional and national competitions—you win simply by causing the opponent to move one foot or by causing him to fall down. For a casual observer, it seems to be a game of balance, but it is much, much more and represents the application of movements in a tai chi form. The fighters must be completely relaxed and just flow until that split second when an attack happens. The typical twe so defense is to simply go limp. Think about it: If an attacking opponent is pushing you and you go limp, your opponent's pushing energy may cause him to fall forward. The same is true if he is pulling you. The opponent expects you to resist, but with good tai chi training, you don't. You simply relax and allow your upper body to go with the push/pull and for that movement to make your opponent fall forward or backward.

Although it originated in China centuries ago, contemporary two-handed twe so has all but disappeared from the temples of Henan, which is the birthplace of kung fu. Taiwan is really the best place to see the art practiced as it once was. Because twe so is the fighting component of tai chi, many practitioners are old men. They use the finesse and technique of twe so to preserve their health and to win fights. Now that twe so has become a sport in the continental Asian Games, a good number of muscle-bound young people are diving into the sport with gusto, combining weight training and nutrition with their practice of the art. Twe so may be the saviour of native martial arts in Taiwan.

I watched in awe as opponents squared off in front of each other, executing their graceful fighting style. They crouched down in a very low type of horse stance. They both put up their hands and began making circles, fending off their opponent's attacks. The goal in twe so is to use no energy at all. Twe so would be classified as an internal martial art, one that utilizes chi or internal energy.

The opponents are completely relaxed, and at times their limbs dangle at their sides like a rag doll's, but at the moment of attack, their bodies become rigid as steel. In a split second, they push their opponent over and that's it. You win by knocking your opponent down.

The defense in twe so is to let your body go completely rubbery and limp so that your opponent's attack has nothing to push off of. By having nothing to push off of, the opponent's force keeps going forward and he actually winds up throwing himself to the ground.
The other way to use the defense is to redirect the opponent's energy and allow him to injure himself with his own power and weight. It's also very similar to what happens in *aikido* or Brazilian *jiu-jitsu*.

An old man asked if I wanted to spar. A senior student played referee, and said, "Go!" for us.

As soon as he did, one of the old man's hands turned into a steel pole and hit my shoulder, sending me spinning to the floor. At the time, I weighed 220 pounds and was a member of the official kung fu team in Kaohsiung. I had 25 years of experience in martial arts with numerous fights to my credit. Yet an old man kicked my butt without breaking a sweat. Twe so was definitely magic.

I got up and squared off in front of him again. This time his fingers became steel wire. They wrapped around my upper arm and jerked me down to the ground where I landed face first. I got up and faced him again. This time, I dropped as low as I could, and at the same time, I hit him with both hands in the midsection, spitting out all of the air from my lungs as I would if I were chopping a board or a brick with my hands. He fell backward and later complimented me on my skill. During the next hour, we must have gone 50 or more rounds. That was the only round that I won. Every time I tried to repeat my performance by lunging at him, I actually felt my own energy coming back and being used to attack me. At one point, my right hand hit me in the gut and knocked the air right out of me! The old man took me down with complicated moves, like wrestling or judo techniques with twists, turns and grapples. Other times, he just used one finger to push my shoulder or my chest where I was off-balance, and I would fall over.

When I got to school, I had bruises up and down my arms like when bullies used to beat me up in the fourth grade.

"What happened to you?" asked one of my teachers.

"I got beat up in the park on the way to school," I answered back in Chinese. (It was pretty good at this point.)

"Did they get your lunch money? You better find a new way to school."

"No, I mean an old man beat me up."

"Surely you won't go back again tomorrow."

"Of course I will," I said. Why wouldn't I?

The next day the twe so practitioners were glad to have me back. I don't think they believed that they would ever see me again. They were all willing to help me, but I wanted to wrestle the same old man again. I could not believe how strong he was. His whole body was one huge muscle. He was phenomenally strong under normal conditions, but at the split second of attack, he seemed two or three times stronger. Yet, with all of this muscle and power, if I tried to grab his arms, they went limp. If I pushed on his shoulder, it became jelly, and my own force took me down. He had told me that he was 68 years old.

One of the old man's fellow students came over to me and said, "Our teacher is here. You must ask him if you can train with us."

I turned around and there was this guy standing there who looked like Jesus and was wearing a flowing white robe.

The students' attitudes changed immediately to one of worship as they all fawned over him. The look on his face said that he expected people to fawn over him. There was a younger student, which for tai chi students means he was in his 30s, who followed him and did his every bidding.

I went up to the teacher and said, "I want to study twe so." Really, I thought this was a formality. I couldn't imagine that he would say no. He asked me if I spoke Taiwanese.

I said, "No, but I speak Chinese."

Now, many Westerners don't really understand Taiwan's situation, and it took me a few months to figure it out. In a nutshell, Taiwan is an island off the southeastern coast of China. Its official name is the Republic of China, and the Taiwanese consider themselves as separate from mainland communist People's Republic of China. However, mainland China disputes this claim, and this back-and-forth over the island's status has been a constant source of political turmoil since the mid-20th century. The official language of the island is Mandarin Chinese, but in the south, most people spoke Taiwanese, which is a different language. Generally, the elderly, the uneducated, traditionalists and some diehard pro-independent separatists tended to speak Taiwanese rather than Chinese. So it wasn't completely incomprehensible to me why the teacher gave me a look that said he had no desire to speak Chinese.

He spoke to me in Taiwanese, and his assistant translated it into Chinese for me.

"The master has no time today," said the student. "Good bye."

They turned their backs on me and walked away.

I looked around for all of the smiling people who had trained with me the day before, but they had slinked off to various corners of the training area to get away from me. Luckily, one brave woman made a helpful concession and handed me a business card. I didn't know what it was, but I took it with me. On the one hand, I was annoyed at what had just happened. On the other hand, if worshiping this guy was a requirement for learning twe so, I didn't want any part of it.

The next morning, at 6:30, I headed into town to look for the address on the card. One of the rough things about studying tai chi or twe so is that it apparently can't be done after eight in the morning. Climbing the stairs of the address, I felt some apprehension. What if this was one of those very-Chinese, very-spiritual places where I wouldn't feel comfortable? What if the teacher wanted me to scrub floors for six months to show my dedication? The first thing I saw when I walked in was two heavy bags and a pile of weights.

"I'm home," I said.

It looked like any other martial arts school I had ever been to, in the West. The instructor was not the old, annoying Jesus-guy I had met in the park but a young man, about 36 years old. He was about five feet tall but built like a power lifter. He reminded me of a retired drill sergeant or a high school football coach. The students didn't call him sifu, though . Instead, they called him *lau su*, which means "teacher."

He didn't speak English but at least he spoke Chinese. The first thing he asked me was if I had money, and this was something I could understand and deal with. "I like you," I said in English, once I was certain he didn't understand. (I guess you can leave the investment bank, but the investment bank never leaves the boy.)

Anyway, there was a huge, padded mat on the floor where most of the training took place. Just like in the park, there were people pushing hands. Most of the students were old men, but there was a

Antonio practices *twe so* with a training partner in Taiwan.

core of younger guys, probably about my age. The younger guys were built like linebackers. One of the heavy bags was extremely heavy—about 200 pounds. An old man who was about 70 years old stood in front of this humongous and heavy bag, pushing it with what seemed to be little or no energy at all. The heavy bag rocked back violently as if it had been kicked.

True to Taiwanese style, the uniform pants were traditional tai chi pants, but the shirt was a white T-shirt with the name of the school on it. After I had changed into the uniform, the lau su had me stand in a tai chi horse stance, and then he pushed down on my shoulders with all of his might. I was supposed to squat down and away from the force, twist, then come back up. He made me do about a hundred repetitions on each leg.

In my usual kung fu team in Kaohsiung, we threw over a thousand kicks per day. So, I am no stranger to muscle fatigue, but this exercise was sheer torture. I really felt tears welling up in my eyes. Later that night, my glutes were so sore that I felt like John Wayne after a day in the saddle. (Fortunately, I think the Chinese word for butt— *pigu*—is really cute. So, I enjoyed telling my coworkers, "My pigu really hurts.")

After pushing me down about 200 times, he had me push a heavy bag. The bag weighed at least as much as I did—it was possible that it weighed even more—because it was supposed to simulate pushing a man. So when you pushed it, it swung back, and part of the training was to not let it knock you down. The trick was to drop low and let your arms go limp when the bag or a potential opponent pushed at you, then you were to push him back as you recovered your stance. Of course, the bag won the first several rounds, but slowly, I was able to do it and not get knocked over. Finally, the lau su had me fight one of the older students who was less than five feet tall and very slim. He just beat the crap out of me. The next old man I fought reminded me of Popeye. His skin was ancient and wrinkled, but under his saggy skin there were rippling muscles that could destroy me. After he had thoroughly trounced me, he smiled and said, "I'm 70 years old."

"So am I," I responded. "So am I."

My schedule became really hectic at that point. I went to the tai chi school to learn twe so at about 5:45 in the morning. Then I went to Chinese school, followed by kung fu practice, followed by work. At night I dropped into bed, completely depleted but still dreaming of Shaolin.

While I really enjoyed practicing kung fu and improving my Chinese language skills, I really wanted to get some sparring practice in to keep up my fighting skills. So, I went out in search of a fight. That is how I found Kaohsiung's local fight club.

In a country with no NASCAR racing and tight gun control laws, how do men bond? The answer is simple: They get together every Wednesday night and pound the daylights out of each other at a fight club sponsored by a local kung fu club.

The school was lead by an Australian kung fu teacher named

Sebastian Thomas. He told me, "Before I came to Taiwan, I imagined I was going to live in a small fishing village and study kung fu with an old man under a tree. I would eventually marry his daughter and become the next generation, carrying on his legacy. Instead, because so many foreigners complained about not being able to find a good kung fu school, I opened one."

Thomas' school was called Mindful Phoenix Arts Group. The group taught classes in drama, kung fu, arts and language. They had a comedy troupe and performed comedy sports and traditional theater. Now, they were expanding their teaching to include classes for Taiwanese children, as well as adventure outings for Taiwanese young people. A surprising number of Taiwanese mothers had brought their children to learn kung fu from Thomas. Even when it came to martial arts, I guess the Taiwanese were outsourcing.

I got in the ring with a very large and scary-looking man named Mike, who weighed 242 pounds. Mike was a member of the Kaohsiung Brazilian jiu-jitsu club, one of the foreign-run martial-arts clubs in Taiwan. I held my own against him for a bit, but then he ran into me like a steamroller, knocking me to the ground. He jumped on top of me. When the ref managed to coax the big man off of my prostrate form, he explained, "We allow grappling in fight club."

"Of course," I gasped.

Taiwan, possessing a predominantly ethnic Chinese culture, has historically been very strong in kung fu, particularly in tai chi. In recent years, hard-style kung fu and *wushu* have lost their popularity while interest in the Taiwanese practice of twe so has remained flat. Only taekwondo is gaining; everything else is losing. As a result, the quality of fighters among ethnic Chinese in Taiwan has dropped off dramatically. Yes, Taiwan has earned recognition in international taekwondo competitions, with Taiwanese athletes displaying amazing agility with high kicks and leaps. But as Taiwan made the climb from developing nation to the ninth largest economy in the world, parents pushed their children to learn computers and business rather than fighting. The average Taiwanese kid gets home from school at 9:00 at night and then sits down to do hours and hours of homework. The martial arts among the young are dying.

Many foreigners, meaning Westerners, who live and work in Taiwan seem to be the people most focused on reviving and developing the martial arts. Thousands of English teachers are imported each year and given lucrative contracts, many of which include housing. They generally work only 25 hours per week. In their off-time, many have a desire to practice martial arts.

Thomas said, "Most of us were looking for that old guy who would teach us secret Asian martial arts."

"Did you find an old guy like that?" I asked.

"Yeah, but he just wanted to sell me knock-off electronics at bargain basement prices," Thomas said sadly.

"So, what did you do?"

"I bought a DVD player from him and saved 50 bucks. Then I opened my kung fu school."

The foreign teachers in Taiwan came from a variety of martial arts backgrounds. None of the members of the BJJ club was a certified instructor. They all worked from books and videos, meeting nearly every day to figure out and practice the techniques. In Taipei, another, more organized BJJ group pooled its cash and hired Andy Wang, of The Ultimate Fighter fame and a high ranking BJJ practitioner, to come to Taipei and work as the group's teacher.

Godfrey, a martial arts instructor from France who owns a Japanese martial arts school in Taipei, has now expanded his teaching curriculum to include kickboxing and grappling. Between the various clubs, all led by foreigners, they have managed to organize both a BJJ circuit and an MMA circuit in Taiwan. (In 2002, real fighting was still in its infancy in Taiwan, but the influx of foreigners had breathed new life into a sport that would otherwise have disappeared. (By 2008, pro MMA events featuring international and Taiwanese performers had become popular.)

In each class, among the heavyweight foreigners, some of whom weigh in at 220 pounds, you will always find a few Chinese students, both men and women. The martial arts began in Asia and spread to the West. Now it is being brought back to Taiwan, but it is being transformed and flavored by the many countries where it was temporarily stored.

Cable TV from Japan brings Taiwan all sorts of fighting sports, like the Ultimate Fighting Championship, King of the Cage, PRIDE, K-1, Pancrase, and RINGS. The Japanese, as much as they are mired in tradition, seem to have embraced the new developments in martial arts, and these shows have become big moneymakers. Sometimes, it seems as if Taiwan tends to follow Japan's lead. In this instance, hopefully Taiwan will make it onto the radar screens of international competition.

One of the interesting twists in the development of the martial arts in Taiwan is that foreigners have found new uses for old techniques. The BJJ guys at Phoenix and elsewhere in Taiwan were combining their submissions with the taekwondo kicks widely taught on the island. Many of the foreign martial artists had studied in Thailand, so they were teaching Thai head clinch throws, which were being taught alongside Chinese *sanda* (kickboxing) waist throws. Muay Thai elbows were being practiced on the ground, and tai chi and twe so pushes were being used in dirty boxing.

"Through twe so, you develop such a sensitivity to your opponent's balance," explained one New Yorker I met in Taiwan. "You just wait 'til his weight is right, and instead of punching, you push. Or when they reach for you, you go limp and let them pull themselves to the floor."

In one particular bout, I had a tough time because I was still primarily a boxer. Generally, I would try to close distance to neutralize Asian martial artists' kicks. Once inside, I would punch. But fighting a grappler was problematic because every time I got close enough to punch, he grabbed me and took me down. Once again, being a boxer, I was not used to hitting the canvas more than once per fight. Those body slams took a lot out of me. For the first time in my fighting history, my strategy was to stay as far away as possible from the bigger man, and kick him low.

In between bouts, I often got a chance to talk to Thomas. "What does fighting have to do with arts?" I asked.

"Mindful Phoenix is about teaching people and helping them to grow," Thomas said in his Aussie accent. "That includes teaching them acting, languages, creativity and martial arts. Fighting is part of martial arts. Besides, with no kangaroos to chase, what are men going to do in their off-time?"

Thomas said that the Phoenix fight club was open to women, and they would be welcome to come and fight. Unfortunately, although a few women came to watch, none participated. He also said that the door was open to nonmartial artists.

"We are all here for different reasons," he'd explain. He described how the BJJ team guys were looking for a chance to improve their striking skills, so that they could be more competitive in MMA fighting events. The kung fu guys were looking for an opportunity to challenge themselves and to use the techniques they had practiced in class.

"If someone who has no training wants to come in and try it out, he is more than welcome. But I would prefer he starts out by hitting the pads and moving around a bit first, before getting in the ring," Thomas would say. "What I would hope is that he might not be interested in martial arts when he gets here, but he would be interested in martial arts when he leaves."

The atmosphere of the fight club was definitely positive. Friendships were made very easily among athletes, but even more so among fighters. There is something about getting a fat lip or swollen nose from someone that binds you to your opponent for life. The fight club was never about hurting your partner. It was about helping him practice and get better. It was also, as Thomas believed, a way of teaching martial artists self-confidence. He'd say, "It doesn't help anyone to get in there and get hurt."

I remained in Taiwan for a total of 16 months before I went to the Shaolin Temple. At the end of about 13 months, I severely injured my knee while sparring. The doctors assured me I would never walk right again and would never play sports and definitely not kung fu. I went for treatments of acupuncture and traditional medicine. I made poultices of smelly substances. I sat for hours in my bathroom, bathing the knee in hot water. I wrapped it in bandages and fitted it with braces and slowly began walking across my room. Eventually I could kick very low and slowly with the injured leg. However, I couldn't kick with the good leg at all because that meant putting all my weight on the injured leg.

When I left for Shaolin Temple I could barely stand unassisted and I couldn't carry my own luggage down the stairs to the taxi. Any normal person would have postponed going to the Temple, but I had waited 34 years for that moment. I wasn't about to cancel.

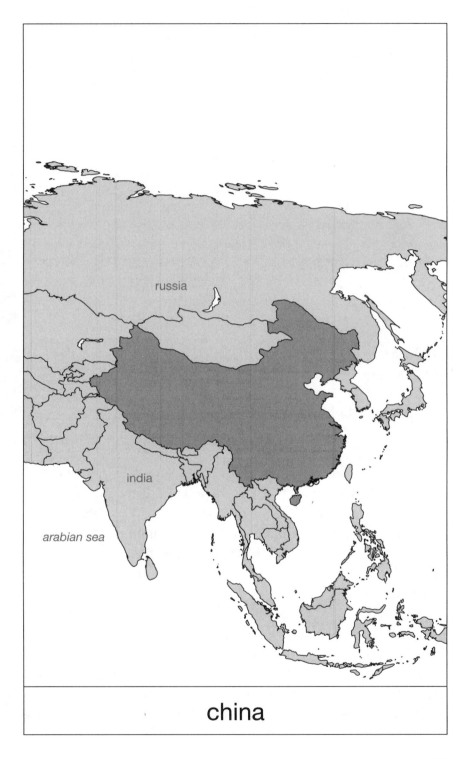

china

chapter 2

"A Shaolin priest can walk through walls. Looked for, he cannot be seen. Felt, he cannot be touched. This rice paper is the test, clean as the cocoon of the silk worm, fragile as the wings of the dragon fly. When you can walk its length and leave no trace, you will have learned."
—*Kung Fu*, the original TV series

MY MOTHER DIED WHEN I WAS A BABY, and as a consequence, I was raised by my maternal grandmother in New York City. My grandmother was easily the toughest person I had ever known. She taught me early on that brains were more important than brawn. She encouraged me to read, learn languages, make up stories and pursue public speaking. She always told me to stand up to anyone and demand my rights.

One day, when I was about six years old, my grandmother was very upset. She told me someone very important had died, but as a child, I didn't understand who Bruce Lee was. Later, she took me to an all-day film festival that commemorated him; it was four full-length feature films, two documentaries, and at least two low-budget Hong Kong movies where Bruce Lee was played by a cardboard cut-out.

I was on the edge of my seat the whole time. Never had I seen or even imagined that people could jump and kick like that.

"EEEEEiiiiiiaaaa!" Even the language of the Bruce Lee films appealed to me. And best of all, I knew that if I could learn all of those special kung fu skills, I wouldn't have to back down to the bullies on the playground.

Shortly after, my uncle introduced me to the TV show *Kung Fu* with David Carradine, and this became my new religion.

So it was and is that, like every other martial artist of my generation, I had dreamed of studying kung fu at the Shaolin Temple. While no one dreams of studying kung fu at a strip mall, this is the reality for what many of us do.

My first and most important martial arts teacher, H. David Collins, talked constantly about the Shaolin Temple and the wisdom that originated there. The Temple seemed as if it were some nirvana that we could never attain.

When I was going to school in Germany, I saw a documentary about a 14-year-old German boy who was the first foreign child to study at the Shaolin Temple. According to the film, his parents flew with him to China, took a train to Henan, and more or less dumped him on the Temple's doorstep.

That documentary changed my life because suddenly I realized studying at the Temple was a real possibility.

Planes are magic. I woke up on the morning of March 3, 2003 in modern Taiwan. Later that same day, I disembarked from a plane in Zhengzhou, the capital of Henan Province of The People's Republic of China. At the airport it was already clear that I'd traveled over more than just distance. That plane had taken me across a cultural divide that was larger than the biggest ocean. Where Taiwan was rich, modern and free, Zhengzhou was, well, Zhengzhou. The airport was devoid of restaurants and gift shops and instead it was full of angry-looking men and women in scary uniforms. The city just disappeared into a very rural countryside. In fact, that is exactly what I was heading toward. The Shaolin Temple was in that undiscovered country.

Outside, I got into the taxi—there was only one—and asked the taxi driver to take me to Dengfeng, which is the village closest to the Shaolin Temple. We negotiated a price of 300 RMB or about $15 USD. It would be at least a three-hour drive without detours, but of course, there would be detours.

I stared out the window of the taxi and took in the sights of the rural Chinese countryside. For hours, I saw nothing but primitive mud-and-brick houses and people toiling in fields. A horse-drawn wagon went by with four poorly dressed passengers. Early March was pretty cold in this northern part of China, and you could see your breath on the window. The taxi had no heat. The frozen landscape outside looked like every image I had ever had of communism. If I hadn't been a die-hard fan of capitalism and democracy before arriving in China, I definitely was before I left.

The taxi driver asked me why I was in China and I told him that I wanted to study kung fu. It was a good thing that I could speak Mandarin because I wouldn't meet one Chinese person who spoke English for the next three months.

"My brother is a kung fu teacher. Let's go get him," the taxi driver volunteered. This response in Asia is pretty common because you have to know someone to get anything done. Or at the very least, you need to know someone who might know someone.

Against my protestations, we drove an hour out of the way of Dengfeng to pick up the cabbie's brother, who was hanging around a training field at an outdoor sports facility. The brother had two other friends who were kung fu teachers, and they wanted to come with us, too. Our twosome became a fivesome, and we pressed on. When I saw healthy-looking boys limping, I knew we were close to the Temple. Seeing the injured practitioners also reminded me of my kung fu team back in Taiwan. The Kaohsiung team had some of the most gifted athletes I had ever seen, but they were always injured.

As we drove through Dengfeng, I could not believe how many

kung fu schools there were. I learned later that there were nearly 40,000 kung fu students living at about 65 schools. At the time, Dengfeng was a small, dusty village with about eight square blocks of shops and restaurants. A few of the 65 schools were located in the town while most were located outside. The government would eventually knock them all down. The surrounding area was all farmland with no development. To get to the Temple from Dengfeng, you took a bus or taxi, which took about 30 minutes.

All along, I had been planning to attend a Shaolin wushu school that I had discovered on the Internet. (Wushu is a demonstration style of kung fu with high leaps, low stances and lots of jumping and shouting. It's the impressive style that Jet Li mastered prior to his stardom.) The main reason I had chosen the school was because it was the only school with a Web site that seemed legitimate, was mostly populated with Chinese students and had reasonable prices.

Around 8:00 p.m., we passed a massive kung fu statue that I had often seen in documentaries about Shaolin. A few minutes later, we arrived at the Temple's tall, medieval walls. We were at the Shaolin Temple, it was the realization of a lifetime worth of dreaming.

The Temple itself consists of a high, medieval-style stone wall with a gate. Behind the wall, the Temple is a huge complex of individual temples, stupa, stone statues and carvings, a bell tower and living quarters for the monks. There is also a performance area for the Shaolin shows that are held several times a day for tourists. (A larger version of the show tours the world, playing in New York, London and other major cities.)

The Da Mo statue that I'd often seen in documentaries is high up on Song Shan Mountain. It is a depiction of the Indian monk Bodhidharma who invented kung fu and developed it at the Temple. He is the patron saint of kung fu, and legend says that he meditated in a cave on Song Shan Mountain for several years, thus developing kung fu while watching animals. His meditating statue overlooks the Temple so you can see him when training or walking about the grounds.

Most of the walkways are paved with flat stone bricks, and nothing is heated. One of my coldest experiences was eating breakfast in the monks' huge cafeteria. It was so cold you could see your breath. There was also a parking lot out front where tour buses come on a daily basis bringing Chinese and foreign visitors to look at the famous complex.

The taxi driver leaned out his window and spoke with the ghostly figure of a cloaked monk. A few minutes later, the gates opened, and we drove inside. It looked exactly like it did in movies. I kept expecting David Carradine as Kwai Chang Caine to come walking around the corner. The monks, wearing brown-hooded robes over gray tops and bottoms, looked like they came right out of a scene from the 1986 monastery-set film *The Name of the Rose* (1986).

Our new ghostly-cloaked monk friend took us to his room. Some older monks joined us. With long gray beards and shaved heads, they looked like ZZ Top's Hare Krishna cousins. They asked me millions of questions about Taiwan and the United States. I steered clear of the Taiwan independence issue as much as I could. They also wanted to see my boxing and my taekwondo skills. It amazed me that even at the Shaolin Temple they thought boxing was such an interesting and exotic sport. In Chinese, they often refer to boxing as "American kung fu." They particularly enjoyed seeing my signature feat, which is throwing 180 punches in one minute. I remember reading somewhere that Bruce Lee could do more than double that number.

It was getting late, and we were all hungry, so the first monk took us all out for dinner. I thought monks were supposed to take a vow of poverty but when the bill came, he dug around inside of his clothes and pulled out a wad of cash to pay the bill without batting an eye. I made a mental note to teach him how to play cards later.

One of the many Chinese specialties on the menu was dog meat. Monks are vegetarians so they didn't have to eat any of Old Yeller. I ate some, just to be one of the guys and as a sort of nonspecific revenge for the existence of French poodles. It wasn't bad. It tasted like any other meat except a little gamier than manatee and a bit greasier than koala or panda.

When we went back to the Temple, it was very late. One of the taxi driver's friends, a former student at the Shaolin Temple, took me outside the monks' quarters and handed me a Buddhist prayer book.

He told me to put $200 USD inside the book, go back inside the quarters to see a specific monk, prostrate myself three times before the monk and give him the book.

"If you do that, you will be in," the friend said.

In? Did he mean I could study at the Shaolin Temple? I had been planning to study at one of the commercial schools in the village, but studying at the actual Shaolin Temple was beyond my wildest dreams. But what was this issue with the money? Was this a case of our-philosophies-are-Eastern-but-our-payment-methods-are-Western mind-set I often came across? I just had to put money in a book and hand it to the monk? Yeah, right.

This is one of the oldest scams in the world. The scammer will get you to put money in the book, then he'll switch books, causing you to lose your money.

The taxi driver's friend was getting impatient. He kept up a constant barrage of fast Chinese, explaining and re-explaining what he wanted me to do—as if the issue were that I didn't understand. I understood just fine. I just didn't want to do what he was asking me.

In between explanations, he was alternately pushing my shoulder, and throwing kicks in the air. Whether that was to intimidate me or not, I have no idea, but it made me uneasy because I was certain that one of those kicks could have broken my leg. He was standing close enough for me to knock him out with a punch. But then what? If I hit him, I probably wouldn't get to study at the Shaolin Temple. The others would still rob me, and I would lose my money anyway.

Suddenly I found myself in one of those situations only I can find myself in. I was in mainland China. I wasn't registered with the U.S. Embassy. I wasn't at the school I had told my family and friends I was going to. Nobody knew where I was. I had no friends. These guys could have killed me, and no one would have asked about the body. In the United States or Taiwan, I always got a little tough with people when I didn't get my way. I knew that if worse came to worst, I could fight my way out of most rooms, but here I would be fighting my way out of a room full of kung fu monks. If you had made a quick call to Atlantic City, bookmakers would have told you that they were giving 5,000-to-1 odds against my survival.

I did as he told me and put the money in the book, but as a compromise, I made sure to keep control of it. If I was going to pay a bribe to get into the Shaolin Temple, I at least wanted the bribe to get to the right person. If bribing a holy man was like God's payola, I wanted to make sure he, like Caesar, got every penny I rendered unto him. In a very ham-handed and laughable way, the guy tried to pull the old switcheroo.

"Give me the book," he said, kneeling down. "I will show you how to hand it to the monk."

If he tried running a scam this stupid in New York City, he'd be left under the boardwalk somewhere with his pockets turned inside out. So once my money was inside that book, he'd have had to use a crowbar to get that book out of my hands. With apparent resignation in his face, he led me back into the monk's quarters, and just before I went inside, he tried to grab the book out of my hands again.

God! Had this guy never heard of Brooklyn? I thought. I handed him my diary instead. I went in, prostrated three times, and gave the book of money to the monk.

The monk nodded approvingly. I saw him exchange a look with the one who had taken me outside. Had they prearranged to steal my money? The other passengers and the driver all stared at the friend questioningly. I guess everyone had been promised a share for their trouble.

"What is your religion?" the monk asked.

"Catholic," I answered.

"To be a monk, you have to be Buddhist," he explained.

"No problem," I said. I wasn't looking to convert. I considered this more like an advanced field experiment in theology anyway. I mean, how was it any different then when I went to temple to see the bar mitzvah of my friend's little brother? It'd also been so long since I'd attended church that Father Fredo would have just shook his head and said, "At least he's attending services."

"Wait here," the monk said. He went outside and whacked up my bribe money with the taxi driver and his friends.

Before they left, the taxi driver had the balls to come and ask me to pay the fare. "Why don't you just take it out of your commission?" I wanted to ask him. But I had become a monk, so I wasn't able to feel anger at anyone anymore, not even some jerk-face moron who tried to steal my money. I felt pity instead.

After everyone had gone, the monk returned and said. "Put your things here." Apparently I would be sharing the room with him and his novice monk. The novice and I hit it off right away. He was 25 years old and a good guy. Also, in the couple of hours I had been there, he hadn't tried to steal from me. I knew we were going to be friends.

It is freaking cold in China in March, and there is no heat in the Temple. I would later find out that even homes are not heated. The monks live in relative squalor. The chambers were generally just tiny, concrete rooms, about twice the size of a "deluxe suite" at Attica with absolutely nothing in them apart from a bed and a desk. Fortunately, the room I stayed in with the two monks had three beds.

While in China, I noticed that the standards of hygiene and sanitation are different to what we're used to in the West. The Temple grounds, at least the part where the monks lived, were strewn with refuse. Unlike in Taiwan and the rest of Asia, you don't take off your shoes when entering a room in China because everyone clears their throats to constantly hawk and spit on the floor. The room the monks slept in was no exception. The floor was always covered with slimy lung goo.

The only things the monks seemed to own, apart from my $200, were the clothes on their backs. The masters—actual monk-teachers—lived inside the Temple while, for the most part, students lived outside it. Some monk-teachers, like the two different ones I would train with, had a handful of special students come to the Temple and train in sight of their quarters. Otherwise, most students trained outside at the schools or dormitories where they lived. The monk-teachers would visit these locations to occasionally oversee training, which was run by a designated jiao-lien, which is a title for instructor. (It translates literally to "teach practice.") Many of the jiao-lien had graduated from the program in the Temple. It is unclear if there is a complete, codified program, but when students left, they were given a certificate. I believe certain students took some kind of competitive test to be awarded a ranking. These higher ranked students could then look forward to better jobs, whether in the Temple, government or elsewhere.

The novice led me through a labyrinth of outdoor alleyways to the communal toilet. There was no electricity, and in addition to being ice-cold, the night was pitch dark. The toilet was just a hole in the ground, overflowing with human waste. There wasn't even a privacy screen or anything, so everyone could see you poop.

We returned to the room where the monk and novice shared their hot water with me. I would learn later that hot water was a rare commodity. The novice would carry a single, one-liter thermos jug to the kitchen every morning at 5:30 and fill it with boiling water. That was the hot water ration for the two of them for the day.

I put on thermals, sweats, thick woolen socks and my Navy watch cap. I crawled into bed, which was really more of a wooden platform, and wrapped up in the blankets they had given me—one over and one under me.

"Tomorrow you will have your head shaved. Then we will begin," the monk said.

Considering that was just my first day at Shaolin Temple, you can imagine why my first two-and-a-half days there felt like years.

It was incredible. I was actually sleeping inside of the Shaolin Temple, in the monks' quarters. I had read online that about 200 foreigners study at the schools around Shaolin annually. Almost none are ever admitted to study at the Temple itself and absolutely none are allowed to sleep there. During my stay at Shaolin, I would eventually meet

Antonio (second to the right) poses with his fellow classmates at the Shaolin Temple.

the only ordained foreign monk, a Mexican named Rafael, who had been at Shaolin for years. Even though he could come and go as he pleased and was well-respected by many of the monks, he was not permitted to sleep inside because of his foreignness—it wasn't yet universally accepted. In contrast, I was permitted to sleep inside because I had effectively paid a bribe.

I trained with the sifu I bribed for two days. (In the West, people understand "sifu" to mean kung fu teacher, but it's actually a term reserved for monks. In Chinese society, any monk, particularly one who is a teacher or advisor, can be called sifu. This has no connection to kung fu.) After two days, he came to me and asked if I was happy with my training so far. I was thrilled.

"How long do you wish to stay?" he asked.

"One year," I said.

"That will be $5,000 U.S.," he told me flatly.

Was this including the $200 USD he'd already stolen from me? I wondered.

The average income in China is about $26 USD a month. Chinese students living at the temple schools pay something like $38 USD a month, including food. Was there any way that I was paying this clown several years' worth of income? I said,-"No way!"

The monk sent me to lunch with the young novice. When we came back, I was told to report to another monk named Shi Hung Fu, who agreed to accept me as a student for a fee of $200 USD per month.

His student, Miao Hai, took me to my new lodgings outside of the Temple. Miao Hai would eventually become my best friend at Shaolin. He and our other training brother Miao Ping would report daily to the Temple for at least half our training. The other half would be near our accommodations.

At the Shaolin Temple training field, students were divided into four groups, each with an instructor. There were two groups of little kids, one of advanced students, and one composed completely of older boys who were part of the sanda (Chinese kickboxing) team. Students generally wore colored tracksuits with the Shaolin name written in English and Chinese characters on them. Monks wore the gray wraparound shirts and trousers I mentioned earlier, and their brown robes in colder weather. The orange robes that many Westerns have seen, students wore during demonstrations. Otherwise, they didn't wear them. Students also sometimes wore gray wraparound outfits inside the Temple's halls when performing religious duties, such as ringing the gong, lighting incense and collecting donations. Everyone's head was shaved, even mine.

As proud as I was to wear a Shaolin uniform after a lifetime of martial arts training, it was little protection from the biting cold. I would wear four layers of T-shirts, thermals and sweatshirts under my tracksuit. Of course, all the hard training caused all the layers to get soaked in sweat. When we stopped to eat, the wet clothing would make me colder. I tried various experiments, like taking off and putting on layers of clothing, but somehow, it just never worked. Most of us students also wore a thick, woolen cap to protect our bald heads from the frigid wind. But they still got chapped, and at the end of the day, huge chunks of scalp snowed down on us like soap flakes.

Before each training session, we stood in military formation to count off. Although my Chinese was good, I would usually miss the count. It would go something like this " … 14, 15, 16 … " Then, when it got to me, I would say "35" or something equally as wrong instead. Despite my time at the foreign language school in Taiwan, I apparently hadn't learned the words for left and right either. So, when the jiao-lien called for students to drill or march, I'd inevitably turn the wrong way, destroying the formation and bumping into my friends. If the sifu wasn't there, we all got a huge laugh out of it. If he were prowling around, my training brother Miao Hai would lower his voice and do the count for me. At the command "left face" or "right face," he would tap me on the appropriate shoulder so I would also know which way to turn.

I had been assigned two training brothers, Miao Hai and Miao Ping. Training brother or *lien sen di*, means a person who trains under the same master as you. When you finish your training, you receive a book or certificate that names your master. Anyone who has that same master is considered your lien sen di, but the Chinese also use "training brother" to mean a student of your master to whom you are extremely close. And this definitely happens when you train; you can see these people 24/7 over a period of years. For most of the young guys, they had spent more of their lives with their training brothers than with their real families. It's an important distinction to call your fellow practitioners "brothers." It is supposed to be a lifelong bond.

Miao Hai was 21 years old and had been living in temples since he was 15. He loved kung fu but was ambivalent, at best, about Buddhism. A master of going through the motions, he taught me how to light the incense and do prostrations without thinking. In the evenings, when we had eight hours of training behind us, he would ask me to teach him boxing. We'd also go round after round of sanda, fighting bare knuckled out in the training field.

Miao Ping, on the other hand, was a devout Buddhist. He

was 24 years old and one of the only students who could read and write Chinese well. Any time the boys needed to write a letter, they would ask Miao Ping to do it for them. Where Miao Hai was a purely physical being, my relationship with Miao Ping was more intellectual. We would have long debates about religion and even about the Chinese government. At times, he surprised me with his candor, admitting the failings of the Chinese system. At other times, he frightened me by repeating, without a moment's hesitation, what the party had instructed him to think.

Training was difficult. After a week I was still passing out right after dinner. Some nights I didn't even make it through my evening meal before collapsing. The fields I practiced in—one at the Temple for special students and the other near the house where I lived— were cold, barren and windswept. Flurries of snow still hung in the air as we practiced on the frozen, muddy ground. We were up at 5:00 in the morning. At 10 a.m., we still had two hours to go. And I wouldn't have had any coffee yet. Actually, I hadn't had any coffee since arriving at the Shaolin Temple two weeks earlier.

In place of my warm brew, I kept warm by practicing *u bu chuan*, the five-step form, over and over again for hours.

Every day for the previous two weeks, I had practiced a single kung fu form, u bu chuan, the five-step form, over and over again, for hours. My thighs were so sore from constantly squatting in horse stance that I often thought I would cry. The five-step form goes something like this: From horse stance, I had to balance on my toes and press up with one foot in the air; the up-in-the-air knee was against my chest, and both my arms were up and over my head. Next, I had to drop low, meaning my up-in-the-air knee was now down on the ground, into u bu stance; my head was not supposed to be higher than the instructor's waist. It was sheer torture. My muscles screamed.

To keep my mind busy during the interminable hours of repetition, I would try to calculate how many times I did the form in a single day. It took roughly three minutes to get through the form. That meant 23 forms per hour. If I practiced 8 hours per day, then

I did u bu chuan 160 times per day.

U bu chuan wasn't our only exercise. At the beginning of each training session, and there were three sessions per day, we did a common Shaolin routine of kicks. In this exercise, you stand like a tightrope walker and hold your arms straight out to your sides. Then you kick across the field with the intent of keeping your kicks as straight and long as possible. There are several ways to do the kicks. The first is straight up to your nose. The second is in an inward semicircle, which hits the opposite hand. The third is the same as the second, except the kick goes in an outward semicircle, and the right foot hits the right hand while the left foot hits the left hand.

The final step is where you set your hands over your head and kick them with straight, overhead kicks. You do a million reps of each—right foot, left foot, right foot, left foot, etc. When you hit one end of the field, you turn around and come back, kicking on the orders of the jiao-lien, who might make you do that for an hour.

To take my mind off of the pain, I would try to calculate how many kicks we did in a day. First, we'd get in line at double arm intervals from one another. At the command of "*Zo,*" we'd make our way, approximately 65 feet across the training field while literally throwing a front kick over our heads. At the far end of the field, we'd turn around and kick our way back. After we had made five round trips, we'd do the identical exercise, but with a round kick to the left side followed by a round kick to the right side. If each kick brought you 3 feet closer to the far end of the field, then it must have taken 20 kicks to cross the field. Twenty kicks each way—that's 40 kicks! Multiply that by five trips times three kinds of kicks. That was 600 kicks. If I multiply that by three sessions per day, plus all of the different kinds of kicking forms we did in one day … well, it was a lot of kicks.

Occasionally, after doing u bu chuan for too long, I would just pop out of position to curse.

"Make up your mind!" I shouted at a jiao-lien.

"If you want me up on one foot, then that's fine. You want me down on the ground? That's OK too. You want me kicking? Great.

But no more of this constant up and down! I'm getting motion sickness, already."

The instructors were all young jiao-lien who had graduated from the ranks of the students. They tended to be about 19 years old on average. Most had very little knowledge of the outside world. Once they became instructors, their lives didn't change much. They continued to live in Dengfeng Feng in barrack-style dormitories and keep the same schedule as the students. They were as up-for-a-laugh as any of my other Chinese friends. When I would lose my cool and start dancing around, cursing and complaining, they would usually crack up.

Being the only foreigner in the Shaolin Temple school, I was generally the source of much amusement. The students ranged in age from 6 to 24. They loved to see me struggling, at age 36, with kung fu positions they found so easy to do. They also got a kick out of watching me shave in the morning, thinking it was an exotic display of foreign culture.

If I really wanted to make them laugh, all I had to do was start writing in my diary. They found it inconceivable that anyone could write so many English words.

Normally, the jiao-lien would let me decide when I needed a break, but when a sifu was there, the mood changed to one of serious intensity. The sifu would march out onto the training field in his heavy robes and tall fur hat and begin shouting orders and making corrections. He carried a three-foot long cane with him and would beat anyone mercilessly who he found making even the slightest mistake.

My face and hands were often completely numb from windburn. Many of the students had open, festering wounds on their ears from prolonged exposure to the cold. The arctic-like air burned deep in my lungs, making me feel like a chain smoker. Once, I stopped for literally two seconds to catch my breath. A sifu saw me and began screaming.

"*NII, LIEN GONG!*" he said. You, practice!

It could be because I looked so different from everyone else that he was able to pick me out of a sea of 70 students. As a foreigner, it is hard to get away with anything in China. You don't exactly blend into the crowd.

A *sifu* teaches Antonio kung fu at the Shaolin Temple.

During my three-month stay at the Shaolin Temple, two significant pieces of government legislation occurred that would greatly affect the future of kung fu in China and around the world.

The first was that the entire Shaolin Temple village was to be vacated. Every building, with the exception of the Temple itself, was emptied of its inhabitants. Then the whole town was razed to make way for new construction. This forced all of the schools to move further away from the temple. Most of them, of course, chose to move to Dengfeng village so they would still be as close as possible to the Temple.

The second case was definitely a landmark one because the government allowed the name "Shaolin" to be put under trademark and copyright protection.

In one of my meetings with the foreign monk Rafael, he explained that the Temple administration won a court case and obtained the right to trademark the term "Shaolin." Now only schools and businesses endorsed by the Shaolin Temple could bear the term "Shaolin." The hope was that it would reduce the number of fake schools and false Shaolin Temples. As I understand the legalities, only the original Shaolin Temple near Dengfeng and the Southern Shaolin Temple in Fujian province are permitted to use the Shaolin name. There is, however, an artificial temple—currently named Northern Shaolin Temple—that, as far as I know, has no connection whatsoever with the original Shaolin Temple. This is a temple, which I believe is owned by the Chinese government and only admits foreign students. At Northern Shaolin Temple, kung fu is taught in English for $500 USD a month. This Northern Shaolin Temple is the only school that has a strong presence on the Internet. It will be interesting to see if this one, too, will be required to change its name.

Rafael also let me in on a few other things.

For example, when I told him about paying a $200 USD bribe my first day, he said, "Historically, Shaolin Temple has always been a den of bandits, thieves and revolutionaries. Why do you think the government burned it to the ground so many times?"

For a guy who had grown up watching David Carradine play the philanthropic Caine in the TV series *Kung Fu* (1972-1975), this was pretty heartbreaking. People had warned me that the Temple was a phony that was only established to steal money through the Shaolin name. After having lived there for three months, I have to say that I found the monks definitely fixated on money.

Although I was angry about being taken advantage of, my time at the Temple was a singular experience, which few Westerners would ever have. Authentic or not, I did practice kung fu for eight hours a day. I lost weight, got into shape, increased my flexibility, improved my Chinese and made a lot of new friends, which were the reasons I had gone to the Temple in the first place. I found everything I was looking for. As for the money that was stolen from me, it totaled less than $500 USD dollars—even my second sifu Shi Hung Fu was not above reproach.

Although $500 USD may seem like a lot, the difference in price between studying at one of the many schools which cater to foreign students, versus studying a completely Chinese program, as I had, would have been about $1,500. So, even including the cost of the theft, I came out ahead, financially.

The most common questions people ask me are, "Would you do it again?" and "Would you recommend the Shaolin Temple to others?" The answer to both of those is "yes." I have plans to go back to one of the larger schools in Dengfeng to study sanda exclusively. As for recommending the Temple, a foreigner could have a very rewarding experience there as long as he understands what he's walking into.

For a foreigner looking to study in Dengfeng, the options included programs as short as one week where you would literally live in a hotel, eat fine food and commute to an English-speaking teacher each day. In this scenario, your training partners would most likely be German, American or Canadian. These programs could cost hundreds of dollars for a day.

The cheapest option is to do what I did: Walk into the Shaolin Temple and ask to be accepted as a student. I negotiated $200 per month for room, board and tuition. I slept on a wooden plank in an unheated concrete dormitory with no running water. The only toilet was an open trench in front of the building. The food was practically inedible. When I left the Temple, I hadn't had a shower in five weeks. The experience was hard. But when I left, I knew I had had an authentic experience.

After my book about my stay at the Shaolin Temple came out, a lot of people from all over the world wrote to ask how they could study there. Here's some general advice:

• **Learn Chinese.** I have trained all over Asia in places where I didn't speak the language. Not only does this hinder your learning, but if you lived at the Shaolin Temple for a few months, you would go insane being unable to talk to people. Also, don't kid yourself that you will just "pick up" Chinese. Chinese is one of the hardest languages in the world. You'll need to study up. Trust me.

• **Go to Taiwan. Get a Job. Save Money.** Taiwan is a brilliant place to start your journey to China. It is different enough from America that it will seem like a big adventure, but not so different that it will crush you with culture shock. If you get homesick in Taiwan, you can hang out with the more than 60,000 other American expats. When you need some familiar food, you can go to McDonald's or Starbucks. It's also easier for Americans to get a visa to go to Taiwan than to China.

If you have a college degree, get a job teaching English in Taiwan. You'll find listings and applications online at ESL mainstays like Dave's ESL Cafe. Teaching jobs in Taiwan usually pay about $1,800 USD a month, and many of those jobs include an apartment and a contract bonus equivalent to one month's salary. The job even reimburses you for your plane ticket, usually. Most foreigners will find that they can save 50 percent of their salaries in Taiwan, and that means you can save up much better for Shaolin than you can at home. The job will probably only fill about 25 to 30 hours of your week. You'll still have plenty of time to study Chinese or learn kung fu. (Note: Some jobs require an ESL certificate, but you can earn that through an online course rather cheaply.)

• **Prepare for Culture Shock.** Living conditions at the Dengfeng Shaolin Temple are terrible. It is dirty, smelly and the food is bad. This is the cost of getting great kung fu training. Living in Taiwan first will help you acclimate to the Chinese culture and, of course, prepare your language skills. Also, studying kung fu in Taiwan will give you an idea of what to expect when you get to China.

• **Get There.** The Chinese government is constantly changing visa regulations. When I studied at the Shaolin Temple, you could get a three-month tourist visa and renew it twice without leaving China. Last year the best visa you could get was only one month. Don't worry too much about visa rules. The travel agent will know the latest information and can help you. You will enter China on a tourist visa. Once you get to the temple, if you want to stay longer, the temple can help you get a six-month or one-year student visa.

• **Find the Temple.** The actual Shaolin Temple is near Dengfeng village, in Henan province of China. (Don't confuse this with Yunnan province. People often do.)

There are about 60 monks at the temple. A good number of them are primarily religious monks, but they have all studied kung fu and Buddhism. The kung fu monks often are associated with schools of students living outside of the Temple. When I studied at Shaolin Temple in 2003, there were nearly 25,000 kung fu students at 65 schools around Dengfeng. Many of those schools have been forcibly evicted because of the legislation I mentioned earlier. They have reopened but are no longer within walking distance of the Temple.

Be careful! The Shaolin Temple in Henan has always been called The Shaolin Temple, and it is the one you have heard about and seen in movies. The Southern Shaolin Temple in Fujian province was reopened around 2007. Now that there is a Southern Shaolin Temple again, some people refer to the original Temple in Dengfeng as The Northern Shaolin Temple. The problem with this is that the Chinese government also opened a faux temple in Northern China, which charges about $600 USD a month and only caters to foreign students. The official name of the fake temple is The Northern Shaolin Temple. The Northern Shaolin Temple has a Web site and even accepts reservations by e-mail. So, if you are doing research, be sure to look only at the Shaolin Temple in Dengfeng, Henan.

• **Find a School. Pay a Reasonable Fee.** China is still a developing country where English and computer literacy are not commonly found. So, if you find a Web site written in English, it probably isn't advertising an authentic experience. The programs advertised online are designed for foreigners. They cost a lot of money. Many of them have students living in three-star hotels and training only two or four hours a day. If you want a real experience, go to Dengfeng on your own. Get a taxi driver to take you to a number of schools and choose one that appeals to you.

The programs advertised online are expensive. Some charge $40 USD a day. I met a foreigner who paid $1,500 USD for a week. I paid $200 USD a month, including food, room and training. The average monthly salary in China is about $40 USD a month. Chinese students pay about this much per month to study at the Temple schools. So, there is no reason why you should pay as much per day as they pay per month. Stick to your guns, be firm and negotiate. Don't overpay.

If you are planning to stay several months, only pay monthly. Don't hand someone thousands of dollars the first day. Negotiate as if you were staying six months, then just pay each month.

• **Be Aware of Training and Living Conditions.** Conditions and training will vary from school to school. Most schools were focused on wushu because of the 2008 Summer Olympics in Beijing. There are schools that also focus on tai chi, sanda and other Chinese arts. Larger schools even have taekwondo and kickboxing classes. Some schools go to competitions outside of the temple. I didn't see any judo practice but I wouldn't be surprised to learn that they had judo programs, especially because many students come to Shaolin dreaming of the Olympics.

As a rule, you can expect to sleep in a military-style dorm. In some schools, they have as many as 30 students in bunk beds, sharing a room. Since there is no running water and most students only have two uniforms, you can imagine what it smells like. In winter, it is bloody cold in Henan, and buildings are not heated at all. And of course, you will be training outdoors. There is nothing worse than training in the bitter cold, sweating up your clothes, freezing your face and hands and then coming inside and discovering you are too wet and cold to sleep.

You will be woken up by a whistle at around 5 a.m. You will fall out into a formation and count off. Next, you will go running. After running, you will have a training session, which will focus primarily on stretching but will also include some exercises.

You will eat breakfast around 7 a.m. and train until lunch. Breakfast will probably be *shi fan* (rice water) and maybe parched shredded potatoes. (You know when you use a carrot scraper? How the carrot comes off in paper-thin streamers? That's what the cooks do to the entire potato. Then they dump boiling water over it and serve it over rice.) Semi-cooked, dirty potatoes and rice is about as pleasant and nutritious as you might expect. If you're lucky, you might also get bread rolls called *manto* and rice. Don't expect tea in China. In rural, poorer areas like Dengfeng, you will drink boiled water.

After breakfast, you'll participate in morning training, which consists of kata-like forms or kung fu techniques. They will most likely include another session of exercises and stretching.
Lunch will be rice and parched shredded potatoes.

After lunch, you will sleep for about two hours. When you wake, you will do kung fu until dinner. After dinner there is another training session of one or two hours. Lights out is at 9:00 p.m.

So what do you get out of the experience? Many people criticize the modern Shaolin Temple because they say it teaches a watered-down and artificial version of the classical arts. This may or may not be true. I don't really care.

What you will get out of your trip is a phenomenal cultural experience that you'll never get anywhere else. Aside from the fact that you're fulfilling a childhood dream, you will be completely immersed in a foreign culture and language. Even teaching ESL in Taiwan isn't the same because you will be playing a role that is not naturally part of Chinese society. But in Shaolin, you are a Shaolin student. That is very Chinese. In fact, you'll be having a Chinese experience that most Chinese people never have.

As for training, many people assume that I was disappointed by the fight training at the Temple. This is true—the monks aren't fighters, and because I am a fighter, I had to go elsewhere for real fight training. However, the Shaolin Temple is pretty much the only place in my experience where you can get 8 to 10 hours of training per day 7 days a week. Compared to "intense" Western schools, one day of Shaolin training is equivalent to one or two weeks of training in the United States.

Studying at the Shaolin Temple definitely increased my flexibility, strengthened my stances and improved my stamina. When I left, I could hold a horse stance for a full hour with students hanging from my arms. Of course, I also learned Shaolin kung fu forms and kicks.

For me, the Shaolin Temple was a life-changing experience that defined who I am and who I would become. But most importantly, I walked where David Carradine did not.

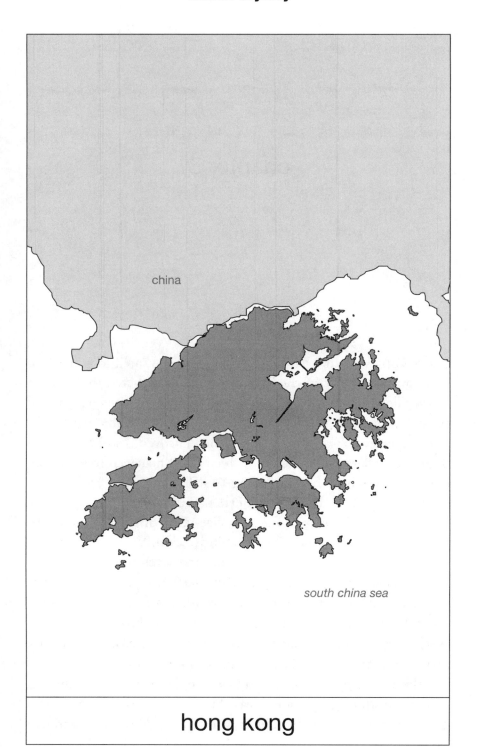

china

south china sea

hong kong

chapter 3

I LEFT CHINA DURING THE SARS EPIDEMIC. I wanted to go back to Taiwan, but when I reached Hong Kong, I discovered that Taiwan wasn't allowing anyone in from China because officials were afraid of contamination. This left me stranded in Hong Kong, one of the most expensive cities in the world. When I arrived, I still had several thousand dollars in my account, which I had managed to save from my teaching job in Taiwan. When I finally got out of Hong Kong several months later, I had $60 USD left. That would be the beginning of "broke times" for me. The next five years of my life would be punctuated by mad scrambles after elusive cash. With the exception of a year I spent teaching in Cambodia and seven months in Korea, I would never even have an apartment again. Everything I owned fit in two backpacks. Later, in Burma, I would have an accident on my way into the war zone and lose one of those backpacks. After that, everything I owned would fit into one. It wasn't exactly by choice that circumstances would turn me into a minimalist.

The Separately Administrated Region of Hong Kong is comprised of three distinct geographic areas: Hong Kong Island, the Outer Territories, and Kowloon. Hong Kong Island is the metropolitan hub; it is about the same size as Manhattan and is the image most people have seen on television. The average income in Hong Kong is $4,000 USD per month compared to $30 to $50 USD in China.) The Outer Territories are made up predominantly of separate and smaller islands. They are the residences of many people who work on Hong Kong Island. Kowloon is unique because it is physically located on mainland China, but it is part of Hong Kong SAR. This means the people who live there have a Hong Kong passport and are decidedly richer and freer than people who live in mainland China. In contrast, mainland China can look into Kowloon, but they need a visa to enter.

For over 100 years, Hong Kong was under British rule. In 1997, Britain handed Hong Kong back to mainland China, and China agreed to rule it as a separately administered region, thus allowing Hong Kong to maintain a separate financial system and many of its freedoms and rights.

In Hong Kong, I felt very much out of place. I was a bald stranger making my way along the fashionable shops of Causeway Bay, wearing my worn out Shaolin Temple training uniform with my fighting sticks hung over my shoulder. I looked like Caine from the TV show *Kung Fu*, except he was a Chinese man in America while I was an American in Hong Kong. While I'm not tall for a Westerner, I weigh about 200 pounds. I'm also heavily built in the shoulders and thighs, thanks to all my martial arts training. It often makes me feel like a bald-headed gorilla among my Chinese friends.

In Hong Kong, I had a lot of time to think and write about the experiences I had in China and Taiwan. I also had to create a training program for myself because I had no money to hire a coach or go to a gym.

During the first few days of my time in Hong Kong, I'd go to Victoria Park to practice kung fu. The old men would stop their tai chi long enough to greet me.

"*An dong ni hao*," they'd say with a smile, pleased I could speak to them in Mandarin. ("An dong ni" is the Chinese pronunciation of my name.)

"*Wo mae i tian hun hao*," I'd say back, which means I'm always really good.

Because I was so used to practicing martial arts all day, I would begin my two and a half hour training routine with the kicking drills I learned at the Shaolin Temple. It was the distinctive Shaolin look of the drills that originally brought the first of the old men over to talk to me. They asked where I had learned them and why I was here. Because some of them knew u bu chuan, we'd practice together. While many of them had experience in kung fu, their real passion was tai chi.

By my third day, I'd developed my routine of training for two and a half hours each day in Victoria Park. By the end of the first week, all of the old men knew me. The owner of a Vietnamese restaurant, who saw me pass by in my uniform every day, called me in to have lunch with him. Because of the epidemic, business was down, and he had time to talk to this strange monk from Brooklyn. Soon, I knew all of the business owners around Causeway Bay. I made a lot of friends, and they all took good care of me.

As I watched my bank account dwindle, I considered getting a job. But I was so hopeful that Taiwan would lift the travel ban any day that I'd decide to wait another day and another and another until the days melted into weeks and eventually, months. To pass the time, I began attending the park at various hours, outside of my normal training time, so that I could get a feeling for martial arts in Hong Kong. I also got a chance to compare Taiwanese with Hong Kong culture.

They both came from a traditional Chinese heritage and both had experienced immense economic development over a very short period of time. Like Taiwan, I could see how Hong Kong struggled to maintain a balance between preserving the old ways and embracing the new, especially in regard to martial arts.

For example, I often noticed a number of Mandarin-speaking kung fu instructors teaching school in the park on weekends. Just like hockey moms in the United States, the mothers stood on the sidelines, dutifully watching and waiting for their children. In talking to the moms, I discovered that most of the children only had kung fu lessons on Sundays because they spent the rest of their time studying. Several of the mothers said they enrolled their children in kung fu as a means of forcing them to practice Mandarin. (Cantonese and English are the official languages of Hong Kong, but after reunification with China in 1997, the region was pressured to change to Mandarin. Because trade with China is so important, the level of Mandarin in Hong Kong has probably improved 300 percent since then.)

In Taiwan and Hong Kong, the largest martial arts demographic is the elderly. Every morning in countless parks, they gather to practice tai chi, chi gong and sometimes *wing chun*. The simple, repetitive movements of chi gong shut off mental channel surfing and empty the mind of all thought, desire and ambition. The subtle flow of tai chi is clearly meditation in movement wherein your end goal is to go nowhere. In a time of tremendous technological leaps and socioeconomic advancement, this martial arts practice brings peace and quiet to the Asian lifestyle. These martial artists find a way to balance the mind, body and spirit.

For the first time in years, I had absolutely nothing to do each day. So I'd walk around Hong Kong thinking, then I would sit down somewhere and write.

I wrote about a lot of things, like the parallels between Hong Kong, Taiwan, China and the West, especially in regard to the martial arts and athletic ability. For example, the countless hours of training at the Shaolin Temple taught me an important lesson. I realized that I could build huge muscles without lifting weights. Most of my training brothers at the Temple had had perfect Bruce Lee bodies—muscles carved out of stone, no body fat and amazing flexibility. I realized that they got that way because of the countless repetitions of various exercises, which used only their natural body weight for resistance.

Western fighters do push-ups, lift weights and hit the heavy bag to build up strength. When you lift weights, you generally lift in sets, like three to eight or maybe 10 or 12. This builds strength very quickly, but so does taking steroids and eating insane quantities of beef. When I was young and boxing, I weighed around 200 pounds. I trained with weights. I took hormones. I ate 300 grams of protein per day, meaning I consciously sat down to eat several pounds of steak, pork or fish every day. I would sometimes eat two or three cans of tuna and a whole loaf of bread at one sitting. I put eggs in every dish I cooked and ran through more than a dozen per day. Between meals and with meals, I also drank high-calorie shakes.

The result was that I was very, very strong. Before a fight, I would diet for several weeks, step up my running and cut my weight by as much as 30 pounds. You can do that in your early 20s. But you will pay the price in your late 30s. There is evidence that proves former wrestlers, bodybuilders, boxers and other athletes who "cut" weight permanently alter their metabolism, and the body cannot process food as it once did. This can cause problems in nutrition uptake, cause weight gain or induce muscle loss. I now have permanent problems with my weight. I also have some joint and ligament problems from lifting too much.

In the West, we think of athletes as being healthy people. But many Western athletes only look healthy. In the end, they destroy their bodies. How many 60 year olds do you see playing professional football? The Chinese, on the other hand, take a much healthier, holistic approach to training and exercise. They are always working on an unlimited timeline, building strength slowly over a period of years. It is no secret that the best tai chi and chi gong practitioners are the oldest.

If you walk into a park in China, Hong Kong or Taiwan early in the morning, you will see literally thousands of people, most of them older, doing either tai chi or chi gong. These practitioners would probably never refer to themselves as athletes and most are not even martial artists, at least in the Western sense of the word. They are people who have grasped the health benefits of the Chinese arts. You will see people in their 70s holding stances and moving through positions which many people in their 20s could never dream of doing. Even if you dismiss the purported internal benefits of Chinese arts—such as lower blood pressure and increased circulation—it is obvious that these older people have more joint flexibility than others at their age.

No matter what Eastern martial art we discuss—chi gong, tai chi, classic kung fu—the two factors that build strength and ultimately health are 1) repetition; and 2) using body weight as resistance. In all three arts, practitioners do thousands and thousands of repetitions, using only the air as resistance. It takes longer to develop strength this way, but it is much healthier. There are no injuries, and if you want to quit, you can just quit.

Bruce Lee trained every second of every day. He is purported to have had a punch pad on the steering wheel of his car that he would hit when he was stuck in traffic. If he was at a party, he would stand in the doorway and do isometric exercise, pushing on the door frame to build his muscles. He did do some weightlifting after he came to the United States but that phenomenal, world-class physique came mostly from doing countless repetitions every day for 20 years.

My tai chi teacher in Taiwan would also practice his tai chi all day, literally pushing the air thousands of times per day. He would push-step across the floor. He would circle his wrist away to break a hold even while waiting for the bus or watching us practice. As a result, his grip was like iron. His shoulders were twice the size of mine. Because he built his muscles for a particular move, it was impossible for him to become muscle bound; they were developed exactly as they needed to be for the move. He performed the moves perfectly because he did them so many times. He did all this without ever having touched a weight in his life. He had also certainly never taken hormones.

My best friend in Taiwan, Lou Che Wei, told me how his father, who is a tai chi instructor, does hand circles while reading. And what does he read? Books about tai chi, of course.

In China and Taiwan, I learned to throw all of my punches in the air instead of against a bag. This way there were no injuries. If you do 5,000 punches in the air per day, you will feel the burn in your muscles. We would sometimes get in a very deep horse stance and do hundreds of curls without weights on each arm.

My Kaohsiung teammates would stand completely still and very, very slowly take 10 to 15 seconds to complete a single kick with perfect form. For every 10th kick in the set, they would execute it in 30 seconds to one minute. By kicking slow, you can kick fast. It takes more control to kick slower, which allows your muscles to develop.

What I learned from this slow, air-resistant and repetitious training is that it gives you more control over a technique, gives your muscles time to develop, negates the need for a warm up or cool down, prevents injury and saves you money because you don't need a gym membership. Doing a technique like a kick too fast or high can rip tendons. If you can kick slow, there's no doubt you can kick fast. So build strength slowly. Use your body for air resistance. Take a page from Bruce Lee and train constantly. Every second that you're not using your hands, you should be training with them.

My training occupied my mornings. In the afternoon, I'd sit in Starbucks writing the book that would eventually be published as *The Monk from Brooklyn*. Because I only had a 90-day visa to stay in Hong Kong, I would do "visa runs," meaning I would travel to Macao (another SAR) in a high-speed boat, have lunch and come back to Hong Kong wherein I would receive a new 90-day visa. But despite that and the countless number of foreign expats living in Hong Kong (Americans outnumber the British and Filipinos are one of the largest groups), I was often lonely. Money was always a problem, I was too broke to go out and, having lost my taste for alcohol, I was uncertain of what to do with myself. I wandered the streets, as I would have back in New York.

Toward the end of my first month in Hong Kong, I walked past an alley and saw a large group of people having a street party. They were laughing, drinking and dancing to Latin rhythms. One of them, who seemed to be the leader, saw me standing at the mouth of the alley and invited me to join them. It turned out that they were all members of the local workers union for Filipino immigrants living in Hong Kong.

Being that I felt as displaced as they did and that we were all Roman Catholic, making us sort of Latin, they invited me to join the party and gave me an open invitation to join the union.

They also invited me to study arnis/*escrima* with them, which are Philippine martial arts that use fighting sticks. In addition to my kung fu practice among my Hong Kong friends, I was now a student of Philippine stick fighting.

The arnis/escrima club in Hong Kong was a lot of fun. Dan Inosanto is the universally accepted master of the art and had been a hero of mine for years. Inosanto is also well-known as the *jeet kune do* student of Hong Kong native Bruce Lee. Today, Inosanto is one of the most respected JKD instructors because he is one of a handful left of students who were trained directly by Bruce Lee. These Filipino workers had brought Inosanto's original art to Bruce Lee's birthplace. I liked how that made a complete circle.

My arnis/escrima instructor Ricky was great, but there was no one for me to fight at the club because all of the students were beautiful young girls who had come to Hong Kong to work as domestic help. I wouldn't have felt comfortable kicking one of them in the head. I also got the impression that while the modern citizens of Hong Kong enjoyed watching kung fu movies, they weren't as interested in practicing martial arts.

For example, the family who owned the guesthouse I stayed at often enjoyed speaking Mandarin to me. They liked to ask me lots of questions about my training in Taiwan and at the Shaolin Temple.

"That was always my dream," the owner's son confessed. "I wish I could go study in the Temple."

"You can," I said simply.

"Of course I cannot," he said, with no other explanation.

I didn't understand why it was an impossible dream. It seemed easier for a Hong Kong Chinese man, or any Chinese at all, to study at the Shaolin Temple than it was for an Italian-American guy from

Brooklyn. From my time in China, I knew there wasn't a huge influx of Hong Kong students studying kung fu on the Chinese mainland. Even though the Chinese government announced its intention to open Shaolin temples all over the world, starting with Hong Kong and Taiwan, my Hong Kong friends were skeptical. They laughed, "What Hong Kong parent would pull their kid out of school to go live in a temple and learn kung fu?"

So I continued to prowl the streets of Hong Kong, looking for a place to fight. I also made a pilgrimage to Kowloon, assuming there would be a Bruce Lee memorial there. But there was nothing in 2004 when I visited—no school, no statue, not even a plaque. Thus, I didn't bother looking for a Jackie Chan memorial. (Since then, I've returned and am happy to report that there is now a Hollywood-style "Avenue of Stars" with movie-star handprints and a massive statue of Bruce Lee. There is also a plan to open a Bruce Lee museum on the site of his former home.)

Eventually I found, or so I was told, the only mixed martial arts fighting team in Hong Kong. The team was called Fighting Fit and consisted almost entirely of expats. Much like in Taiwan, foreigners had flocked to Hong Kong, looking for ancient Chinese culture, but instead, they found the locals had traded it for economic development.

There was another circle that I noticed: Westerners were returning ancient culture to Asia little by little. For example, I had found a BJJ team in Hong Kong. Brazilian jiu-jitsu left Japan as *jujutsu* over a hundred years ago, was developed in Brazil and was finally returned in its contemporary form to Asia by foreigners.

Near the end of my stay in Hong Kong, the guesthouse family passed along free tickets they had received for the traveling show from the Shaolin Temple. Knowing how much I loved kung fu, they gave their tickets to me, and one of my Hong Kong Chinese friends, Joseph, went with me. The performance was not sold out. The audience was comprised mainly of small children who had come with school groups.

The first performance was by a kung fu club representing

Hong Kong. They were good. In fact, they would have been called excellent anywhere else, but next to the monks, they were nothing. I understood that the Hong Kong team was made up of high school and university students, which meant they knew how to read and write in addition to performing kung fu. But the Shaolin monks knew nothing apart from their kung fu, which meant that their performance was perfect.

During the performance, I recognized one of the older monks as a healer who had helped me with a knee injury while I was living at the Temple. After the show, I went backstage with Joseph to greet him. We talked for a long time, swapping stories about the Temple. He told me how excited he was to be going to America next. Afterwards, Joseph told me that he hadn't understood a word of what we had said. Even though he was Hong Kong Chinese and spoke excellent Mandarin, he didn't understand the Shaolin dialect, which had become easy for me to understand.

It was at times like these that I felt very lucky because I was experiencing things that not only few Westerners did, but what few

Antonio trains with *arnis* instructor Ricky in Hong Kong.

Asians experienced, also. Joseph was a citizen of the People's Republic of China but he had never seen Shaolin monks before, certainly didn't know any by name and didn't speak their dialect. Maybe I had no money and my life seemed uncertain, but that day I gave another prayer of thanks for the wonderful journey I was being blessed with.

Shortly after the monks left, the travel ban was lifted. After four months, I was finally able to return to Taiwan, but Hong Kong will always hold a special place in my heart because it really forced me to study and consider martial arts and life.

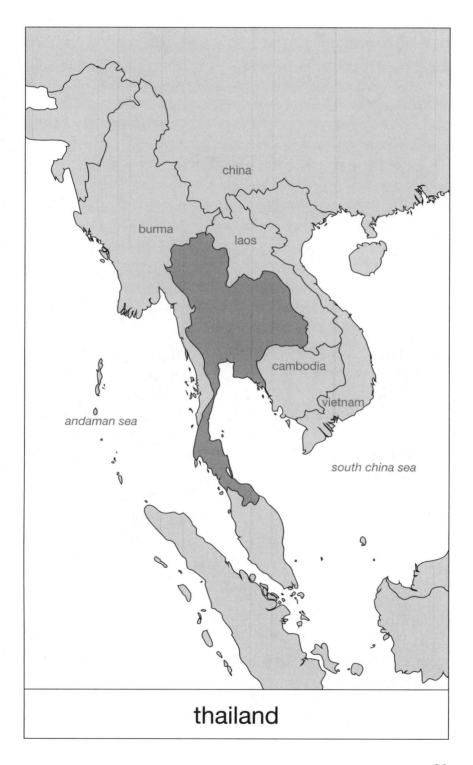

china

burma

laos

cambodia

vietnam

andaman sea

south china sea

thailand

chapter 4

FROM HONG KONG, I RETURNED TO TAIWAN with less than $60 USD in my pocket and nothing in my bank account. My old landlord in Kaohsiung was willing to give me an apartment and accept payment at the end of the month. My best friend, who was a former monk, Lao Che Wei, kindly lent me a bunch of cash so I could get started. I found a job teaching school and signed a one-year contract.

After the intensity of study at Shaolin, I found it impossible to go back to any of my former kung fu teams and train part-time. And after the unrestricted intellectual freedom of Hong Kong, I found it impossible to occupy my time with work instead of with writing. I wrote later and later into each night. I bought a bicycle and ran out on mad adventures. Eventually, I quit my job and spent 10 days riding my bicycle all the way around the island of Taiwan.

I started writing for magazines and decided I wanted to be a full-time writer. My average monthly income, however, was about $250 USD.

When my two-month Taiwan visa was up, I had to get a new one. The rule in Taiwan is that you can't renew or extend a Taiwan tourist visa in Taiwan. So, you have to leave Taiwan and go to a Taiwanese economic office in another country and apply for a new visa. The closest place to fly from Taiwan was Hong Kong so I liquidated the last of my Wall Street investments and flew back to Hong Kong to deal with the two-day visa process.

I stayed in the same guesthouse I lived in, and the guesthouse family not only welcomed me back with open arms but handed me a bunch of mail that had come in my absence. It's funny that while I love Hong Kong, I'm always there because I'm stranded, broke or dealing with visa eligibility for some other country. I would like to visit Hong Kong and stay awhile under pleasant circumstances.

The Taiwanese government doesn't like foreigners to hang around the island without doing anything. If you want to stay longer, you have to find a job, and that job needs to sponsor you for a one-year visa and work permit. I didn't have a job. Instead, I had trained, gone on adventures, written articles and worked on my book while looking for a publisher. While the Hong Kong office would have renewed my visa, the employees at the Taiwanese visa office warned me that this was the last 60-day visa they would issue me. These people get really good at recognizing faces and names. If they see you come through too many times, they assume you are living or working illegally in Taiwan and will put a big red stamp on your file, banning you from entering Taiwan for up to a year.

Two months later, my second visa was up. Leaving Taiwan was going to be problematic, however, because I didn't have any money to buy a ticket out of the country. This is where some people—those who take too long to decide on a job—get in trouble. In my case, I wasn't looking for a job but just a way off the island.

Luckily for me, my sister's husband was in Taiwan on business and needed a translator for a few days. He was very kind and bought me a one-way ticket to Thailand. I closed up my apartment, promised Lao Che Wei that I would pay him at some point or have a bad reincarnation, and I left.

✪

I had only been to Thailand once before. When I was living in Taiwan, an ex-girlfriend of mine was on a joint U.S./Thai military exercise, and I had flown to meet her in Bangkok. Now I was headed back to Thailand where I didn't speak the language and where I didn't know anyone. But I knew that I wanted to go study at Thailand's last muay Thai monastery.

Muay Thai is a kickboxing art that is the national sport of Thailand. It uses kicks, punches, elbows, knee strikes and stand-up grappling. Similar arts are practiced in Cambodia, Laos and Burma, and there is a centuries old feud between Cambodia and Thailand over who invented it, but more on that later.

The earliest records of muay Thai date back to the 15th century when the art was practiced by military leaders and professional fighters who represented their individual region in competitions. Each teacher in each region practiced a particular style of muay Thai, and large-scale competitions were held to see which style or which teacher was best. These fights had few rules, and the men's hands were wrapped in cords.

During the 1920s and 1930s, the art was refined into a professional sport. The first stadiums were built, and the ring and gloves were added. This period is really the birth of modern muay Thai. Today, muay Thai is a big professional sport in Thailand with somewhere between 60,000 and 90,000 professional fighters. In the West, we would expect good professional fighters to have worked their way up from the amateur circuit, but in Thailand, there isn't much of an amateur muay Thai circuit. For the most part, Thai people can't see the point of getting beat up for free. As a result, there is nearly exclusively professional muay Thai.

Most muay Thai fighters live in camps in which they train twice a day and fight every three weeks or so to earn money. In big cities, the fighters might live at home with their families and commute to the gym each day. But in Thailand, there was only one muay Thai monastery, and it sounded like a unique and interesting place.

I had read about the muay Thai monastery shortly after arriving in Taiwan two years earlier. Because the story was so interesting, I filed it away in a book with the vague notion of someday going there for training. On the night that I was packing to go to the Shaolin Temple, the yellowed newspaper clipping fell out of that old book, reminding me about the monastery. I flipped on the television for background noise, and whether by fate or the Hand of God (or the benefits of a deluxe cable package), Star Network was running a documentary about Wat Acha Tong.

Known in English as the Golden Horse Monastery, Wat Acha Tong had been home to orphans and other displaced persons, many recovering from *yaba* (meth) addictions, since 1991. In the ancient tradition, the abbott Pra Kru Ba taught the arts of muay Thai, meditation, prayer, horsemanship and farming as a way of purifying the body and soul. The rigorous program was designed to create physical and spiritual harmony and keep young people off the streets and away from drugs. When the boys—and when I say boys I mean small children to young men in their mid-20s—felt ready to leave the program, they would have many career options in farming, animal husbandry, the military, the police or as professional muay Thai fighters.

I would eventually wind up spending three months at the monastery, discovering that I was only the second foreign student ever to study there. The first one, also an American, had quit after five days, saying the program was just too painful. After my time there, I couldn't blame him. Studying with Pra Kru Ba (*pra* means "monk" and *kru* means "teacher") was one of the hardest things I have ever done. But the gifts I gained of learning and personal growth were invaluable, and Pra Kru Ba never asked me to pay a single cent for my food, lodging or training.

I left Taiwan and returned to Thailand determined to find Pra Kru Ba and study in his monastery. I flew to the northern city of Chiang Mai and then took a bus to Chiang Rai, which is still further north, because all I knew was that the monastery was somewhere between Chiang Rai and the Burmese border. At Chiang Rai I got on a bus that went to the Burmese border to the small Thai city of Mae Sai. I walked around the streets of Mae Sai, showing people a grainy photograph of Pra Kru Ba, which I had printed off the Internet.

"Do you know this monk?" I asked countless people. Finally someone suggested I take the bus halfway back to Chiang Rai, get out at the small town of Mae Chaem and ask around again.

At a Mae Chaem gas station, I found a man who didn't speak any English but who clearly knew Pra Kru Ba. He drove me into the mountains on his motorcycle and dropped me off in the middle of a group of thatched huts.

A novice monk led me down a path to an open hut where Pra Kru Ba was laying on his bed recovering from a recent illness. He looked up and was as surprised to see me as I was to finally find him.

With the little English that Pra Kru Ba had at his disposal ("Speak Thai?"), we figured out that we had no common language. So we did what men do when they want to interact: We fought.

Actually, Pra Kru Ba instructed the novices to take me to the other side of the monastery where a fighting ring was located. He put me in with a guy named Payong, who would become my training brother. We went two rounds of boxing, which I won easily. Then we were supposed to fight two rounds of muay Thai, but I only lasted one. I was black and blue from head to toe.

Despite the language barrier, I made Pra Kru Ba understand that I wanted to stay and train with him. After an ice-cold bucket shower with mountain water, Payong took me to his hut and we slept.

✸

Wat Acha Tong is not so much set on the top of a mountain as across the tops of two mountaintops. The fighting ring I sparred in on my first day and the training area are on one peak, which also includes the main horse stables. The main temple and living and sleeping quarters (a collection of individual huts that housed two to three people) are on the opposite peak. The monastery's sacred cave is further up that mountain, overlooking the main temple area.

Antonio poses for a picture with Pra Kru Ba in Thailand.

I wound up staying at the Wat Acha Tong for three months. At the time, there were more than 30 people living there with more than 100 horses. Among the residents were Pra Kru Ba and another adult monk. There was Maii, the house mother, who was also Pra Kru Ba's sister and a dedicated Buddhist laywoman. There were 14 novice monks in residence. (As novices, they weren't true monks because they didn't have to follow all 227 rules of monkhood. However, they did have shaved heads, wore orange robes and lived harsh lives full of religious instruction). There were two women who came and went from the monastery daily; they helped prepare food and cut hair. There were several drivers with trucks who helped us with our daily farm work; these men were men who had done bad things and/or had bad experiences with drugs or violence. They were dedicating themselves to hard work and servitude to balance their karma. The rest of the residents were guys who ranged from 15 to 30 years of age. These men weren't monks and didn't shave their heads but they lived lives of strict discipline, hard work, prayer and muay Thai. I became one of those guys.

A typical day in the monastery typically began when the rooster woke all of us around 5:00 a.m. If I had had a gun, we'd have had fried bird for dinner. Payong would always be up first and doing his morning prayers on the small prayer mat in our thatched hut. Because I was now a part of the monastery's daily life, I'd fall on my knees and grudgingly do my prostrations, too. While I prayed a lot better after coffee, Payong seemed to pray well day or night.

After doing this, Payong would light a candle because it was still dark. Together, we would climb uphill to the main temple that had the monastery's patron golden horse. We'd sweep the shrine's floor, light candles and incense and do more prostrations. We'd sip holy water before going past the statues and up the mountain to enter the sacred cave.

The cave is where it all began—where Pra Kru Ba meditated for a period of years, eventually having a vision that he should build the monastery. It was the same story as Da Mo (Bodhidharma) at the Shaolin Temple. Concerned about the welfare of the monks, Da Mo climbed Song Shan Mountain and meditated for a period of years until he had a vision telling him to create kung fu and teach it to the monks. So it was with Pra Kru Ba. He had meditated alone in the sacred cave until he had a vision of building Wat Acha Tong to teach muay Thai to troubled boys. While Pra Kru Ba was real and tangible, the sacred cave had an eerie and powerful feeling about it.

At some point, Pra Kru Ba would call us all together into the clearing by the temple, which was surrounded by sacred statues of Hindu gods and ancient muay Thai warriors. We went through more prayers and meditation, followed by muay Thai training. Then we took Thai showers, meaning that we stood beside a 20-gallon drum full of mountain water and used a dipper to dump the icy water over our heads repeatedly until clean. This was a feat of bravery in itself because the mountains were very cold in the morning. It took a lot to strip down, dump cold water over my head, lather up with soap and dump, dump and dump water over my head until finished. By the end, I would be completely numb and shivering. We bathed like this at the start and finish of every muay Thai session, prayer session and audience session with Pra Kru Ba. We probably bathed three to five times per day at the monastery, depending on how many meetings we had with Pra Kru Ba. I never got an accurate count, but in many of my memories of the monastery, I am cold and wet but clean.

Breakfast wasn't until 9 a.m., but Payong and I would often come snooping around the kitchen for a treat, which Maii would give us. Some days it was sweet porridge. Usually, it was a cup of coffee for me. Fortified with caffeine, I would be ready to take on my daily prayers.

Religion at the monastery was a very real part of everyday life. In China, it was a given that Buddhism and martial arts were inseparable, but the religious aspect was not even a secondary thought in daily life. In Taiwan, the best tai chi and kung fu teachers are deeply religious, often monks, and more likely than not, practitioners of traditional Chinese medicine. In Thai culture, it took me some time to acclimate to Theravada Buddhism, which is very different from Chinese and Taiwanese Buddhism; it is closer to Hinduism. Monks are required to follow the 227 precepts, or prohibitions. Normally, monks aren't supposed to do physical labor and are strictly prohibited from practicing muay Thai. But forest monks, like Pra Kru Ba, were given special permission because farm work and other labors were necessary for survival. As for muay Thai, it took a long time for him to obtain official recognition for his work and the necessary permission to carry on with it. To the best of my knowledge, he is the only monk who has been granted permission to teach muay Thai. Even though the deepest and most ancient roots of muay Thai are closely related to Buddhism. The ancient fighters practiced meditation and prayer. They believed that the fighter who purifies his soul and body would be victorious in battle. That's why muay Thai fighters are often religious people who spend time in prayer and consultation with monks, and this was why Pra Kru Ba saw muay Thai as a natural fit to the temple life.

Some days, the first training session was held after breakfast. On those days, Payong and I would jog to the muay Thai ring on the opposite hillside. There we would meet our other training partner Daescho, as well as other boys who were living at the temple.

"Many of these boys used to be addicted to yaba," Maii explained. "Pra Kru Ba hates drugs. So he and the boys ride their horses to the mountain villages, telling the boys not to take drugs. If there are any boys without parents, he brings them back to the monastery, and they become like his sons." Some of the guys, like Payong, used to be child monks before. Now that they were in their late teens or early 20s, they lived and worked at the monastery, training, praying and serving.

At the ring, we'd strip down to muay Thai shorts. We wore no shirts in spite of the cold mountain air and we would begin our routine. We'd do several rounds of knee and elbow strikes on the bag. As I was new to muay Thai, the scabs that always formed the night before would open up. I'd have blood dripping from all four limbs.

Our trainer Hote or Pra Kru Ba would teach us. Maii would supervise the training, standing by to bandage our wounds or yell at us if we weren't training hard enough. Sometimes she'd hit boys with sticks to make them practice.

Maii was tough, but very loving. For example, once one of the kids upset her so she beat him, rather expertly, with a practice sword. This was nothing like the nuns back at Catholic school who hit me with a ruler. Maii picked that sword up with two hands and swung with all of her body weight. Crack! Crack! I was reminded of Obi Wan Kenobi from *Star Wars* (1971). But there was no malice in Maii. Later, when she was handing out cookies, she also gave one to the boy she had punished.

Sometime in the morning, the trucks came to load us muay Thai fighters and novice monks into their rears to take us to work—farming the fields and cutting feed for the horses. The older boys, who generally weren't monks like me, wore regular clothes. The child monks all had their heads shaved, went barefoot and wore orange robes. We generally ate our lunch at noon out in the fields where we were working.

Because monks aren't allowed to handle money, Maii took care of the finances for the whole monastery. She sometimes came with us to pay for gas or repairs for the trucks. Sometimes the trucks dropped her off at appointments in town or along the way to the fields. She would buy supplies and occasionally buy us a treat if she had extra money.

Maii could also speak a little English, and over the months as I learned Thai, we were able to communicate in the two languages. Because of this, Maii would often point out certain boys to tell me their stories on these car rides.

"This one has no parents. That one was too small and couldn't work enough so his family didn't want him. That one was the seventh of eight children. The family couldn't feed him, so they sent him away."

On one such excursion, we stopped for gas, and Maii handed the receipt to one of the 20 year olds.

"What is this word?" she asked him in Thai, pointing at a word on the receipt.

His lips stammered as he slowly sounded out the word.

"Liters," he said.

"And this one?" Maii asked.

Again, there was a long pause.

"Price per liter," he said.

"And this one?"

"Total."

"Do you know what is total?" she asked. The boy looked down, embarrassed.

"This is the amount of money you have to pay the man," she explained. She handed him some Thai baht notes.

"You go pay," she said.

After the boy was gone, Maii told me,: "He has no family, and he never went to school. So, now I teach him to read." That was how I learned that Maii basically taught all the things many of us take for granted because we learned them from our parents—how to cook, how to use money, how to drive a car, etc.

In the fields, we'd use a huge Thai *daap* (machete) to cut corn stalks, which would be used to feed the horses. We cut all day, breaking only for meals. Working was a constant and back-breaking affair. We spent hours and hours riding the truck from field to field, cutting stalks, filling trucks, riding back to the monastery, unloading the feed, riding back to the fields, cutting stalks, filling the trucks and so on.

Every now and then, Maii would make my heart soar by telling me that I would get off work early and visit Pra Kru Ba instead.

I would usually find Pra Kru Ba seated beneath a tree beside the main horse stables. He had been ill lately, spending a lot of time in bed, for which he seemed embarrassed. Even in his slightly diminished state, however, his power was unmistakable. His upper body was heavily muscled and every inch of it was covered with holy tattoos. He wore a smile, as if it were part of his uniform. His eyes always gleamed with the wonder of a child on Christmas morning. He lived so enthusiastically, as if he were seeing the world for the first time. Seeing me approach, he smiled even brighter. I was always amazed that he had once been a soldier and a professional muay Thai fighter.

"Show me what you have learned," he would command.

I'd throw kicks, elbows, knees and punches. Testing me, Pra Kru Ba called out the names of each move in Thai. I was always faced with two problems. One, I sometimes forgot the move, and two, I sometimes forgot the move's Thai name.

After dark, I would return to the monastery to bathe. Then the whole family of monks, workers, muay Thai fighters and I would gather in the community room and watch a Thai TV show about the king of Thailand. Everyone in the monastery loved the show so much that all activity came to a halt each night at 7:00. Even Pra Kru Ba watched with interest, making pointed comments and occasionally laughing for no reason at all. He'd often look over to see me writing in my diary instead.

"Antoni," he'd say. (He called me Antoni, Tony, Muay Thai Tony or Tony Muay Thai—never Antonio.) "After you leave here, please don't forget us."

"I will never forget you," I promised.

The show would end. We would share our dinner together—novices, truckers and fighters; the monks didn't eat dinner.

Payong and I would go back to our little hut to say our prayers before bed. Lights out was at 9:00 p.m., but at 1:00 a.m., a novice monk would come to wake Payong up for "evening" prayers, which meant sitting on the floor of an unheated mountain monastery for three hours, chanting. Much as I was a part of the monastery's everyday life, this was the one part of training I would pass on. Otherwise, the day would start all over again.

Pra Kru Ba at Wat Acha Tong in Thailand.

In Thailand, there are nearly 90,000 professional fighters, and muay Thai is the country's most popular sport. The martial art utilizes kicks, punches, elbow and knee strikes and stand-up grappling. The main kick is the visually impressive roundhouse, but the kick hits with the shin rather than the foot. The kick's goal is to smash your opponent's thighs, ribs or head with your shins. With hand tools, the goal is to cut the opponent's face with your elbows. In professional fights, you get points for grabbing the opponent by the head and/or neck and throwing him to the ground. The professional fights are five rounds long. They are fought in a regular boxing ring and fighters wear boxing gloves. There are judges, and you can win by knockout or points. Muay Thai is probably the most brutal stand-up striking art on the planet, with the exception of its close cousin Burmese *lethwei*, which doesn't use gloves or rules. In Burma, head butting is still legal while in Thailand it is not.

In Thailand, muay Thai fighters are referred to as boxers. And because Theravada Buddhist society is quite stratified with a specific caste system, boxers are considered a caste. This is why it's sometimes difficult to be a foreigner—there is no caste for you. In spite of that, I was easily accepted into the boxer caste, which meant I held a position in Thai society. I worked on a farm. I studied with monks. I lived a real Thai life that many foreigners rarely experience. As I mentioned earlier, foreign English teachers occupy a role designated specifically to foreigners, but if you live as a boxer in a Thailand monastery, you are living Thai.

From time to time, the nonmonks like Payong, Daescho and myself would participate in fights to earn money for the monastery or the poor hill-tribe people. The majority of the competitions were in Chiang Rai, but my training brothers had participated in fights in Chiang Mai and Bangkok.

Before my first professional fight in Thailand, I thought a lot about the differences between Western boxers and Thai boxers.

For instance, when I was a young, Western boxer in the United States, the most I ever made for a fight was $150 USD. I only got that much because the promoter cut the money for the tickets sold in half. Because I come from a big family, my tickets generally got bought. For that paltry sum of money, I trained and sparred for countless rounds and fought literally hundreds of challenge matches for free. Whenever the big night would come, I'd climb into a ring, face a strange opponent that I had nothing against and pound at him for three long rounds while taking his similar beatings. The recovery time necessary after a fight like this is about two to three weeks. That gave a small-time boxer like I me an income of about $300 USD a month. In Thailand, I'd learn that muay Thai boxers earned about $12 USD a month.

But in the United States, my story is rare for a fighter. I was fortunate. I managed to get myself an education, travel and make a life for myself as a writer. Most of my training partners from that period of my life didn't end up as lucky. They were physically wrecked, hooked on drugs or alcohol and/or doing time in prison. At the very least, they drifted away and into obscurity. In retrospect, it's easy to feel sorry for myself and the scores of boys who tried to use boxing as a way out of poverty. But on a chilly December night in Chiang Rai, my eyes were opened.

While foreign boxers are commonplace in Chiang Mai and Bangkok, they are rarely seen in rural Thailand. I was the first foreigner ever to train in this forest camp, located in the jungle, 60 kilometers north of Chiang Rai. At first glimpse, the hill-tribe boys who occupied the monastery were not very different from the desperate poor of Appalachia or the ethnic poor of America's inner cities. They were uneducated. They came from broken homes, born of parents who were also uneducated. Many of them had had brushes with drug addiction and with the law. At birth, no one expected them to get any further than their parents had, and their parents hadn't gotten very far at all. They saw fighting as their only chance of ever amounting to anything.

I also learned that the youths of the Thai/Burma border faced a slew of additional problems, which many of the disenfranchised youth in American will never face. First, many of them belonged to ethnic minorities from the Burmese side of the border. These ethnicities were already denied Burmese citizenship because of the military junta, and that officially classified them as "stateless persons" in Thailand. Because of their unrecorded births in remote hill-tribe villages and because of widespread illiteracy among the adults of their world, they had never been entered into "the system." They had no passport, no identity card and no social security number. At age 17 or 20, it would be nearly impossible for them to enter the system. This meant they could never be policemen or soldiers, or ever hold a legitimate job. And of course, even if they possessed the relevant skills, the doors of the universities would be closed to them.

The only bright note in the face of these problems is that the boys' scope was so small that they didn't understand that they were stateless. They had never needed an identity card so they didn't feel the loss when it was denied them.

The loss that they did feel, however, was the loss of family. The boys living in these types of camps are loosely referred to as orphans, but in the strictest sense of the word, they aren't orphans at all. Often one or both of their parents are still alive. The boys are simply unwanted. Whether for economic reasons or because of a remarriage, the parents will often deposit their unwanted sons at the nearest temple or Thai boxing camp.

Aside from the fact that Thai boxing training is infinitely more painful than training for Western boxing, by the time these boys even got in the ring they had endured more than their share of hard knocks.

With only a week before an official fight, Pra Kru Ba suspended our usual 10 to 12 hour work and training day in order to bless us for the competition. Payong, Daescho and I joined 10 other fighters at the main temple, which was really an outdoor concrete platform with an altar for prayer. We were dressed in our uniforms, shirtless and barefoot. We stood at rigid attention, shivering in the cold mountain air. We held incense to our foreheads and did prostrations in the dirt, reciting our prayers.

Pra Kru Ba, a veteran of more than 50 professional fights, gave each of us three lighted candles, which we arranged in a circle around the main temple's stone altar. The glow of so many candles gave the ceremony a supernatural feeling. It reminded me of *Kung Fu* when David Carradine's character was often shown training by candlelight at the Shaolin Temple. But this wasn't television; this was real. I never saw anything like this at the real Shaolin Temple in which Buddhism and its rituals were almost extinct. Here in this jungle temple, it was alive and well.

We knelt for more than an hour while reciting our prayers. When we finished praying, we meditated. The cold, rough stone dug into the flesh of my knees, which were already scabbed and bloody from weeks of training. When meditating, Pra Kru Ba said that great instructors from the past would come and teach him. In one of my private audiences with him, Pra Kru Ba told me that the best fighter would be the one who practiced physically and meditated daily, rehearsing the moves physically and mentally. "You must visualize every aspect of the move," he instructed. I usually just felt pained, cramped and glad when meditation was over so I could straighten my legs. After the blessing, all of us fighters stepped off the temple platform and began warming up in the open jungle.

Later in our private time, Pra Kru Ba chastised me about my meditation. "When you meditate," he said, "You look sad." To him, meditation should be an empty and, thus, joyful experience. To me, it was too much standing still.

We were fighting as the main entertainment for a county-fair-type event on two consecutive nights. While I had trained and prepared with the team, I had no fights planned during the competition. But on that first night, a promoter noticed me—the only Western face in the crowd—and immediately asked if I wanted to come back and fight in a boxing match the next day. I quickly agreed, because I always believe it's better to cover a story from inside than from out.

The promoter made me strip off my shirt in the cold night air and shadow box in the ring while the crowd cheered wildly. For many of them, mostly farmers from remote villages, it was probably the first time they had seen a foreigner at all, much less seen one box. I was immediately given the fight name "Toni Farang." "Toni" is what the Thais called me because they could write and pronounce it in Thai. "*Farang*" means foreigner. The promoter worried that if he wrote "Toni" on the fight card, people would think I was Thai. But if he wrote "Toni Farang," everyone would know I was a foreigner, and that was a huge attraction.

On the second fight night, I watched Payong destroy his opponent. Payong had been abandoned by his mother when she remarried. In spite of having had a hard home life, he was always laughing. No matter how low my mood would sink, Payong could cheer me back up with his silly antics and off-key singing. When the bell rang for the first round, there was no trace of the comical, good-natured guy who shared his bamboo hut with me. Instead, the peaceful Payong had been replaced by the most vicious fighter I had ever seen. I have personally fought in and witnessed hundreds of matches around the world, but I never before saw the crude violence that Payong unleashed on his opponent. The fight got stopped in the middle of the second round when both the referee and the corner trainer felt that Payong's opponent had had enough.

I couldn't help wondering if the anger he had displayed in the ring was the result of his abandonment. Was there some deep specter of pent-up aggression lurking inside of him? Would he someday crack? Climb up a bell tower with a rifle? Enter a marketplace with a gun? Because most of the boxers had similar or worse stories, were they all just little time bombs waiting to go off?

One thing about small-time fighting is that it is very disorganized. In Thailand, it was disorganized times 10. While I waited for my turn and shot pictures of the fights, people were coming up to me, grabbing my calf muscles and feeling my biceps. They discussed which way they were betting in the Toni Farang fight. People crowded in on me, making it impossible to breathe. By the time I realized that my name was being called, my opponent was already in the ring waiting for me.

With no time for a warm up or a rub down, I just began stripping off my clothes while the crowd pushed and dragged me to my corner. Luckily, Hote, an ex-muay Thai boxer and the monastery's trainer, had enough good moves left in him that he was able to fight his way through the crowd and stick some gloves on my hands, or else I would have had to fight barehanded.

The ring announcer was shouting for me to get in the ring or get disqualified. Half the crowd was trying to push me up the steps. The other half was still feeling my muscles and trying to get me to pose for photos.

"No weigh-in?" I shouted to Hote over the din.

"Now boxing!" he cried back, desperately trying to pull me into the ring.

"What about hand wraps?"

"No time," he said.

I had visions of nursing broken knuckles the following day. Even after I climbed into the ring, people were still holding onto my legs. Someone else was trying to force a huge basin underneath me. It nearly knocked me off my feet. After bruising my calves on the basin, they gave up assuming that I would know to step into it and began dumping ice-cold water all over me. Apparently, stepping into a basin and getting water dumped over you is something they do in Thailand, but I was so cold to begin with that my muscles began cramping. And now the ring was wet and slippery.

A bell rang. I wasn't sure if it meant to come out fighting or to come out and get the instructions. The referee was shouting at me in Thai. The crowd was shouting. There were instructions coming over the P.A. system. I looked to Hote, hoping he would tell me what to do, but he just shrugged.

"Thanks, man." I said. A good corner man can make or break the fight for you. In small-time fighting, you get small-time corner men.

I tried to take a step, but people had climbed up on the ring apron and were still holding on to my ankles. I ripped my legs free and walked warily to the center. This was the first time I saw my opponent. He was the biggest Thai man I had ever seen in my life. In fact, he was the biggest man I had ever seen in my life. He was at least a head taller than me and easily 40 pounds heavier. Another thing about small-time fighting is that the fighters have been through so much, you don't usually get an attractive opponent. This man was no exception. He had a forehead so big that it blocked the sun. He looked like he had just stepped out of Darwin's Evolution of Man, somewhere between Cro-Magnon and Neanderthal. He wasn't just ugly. He was circus ugly. People would have paid money to get a look at his mug in a freak show only to lose their lunch afterwards. Because small-time fighters have to fight constantly to make some semblance of a living, he actually had open cuts all over his face.

I was nearly intimidated by his battered appearance, until I remembered a scene from that great American Western *The Magnificent Seven* (1960), where our heroes are looking to hire good gun fighters. They see a man with scars all over his face, and someone says, "We should hire him. He is very tough." But Yul Brynner's character says, "No, we should hire the man who gave him those scars." I breathed a sigh of relief. I was ready.

My opponent smiled at me, revealing a mouth devoid of teeth. A mouthpiece is optional in Thailand. I guess it would be optional anywhere if you had no teeth; I wanted to keep mine so I was wearing one.

The fight went really well for me. I hit my opponent about 300 times. He hit me about 6 times. We observed international, Western boxing rules of three three-minute rounds with one minute in between each round. The real battle was always in the corner where people kept grabbing me and yelling things at me. Whenever the bell rang for me to go out and fight, I felt relieved. It was all so confusing that at the end, I didn't know who had won. I just knew that my opponent had gone, and they'd asked me to stay in the ring and take pictures with my arms over my head.

Later, lying in our hut, Payong and I talked about the fights, too excited to sleep.

"You were great," I told him, pantomiming all of his excellent kicks and knees.

"Toni was great," he said, and swung his fists like a mad man.

We joked about my opponent's lack of teeth. We also had a good laugh, imitating how Payong's opponent was knocked down 25 times.

"Payong is happy," he told me, "Mother and Father happy." Payong's mother and stepfather had shown up at the fights. I had heard that many of the parents did this, coming around to take most of the winnings from their sons. In this case, Payong had won 300 baht ($9.00 USD).

"Mother and Father say Payong can go home now," he told me with boyish delight.

My stomach turned. They kicked him out when they thought they had no use for him. Now that he looked like a moneymaker they wanted him back. I lacked the vocabulary to tell Payong what I was thinking and wondered if it would have been right to interfere in the first place.

Suddenly, Payong's face turned sullen. "Is Payong good?" he asked, sounding like a hurt little boy.

"Of course Payong is good," I said. "Payong was fighting like this," I said, kicking and punching frantically.

He became very quiet and asked again in a timid voice, "Is Payong good?"

It hit me what he was asking. He wasn't asking about the fight. He wasn't asking if he had fought well that night. He was asking if Payong was a good person. Ultimately he was asking me, "Is Payong a good enough person that he deserves better than to be abandoned by his family?"

I cursed my lack of vocabulary. Hoping that my tone would convey what my words could not, I said, "Yes, Payong is good."

He looked at me for a moment, as if deciding if I were telling him the truth. Then a smile spread across his face, and he burst out in his usual laughter. "Payong is good," he chuckled. "Payong is good."

Antonio and Payong do a little friendly sparring in the Thai fields.

❂

Payong moved out a few days after our fight. With Payong gone, the monastery became a lonely place. It was time for me to go, so after three months and two weeks at the monastery, I went down to Chiang Mai and lived in a two-dollar a night guesthouse while I worked on my adventure writing. I never had enough money. Friends had to send me small donations via Western Union. I sold my books. I did everything I could to survive and to keep writing. I did a lot of stories on tribes in the jungles just so I could stay there for free. One night I was surfing the Internet, looking for obscure martial arts, and I found an entry on a Web site that listed the Cambodian martial art of bokator. There was no other information on this martial art anywhere on the Internet, only the name bokator. I also found an entry about a Laotian martial art called *ling lom*.

I sent e-mails to martial arts and sports associations in Laos and Cambodia, explaining that I wanted to come, train and write about ling lom or bokator. Laos didn't answer me, but someone from a Cambodian martial arts association invited me to come and study martial arts. They also instructed me to call the representative from the association when I arrived in the capital of Phnom Penh. So I bought a train ticket, followed by a bus ticket and followed by a horrible taxi ride. Several days later, I arrived in Phnom Penh.

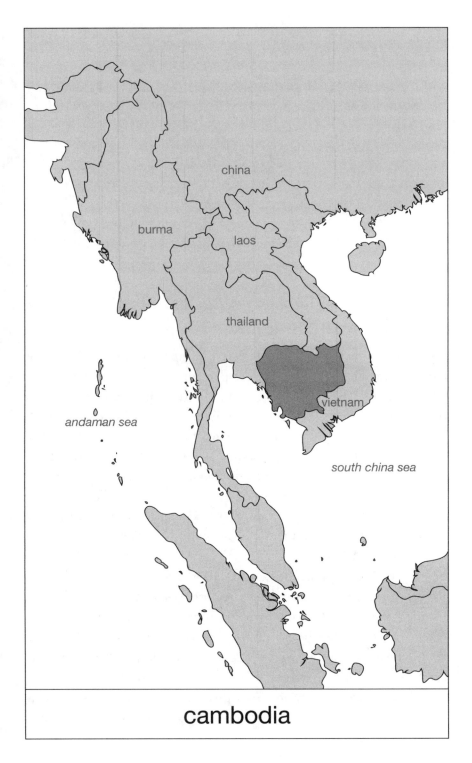

cambodia

chapter 5

NOTHING PREPARES YOU for your first glimpse of Phnom Penh. The city is brutally hot. Less than 20 percent of the streets are paved, which means you generally ride on the back of a motorcycle taxi down bumpy streets that are covered in filth. (This has since changed, but Phnom Penh is still one of the least developed capital cities in the world.) There are beggars, scam artists and desperate people everywhere. Whole families earn their living by digging through piles of smelly refuse that build up in front of house blocks. While the Thai people are soft, kind and smiling, the Khmer (Cambodian) people are harder but with good reason. They have lived through hell.

Between 1975 and 1979, 25 percent of the Cambodian population (approximately 1.7 million) was murdered by the Khmer Rouge government under the dictator Pol Pot. Then, Vietnam invaded the country and drove the Khmer Rouge from power in 1979, but there can be no doubt that the trauma left behind has yet to heal. Khmer Rouge officials who orchestrated torture and executions readily switched sides after their fall from power and have, for the most part, not been prosecuted. (In fact, the political party's leader Pol Pot continued to lead a Khmer Rouge unit and reigned over a Khmer Rouge controlled region of the country until his death in 1997.) Many Khmer Rouge soldiers simply traded their black uniforms for green ones and became the new face of the police and military in this lawless country, which *The CIA World Fact Book* labels as a "failed state." Everything from medicine to education is now provided by private hands and foreign NGOs.

Today, the ruling party is the CPP, the Cambodian People's Party, which has been in power since 1979. The country is no longer communist, but the communist CPP is the ruling party. The monarchy is nothing more than a remnant of an absolute institution, and the king is little more than a figurehead.

The longer you live in Asia, the more you appreciate the relative freedom and safety of countries like Taiwan. In comparison, Cambodia is a harsh place. The average income is $26 USD per month, but to live and support a family of four in Phnom Penh, a breadwinner needs a bare minimum of $150 USD a month. Because the government doesn't provide for its people, anything you need done in Cambodia involves paying bribes.

Even public school teachers survive on the bribes they receive from their students. They refuse to teach students who cannot pay. The police normally don't receive their $10 USD a month salary because their superior officers steal it. They survive by setting up roadblocks and extracting "fines" from the citizenry. Nurses charge money to administer drugs to sick patients in hospitals. Foremen charge a month's salary to a new employee in exchange for hiring him. One of my Khmer friends wanted to work at a hotel, but the foreman wanted $90 USD to hire him. The mother of another of my friends bought him a high-ranking job with the police for $5,000 USD. A high-ranking job means that he now has a position where he can steal a lot. So, the bribe was a good investment.

I knew a police officer whose salary was $50 USD per month, but he owned his own home and drove an SUV. I guess he was better at budgeting than I was. I barely survived on $500 USD a month.

✸

I arrived in Phnom Penh, late in the evening on a Saturday in May 2004. I checked into a cheap guesthouse for $4 USD per night and called the martial arts association. They sent people to pick me up, they came in an SUV. They took me to dinner during which they asked me a lot of questions about where I had been and what I had studied. Finally, they asked, "Would you like to star in a kung fu movie?"

My answer: Why not?

Film shooting began the next morning. I had been in the country for less than 24 hours, and I was already on a set, filming a movie. I played opposite Eh Phou Thoung, the Khmer boxing champion who I would remain friends with for years.

I'm going to digress for a moment to talk about Khmer boxing, also called *bradal serey* (or *pradal serey*), which is an extremely popular sport in Cambodia. Bradal serey translates as "free fighting." Fighters use roundhouse kicks and hit the target with their shins. They use push kicks, knee strikes, elbow strikes, punches and stand-up grappling. That all may sound exactly like muay Thai, but that word is an insult to the Khmer. They believe they invented the Southeast Asian art of kickboxing and that the Thais stole it from them. They base this on the fact that there are bas-reliefs in Cambodia from the 11th and 13th centuries showing men fighting with wrapped hands, whereas written muay Thai records date back approximately 500 years. (Monks and scholars I have spoken to in Thailand believe it is very possible that many of the techniques or refinement of muay Thai may have been adopted from Cambodia. It is certain, however, that there was some type of unarmed combat technique in Thailand before the Khmer influence.)

No matter who is right or wrong, the fact of the matter is that this feud has affected the overall development of sport fighting in Cambodia; it's very much behind that of Thailand or the Philippines, which are countries more open to foreign influence. For example, because the Khmer believe the sport should be called bradal serey instead of muay Thai, they refused to join the World Muay Thai Council and refused to compete in the Muay Thai championships in the Southeast Asian Games. As a result, Cambodia can't fight in internationally recognized bouts. (By 2009, Cambodia did win a victory of sorts. The muay Thai component of the Southeast Asia Games and Asian Martial Arts Games was changed simply to "muay." But obviously, the World Muay Thai Council has no plans to change its name, so at the time of this writing, Cambodia still doesn't compete in big fights that challenge for a world title or at bouts at Lumpini Stadium in Bangkok.)

To a casual foreign observer, it may seem like a lot of to-do about two arts that are essentially identical, but the Khmer don't see it that way. In addition to a deeply ingrained cultural prejudice against the Thai, which is reciprocated, the Khmer refuse to see the similarities between the two arts. It's just easier to avoid the argument whenever possible. In fact, I was told at my gym to not even wear shorts that said muay Thai on them.

But let's get back to the movie.

The argument of whether an action movie star can win a real fight, has been raging for decades. In the 1980s, people would have paid big money to see Sylvester Stallone take on a professional heavyweight contender or watch Arnold Schwarzenegger battle an actual space alien in a no-holds-barred competition. Because movies are how most of the population learns about martial arts, the public assumes these movie stars are the badass fighters the films make them out to be.

However, Keanu Reeves, to his credit, had something different to say when he was interviewed by Jay Leno on *The Tonight Show* about his training for the kung fu hit, *The Matrix*. When Leno asked what Reeves would do if he jumped the star, Reeves said, "I'd run." Reeves then went on to explain that the intense training he'd studied for the movie was cinematic kung fu rather than *real* kung fu.

Now that I was doing a kung fu movie, I got to pose the opposite question: Can real fighters learn to be kung fu actors?

In regards to the most famous real-fighter-turned-actor Bruce

Lee, I knew that he had had a difficult time converting real kung fu to movie kung fu. Cinematically, his first film clips are terrible because of his blinding leg and hand speed; they were so fast that they just showed up as a blur on film. In fact, Bruce Lee was the one who came up with the idea of speeding up the camera during filming. This means that the camera would shoot more frames per second so a kick, which would only have appeared in one frame at normal speed, would appear in several. When the finished film was played at normal speed, all the kicks and punches looked beautiful.

Another issue Lee faced was that his personal martial arts style, jeet kune do, was based on minimalism—Lee's JKD philosophy was to cut away everything that was ineffective or inefficient. This meant his kicks were low and straight and his punches were close and fast. His signature move was called the one-inch punch, which is an amazing feat in itself but not too impressive on film. In movies, people want to see big movements rather than strikes that only travel one inch.

As a result, Lee developed his own movie-style kung fu, filling it with animalistic cries; high, spinning kicks and long and dramatic hand techniques. It has since become the standard for many martial arts films.

My acting debut was in a Khmer kung fu film called *Krabei Liak Goan* (*Buffalo Protecting Child*). I played the villain, as Westerners generally do in Asia. My normal fighting style uses very low kicks, mostly with the instep of my foot aimed at an opponent's shins. I use kicks only as a distraction to be able to move in and punch. I use my upper-body strength to push opponents, crowd them and get them on the ropes of the ring. But there would be no ropes in the film.

Eh Phou Thoung played the hero, of course. He was an extremely popular figure and a household name in Cambodia. He was even known in France and Australia, where Khmer boxing enjoys a following.

The director told me that it was hard converting the heavyweight kickboxer, who had more than 150 wins to his credit, into a kung fu film star.

"For the movies, he has to learn all new kicks," said the director, whose own martial arts background included impressive wins in kung fu.

"In the ring, he only throws roundhouse and push kick," the director added. "But the people have seen that already." After all, kickboxing is on television in Cambodia every Friday, Saturday and Sunday.

All the other fighters in the film were also experienced in Khmer kung fu, which is this odd style of movie kung fu they had invented. It looked like it was largely based on wushu, but it also included high spinning kicks from taekwondo. There were also shin kicks and knee and elbow strikes from Khmer boxing, but otherwise, they never worked on a bag or pads like fighters. Instead, they practiced kicks and spent hours rehearsing choreography for fight scenes.

They could leap and fly through the air with grace and speed. Their kicks were high, spinning, fluid and perfect. Compared to the lean, lithe extras who probably weighed an average 120 pounds each, the 200-pound me looked like an uncoordinated spaz. No wonder I was playing the villain!

The director had ordered that kickboxing champ Eh and I attend classes every day primarily to learn the high spinning and jump kicks for the fight scenes. The fight scenes themselves were written and choreographed on the set during filming. This was different from the normal team members who all had designated partners and had memorized numerous fight scenes so that they would be able to do them for any movie, TV show or karaoke video as needed. The directors would just have to put a handful of the Khmer kung fu team members in front of a camera and yell "action," and the fighters would do the scenes that they had practiced in training.

The champion only showed up for training twice because, as he'd say, "I can kick harder than them." It was true. He could kick harder. He could probably dismantle our Khmer kung fu teacher with one roundhouse kick, but power is the one skill movies don't require.

When it came time for our big fight scene in the film, neither Eh nor I knew what to do. If someone had put gloves on our hands and set us loose on one another, we wouldn't need directions. Yes, I would probably have been killed, but at least I'd go down knowing what was going on. But in a movie fight, it's not about winning. It's about following directions and doing exactly what the director wants. This is so much harder. Bruce Lee once said that fighting was the truest expression of self. I believe this, but movie fighting is all about rigid obedience and expressing someone else's view of the world.

The director demonstrated the series of moves the scene required. Because Eh hadn't trained and I am generally untrainable, he kept the moves simple. I was to throw a left knee, then a right knee at Eh; he would block it. He would swing at my head, and I would duck. Then I would kick at his head, and he would duck. The scene went on from there with other action and plot.

Just that scene took us several hours to film and by the end, I had thrown a head kick nearly 100 times. Sometimes we had to redo the scene because I forgot the sequence: left knee, right knee, duck, kick to the head. Instead I would go: left knee, kick, or left knee, right knee, forget to duck and catch a shot in the face. Eh was supposed to punch me, but he kicked me instead a couple of times just out of sheer reaction. Other times, he missed a block, and more than once, he didn't duck fast enough to avoid my head kick. The more times we re-shot the scene, the harder it was to get my leg that high. I hit him in the shoulder more than once.

Another special problem of fighting in an Asian film was the language. Eh spoke no English, so we communicated in Thai. The director spoke no Thai, so he would speak to me in English and to Eh in Khmer. There were times he made changes to the sequence, told one of us, but forgot to translate for the other. Those lapses always resulted in us hitting each other. I usually got the worst of these exchanges.

Another problem was cultural. Being American, I thought we would go on "three." In Cambodia, you go on "*pram*." At the beginning, I just assumed that pram was three, but pram is actually five. So when I'd hear the director counting three Khmer numbers,

I'd hit Eh when he wasn't prepared to block.

The second half of the scene should have been called "Eh's Revenge." After my character throws a flying kick to Eh's head and he ducks, he beats the tar out of me and kills me with a flying elbow.

If you're planning to come over to Asia to make movies, you should be prepared for a few things. First, you will be the bad guy. Second, you will get beat up. Third, there are no stunt doubles. If they tell you that your character is going to jump off the roof, then that means you are going to jump off the roof. Last, you are definitely going to earn some bruises or worse. In a Jackie Chan biography, the author dedicates a whole chapter to Chan's injuries. It's no wonder that that is the case when they use bed mattresses for high falls and real bullets in place of blanks.

The good thing about Asian films is that everyone in the film really can do martial arts. The special effects are simple, if silly, but the fighting is real. Baby powder is put on the shoes of the combatants so they give off exciting puffs of smoke when kicks connect. Yes, all of the kicks and punches do connect—no tricky camera angles here.

In the climax of my fight scene with Eh, he jumps what seems like 20 feet in the air and crashes down on my head with an elbow. Then while I am staggering around dazedly, he rams me in the stomach with his head. Of course, you have to vomit when you get rammed in the stomach in Asia. So picture me running around the set, doing a fight scene, with a mouthful of black tea to spit out when I get hit. We couldn't finish fast enough.

The movies are their own special world, and while it was a lot of fun to be part of a film, I felt like an animal on a leash. I was never able to relax because I was always wondering whether I was doing the scene right. But like Eh, I had to swallow my pride and admit that years and years of fighting experience were useless to me on camera. I had to start all over again from the beginning. So I guess the answers to the two questions I posed are no and no. It's hard for real fighters to become movie fighters and vice versa. Just remember the next time you're watching a fight film that they have as much to do with real fighting as doctors on television have to do with performing real surgery.

The Khmer film crew of *Krabei Liak Goan* set up for a scene.

During the weeks of filming, I practiced with the Khmer kung fu team in the morning. I saw a mix of many elements in their practice—taekwondo, judo, Khmer boxing, *hapkido* and kung fu. After training in China and Thailand, it was just a letdown to only train for an hour or two a day. Considering the fact that the team didn't train as much, their skills were still impressive. They could leap, jump and do handsprings. They would even practice jumping over the heads of their training partners. Even the instructor, who was 30 pounds overweight, could jump over five standing, lined-up students. The higher-level students could do as many as four or five kicks while standing, without setting their kicking foot back down on the ground.

I stuck it out for a while but I soon turned away from traditional arts once again and returned to modern boxing. I wanted to learn the national sport of Khmer boxing.

At the guesthouse where I lived was a driver named Sameth. He had been a monk before coming to work at the guesthouse, and we became close friends because we were two of the only people living in the backpacker quarter of Phnom Penh who didn't drink alcohol or use drugs. I originally hired Sameth as my driver, but when I saw how intelligent he was, I hired him as my Khmer language teacher. At that time in my life, I supported myself by writing for magazines, so Sameth worked for me as my driver, translator and camera assistant. Anything I needed in Phnom Penh, I always asked Sameth for first, and he would find it for me. So when I asked him to find a place for me to learn bradal serey, he took me to a gym that taught bradal serey and was run by a South African named Paddy Carson.

From that first meeting, Paddy and I began a friendship that continues to this day. I consider Paddy to be the absolute best boxing and kickboxing trainer I have ever worked with.

My training was to begin on a Monday so Sunday evening Sameth took me to watch the fights at a television studio. Each network has its own stadium and ring. They each host fights at least once per week. The fights are broadcast on television but a favorite pastime of the Khmer is to go attend the fights in person at the network stadium. The most popular network in 2004 was TV 5, which had the biggest stadium. For just a few thousand riel (less than $1 USD), the Khmer could watch the fights live. Small boys made their way through the crowd selling warm beer and soda. There was a special section for gamblers who shouted frantically and used hand signals to call out their bets.

It also turns out that most of the fighters in Cambodia are under contract to one or the other of the television studios, which are constantly vying for control of viewers and athletes alike. Once I began my training, my Khmer teammates would tell me that the studio paid them a salary of $20 USD per month to support their training. They generally received about $20 to $25 USD for their fights and fought who and when the studio ordered them to.

The deeper I got into the world of professional kickboxing in Cambodia, the more it made professional wrestling back in the States look honest. In fact, Don King had nothing on the slave contracts and shenanigans going on in Phnom Penh's fight community.

In Cambodia, boxers turn pro at about 14 years old. In the provinces, they can start fighting as early as 7 or 8 years old. In Cambodia, age is arbitrary because of unsubstantiated birth and death records. Even the youngsters get paid for their fights, but they are called amateurs, which means they fight under slightly different rules.

Youngsters fight four rounds that last two minutes each with two minutes rest in between. Adults fight fives rounds that last three minutes each with two minutes rest in between. All fights are scored by five judges. The judges look at such aspects of the fight as dominance and the damage done by effective striking. Knee strikes, elbow strikes, kicks and punches are allowed. Head-butting used to be allowed but is no longer used. In the old days, fighters fought with their hands wrapped in gauze, and matches also went on as long as they had to, until one fighter could no longer stand. These matches often resulted in death. During the colonial days, the French introduced the Khmer to boxing gloves, as well as the concept of rounds. Today, regulation Western boxing gloves are worn in official fights.

Although the national Khmer boxing commission does a fairly good job at keeping an eye on the sport, many of the Western safeguards are missing. For example, a fighter's hand wrappings are weighed in the West. You are only allowed so much gauze. After wrapping, the hands are checked and signed by a commissioner. In Cambodia, fighters wrap their hands with as much gauze as they want, heaping up the extra over the first two knuckles to make their punches harder. In the West, official gloves are used only one time during the fight night. In Cambodia at the end of a bout, gloves and often shorts and groin protection are handed off to the next fighter. If gloves are soaked in sweat, the padding becomes ineffective, and there will be more cuts.

In Khmer boxing, fighters are allowed to throw an opponent. Sometimes, they go into a clinch, and one throws the other. Or, one will block a kick in such a way that the opponent falls. Fighters sometimes wait until the opponent is kicking, and then kick his base leg out from under him. Any of these types of throws count highly with the judges, but they don't count as a knock down. As a rule, judges like kicks, elbows, knees and throws. They generally don't score punches too highly, unless the punch results in a knock down or a knock out.

The rest of the rules are similar to Western forms of kickboxing. For instance, fights are scored on a 10-point must system. This means the winner of a round must be assigned 10 points. The loser gets nine points, minus one point per knock down. A knock down and a slip are two different things. The former means a fighter gets hit so hard that he is almost knocked unconscious. His legs buckle and he falls down. When he gets back to his feet, he has a standing eight count, which means the referee will count to eight and ask the fighter if he is OK to continue. If the fighter is not ready to continue, then the referee will call a stoppage, and the other fighter will be awarded a win on a TKO or KO. If the fighter is ready to continue, then the fight will go on; but the fighter who fell loses one point. If a fighter gets knocked down three times in one round, he automatically loses the fight. A slip, on the other hand, just means someone made a misstep; for example, he slipped in a puddle of sweat or got his legs tangled and fell. There are no points for a slip.

In the West, my hero Muhammad Ali fought in 61 fights over 20 years and boxed in his final fight at the age of 40. In Cambodia, Khmer boxers peak around age 25; Eh Phou Thoung was pushing 30 and, while still fighting well, he wasn't as brilliant as he had been a few years ago. Khmer boxers fight an incredible number of matches over their short career, too. Some fighters in their early 20s have over 100 fights to their name, and some fighters compete two or three times a month.

Back at the TV studio, Sameth and I watched two fighters enter the ring for the first fight. (In bradal serey, each fighter is assigned the "red" or "blue" corner, and they wear shorts that correspond to that color.) The fight was happening in a big arena with the boxing ring in the middle and seats and bleachers on the side, much like it's set up in Las Vegas. Because I was not Khmer, I had paid the foreigner price for tickets, which was more expensive, at $2 USD.

Before the fight began, the two fighters did an abbreviated version of the *wai kru* and *ram muay*, which is a dance with cultural and religious significance that is also performed before muay Thai matches. You hear the exact same traditional music at the Lumpini Stadium in Bangkok before a fight. When I pointed that out, a number of Khmers told me I was absolutely wrong. They were offended that I would suggest that their national sport of Khmer kickboxing even slightly resembled any sport being played in Thailand. So I didn't point out how the uniforms also resembled muay Thai fight uniforms, or any other similarities, but there were many that I noticed.

For instance, when the bell signaled the first round, the opponents felt each other out—kicking, punching and clinching— which is exactly what happens in muay Thai. The rhythm was even the same as muay Thai. The first two rounds were slower because the only way to win in those rounds was by knockout and because the judges didn't record points scored in those rounds. They were just a way for the opponents to get warmed up and size each other up. Rounds three and four were where the bulk of the action took place. Whomever won those rounds would most likely win the fight, unless he got knocked out. Now, round five was problematic. If the blue corner fighter won rounds three and four, the red corner fighter would know that he had no chance of winning. So Red would just take it easy in round five.

Blue would also take it easy, not wanting to take any chances that could upset his victory. In this case, round five would be boring. If Red won round three, and Blue won round four, on the other hand, then the fifth round was make or break. The men would be pounding each other for all they were worth. The spectators would be on their feet the whole time, shouting their bets.

After I got to know a number of boxers, including my teammates and my trainers, they would give me another reason for "sleepy rounds." Because fighters were basically only allowed to fight other athletes contracted to the same TV station, this meant they were fighting their teammates, the people they trained with every day. Since the world of Phnom Penh is so small, you probably wound up fighting the same guy again and again. The only time fighters from different camps faced each other was in national championships, which are held once a year. Because the boxing community in

Cambodia is so tiny, there aren't a lot of opponents to divide into weight classes, which means that the huge-for-a-Khmer, 170-pound Eh has probably trounced the same underweight opponent five or six times.

Later, after I started training with Paddy Carson, I was helping my teammate, Main, prepare for the national championships.

"Are you nervous about getting matched up with someone better than you?" I asked.

"No," he answered. "I already know I will have to fight my best friend."

"Can you beat him?"

"Sometimes," he said. It turned out that they had already fought each other six times.

The fights at TV 5 were great. Just like in Thailand, the boxers had trained from a very young age and had fought once a month or more for years and years. They possessed a strength, toughness and heart I had rarely seen anywhere else.

The next day, I began my training with Paddy Carson.

The first thing you notice when you walk into a gym in Phnom Penh is that every Khmer man, almost without exception, can kick. Everyone, from young boys to out-of-shape, middle-aged businessmen can't resist the opportunity to throw a few deadly roundhouse kicks at the bag when they walk past it. When I first saw this kind of behavior, I found it intimidating. I kept thinking, They can all kick better than me.

The next thing you notice once you start training is that the training is extremely disorganized. None of the gyms I visited had a boxing ring. The only boxing rings were at the TV studios. So the guys never had the experience of training in a ring. None of the gyms used a ring timer, which is an essential tool used by Western boxers in training. We train so that we can time a round in our sleep because kickboxers and boxers live and die in two or three minute intervals. In Cambodia, training was very free form. I may have seen people throw leg-shattering kicks at bags, but on closer inspection, I saw that they never practiced combination kicks or other techniques. After a few hellacious kicks, they would wander off the mat to drink water and chat with their friends. Other more dedicated fighters would stand at the bag throwing isolated kicks all day. The sound was deafening and I couldn't imagine one of those kicks hitting my leg, but still there were no combinations or real strategy; there were just isolated, deadly strikes. Also none of the boxing gyms had weights, so the only cross-training the guys were doing was running.

But with all those deficiencies, Khmer boxers were the hardest fighters I had ever met. After years of training, even a low-level professional Khmer boxer could easily beat me in a fight. In the international fights, when Westerners came to fight in Cambodia, the Westerners usually lost. It always floored us how the Khmer with little or no resources and no scientific approach to training could still produce results. We assumed the answer had to do with the system— Khmer boxers grew up as fighters, so there must be a "survival of the fittest" mentality involved. The pool begins with hopefuls but weeds them down from an early age to find the champions. I always thought that the ideal training scenario would have been a Western gym with Western training available to young Khmer fighters who would grow up to fight twice a month. Think of the superhuman fighters you could produce!

Paddy's gym was somewhat like this. He did his training by the book in which workouts were broken into three-minute rounds with one minute in between. Every day, practice started with three rounds of shadowboxing followed by three to five rounds of focus-pad training for the hands only. All pad work was done in combinations, and Paddy would vary the pace depending on what we were working on that day. If the focus was cardio, we'd throw a high volume of punches with Paddy calling out combinations in rapid-fire succession.

"Give me two. Give four. Give me two, two. Give me five. Give me three, five," he'd call out. (All of the fighters, including the Khmer, knew the English codes for the combinations.)

He did the same with kicks, sometimes calling for as many as 10 consecutive kicks before changing legs. Another cardio exercise was holding onto Paddy's neck and throwing knees into his padded midsection for an entire round. If your pace slowed at all, Patty would hit back. The first time we did this exercise, I only lasted 30 seconds.

Normally, I preferred to train with local instructors in other countries, but in Cambodia, Paddy, who had trained Western fighters in South Africa and Thailand for years before coming to Phnom Penh, was the way to go. Fortunately, I learned all my culture through my teammates who were all Khmer save for one. The fact that the Khmer went to a foreigner to learn their national sport is still amazing to me. When people saw the advantages of Western training methods, Paddy began acquiring his student base.

Because Cambodia was like the Wild West, it wasn't unusual for people to come into Paddy's gym and challenge him (or me) to fight. Paddy would reverse the challenge: If the challenger went with Paddy on the focus pads for one round, then he could fight anyone in the gym. Most challengers sustained their punches for 30 to 45 seconds before wilting.

Paddy also had a lot of experience coaching his students through fights in both Thailand and Cambodia. He explained the most common knockouts in Khmer boxing and muay Thai came from apparent kicks to the head. Sometimes, the knockout wasn't from the shin hitting the side of the opponents head, as it looked, but instead was caused by the top of the foot hitting the back of the opponent's head. This means the leg has to go up and almost over the opponent's head, change direction and then crash down on it. The shin hits the side of the head, but the foot smashes into the back of the opponent's neck.

Because the Khmer start training as children, they learn to win with this kick earlier on in life. It's one of their best tools and it's doubtful you'll win if you try and beat them at their own game.

It was rare to see a Khmer fighter do anything but single punches, generally a long-range hook to the side of the head, because they were such good kickers. Their strength lay in their kicks—the high roundhouse and precision kicks to the ribs or thighs, but their boxing skills were lacking. While they could withstand kicks that would kill a Westerner, those same Khmer fighters were often defenseless against a right hook to the body. Of course, the great equalizer was the elbows and knees, which Westerners could throw from close range. A Khmer won't even see an elbow or knee coming because he isn't trained for it. My teammate Peter, a New Zealander who had been fighting in professional kickboxing in Thailand before coming to Cambodia, definitely found that having superior cardio and superior hands was winning fights for him.

Fighting professionally in Thailand is hands down better than fighting in Phnom Penh. Peter and I both trained in Cambodia, and with the exception of Peter's one fight in Phnom Penh, we both fought only in Thailand. (During my 18 months in Cambodia, I traveled across the border to Thailand to fight twice. Peter and some of the other foreigners also went to Thailand for fights.)

For example, my teammate Peter was fighting, and in the first several seconds of the first round, an elbow strike cut open his forehead just over his left eye. Officials stopped the fight and gave Peter a few seconds to control the bleeding before restarting. Twenty seconds later, Peter had an identical cut over his other eye. After that, he seemed to wake up. He dominated his opponent through the next four rounds, but in Cambodia, the decision is almost always awarded based on damage done. So Peter lost.

Back in the dressing room, he lay on a table while the doctor sewed him up. We asked the doctor how many stitches Peter got and the doctor just sort of shrugged. There were so many that he had stopped counting.

Peter got $125 USD for that fight because he is a foreigner. His opponent, who won, got a small fraction of that amount. In other countries, boxing is seen as a way of fighting yourself out of poverty. In Cambodia, boxing is a way of fighting and remaining poor.

One of our teammates was a 26-year-old Khmer guy called Boss. He told us about his fighting life before meeting Paddy.

"I had been a professional boxer back in my village," Boss said, "but you can't make any money in the provinces. So I came to Phnom Penh. I wound up living on the streets. And, without proper food to eat, winning got harder and harder. In Cambodia, a fighter earns about $25 for winning a fight. How can we live on that?"

Paddy had us training Monday through Friday. We generally did 16 rounds per day of training, which added up to several rounds on the heavy bag, medium bag, pads and sparring at the end of three hours. We were also expected to do 20 minutes of shadowboxing as well as weight training and running. Because of my past knee injuries, I did all my running on a treadmill, but it broke down constantly because I weighed as much as two Khmer.

Because of its tropical location, Cambodia is extremely hot all year, and inside Paddy's gym, the temperature normally hovered in the high 90s. Peter and I estimated that we'd sweat out four or five liters of fluid during a single training session. It was so bad that the Khmer staff had to follow me around with a mop because I'd leave massive puddles of sweat on the floor, and people would slip when they were kicking the bag. Training in that kind of heat, you had to drink two or three quarts of water during the workout. After the requisite three hours of training, I would happily return to my guesthouse, shower, sit in front of the fan and drink fluids for the next several hours. I was never a great fan of air conditioning, but in Cambodia, I was glad to have a fan or I wouldn't have recovered in time for the next day's training.

On weekends, Sameth and I would go to TV 5 and watch the fights. I saw Eh Phou Thoung fight a number of times. He always won. Once, he was fighting a foreigner and he shattered the man's arm with a single kick. I later found a Web site that kept records on how many other people's legs and arms Eh had broken. There were several.

While I continued training with Paddy, I was still looking for bokator.

In a Phnom Penh gym, Antonio trains with Paddy Carson.

Living in Phnom Penh was a constant frustration. It was difficult to get anything done. At that time there weren't any ATMs, and banks weren't on international networks so getting paid for my writing was very difficult. Internet connections weren't great because the Prime Minister's relative owned a monopoly right to provide service to Cambodia and saw no reason to improve it. Internet shop owners said they preferred the slower speed because it increased the time that customers would need to be logged in and they were paying by the hour. Also, there were constant power outages.

In Thailand, you could always get incredible Thai food for cheap. Street stalls sold noodle dishes for as little as 20 baht. However, in Cambodia, you couldn't eat on the streets unless you wanted to get deathly ill. If you didn't like that option, you were forced to eat in restaurants, which got expensive after a while.

People often tried to rip you off in Cambodia. It was easy to get angry at them, but you then had to remind yourself of several relevant facts. First, they had all been through an incomparable genocidal tragedy. Second, there were nearly zero job opportunities. The country had only established a cash economy during the early

1990s. A number of Khmer over the age of 30 had no education at all, and some of those who had a university degree hadn't been to primary school.

This is all made more tragic by the fact that Cambodia is a country with a long and proud history of culture and empire, dating back to the Angkor period that precedes many of the other civilizations in Southeast Asia. Along with their ancient culture, Cambodia has a long tradition of martial arts. For thousands of years, right on up to the present, high-ranking military and police officers were expected to be experts in martial arts and proficient in individual combat, but then came the Khmer Rouge. As with many other intellectual and cultural national treasures, the Khmer Rouge almost eliminated Cambodian martial arts when they killed off the majority of the masters. Things didn't get better during the Vietnamese occupation because they also prohibited the practice of martial arts, under pain of death.

After nearly two decades of decay and destruction, many Khmer are working hard to rebuild this martial-art tradition. Even the film director I worked with on *Krabei Liak Goan* was working hard to revive his country's martial arts. It is no easy task because the country continues to recover from more than 150 years of colonization, auto-genocide and occupation.

There was another obstacle preventing the recovery of this martial heritage in Cambodia: Nothing had ever been written about these arts. As a result, it was impossible to catalogue or preserve the martial arts. Masters wouldn't share their secrets with each other and most of them were pretty old. For example, a Phnom Penh sports magazine ran a story about an 80-something-year-old man who was one of the last people alive who had any familiarity with the ancient art of bokator. However, he had actually only studied the art for two years, more than 60 years ago, before the genocide. He never taught students because the art was supposed to remain a secret. You have to wonder: Did two years of training make him an expert? No wonder it was difficult for Cambodians to preserve their cultural heritage!

There was no lack of interest among young people, however. They all wanted to learn martial arts. In speaking to officials of the Cambodian Martial Arts Games Committee, one problem seemed to be the popularity of foreign arts like taekwondo, karate, judo and Chinese kung fu; they distracted young Khmer from learning their traditional arts. These non-native arts also offered students the opportunity to earn belts and compete internationally in sports where they never really get hit. In contrast, the Khmer arts were more painful because fighters would have to train to fight in order to excel.

After nearly 18 months in Cambodia, I was ready to leave. I had learned a lot and written two books. I spoke Khmer fairly well and had brought my boxing and fitness to a level I had never reached before, thanks to working with Paddy Carson.

Despite making plans to leave the country, I ended up staying three months longer. Why? Because while driving down a street, I noticed a small sign tacked to a telephone pole that advertised:

"Bokator, the traditional Cambodian martial art."

I called the number and made an appointment to visit the club right away.

Bokator is the ancient Khmer martial art from which all modern Khmer martial arts derive, like bradal serey. Today, the name bradal serey has been lost to the world, having been replaced by the phrase muay Thai. "The Thais stole our art," say many Khmer, who believe that the bas-reliefs carved on the walls of Angkor Wat temple prove that the origin of Khmer boxing predates muay Thai. While the name may have been stolen, the art of Khmer boxing is very much alive and thriving as a professional sport, enjoyed all around the world. This, unfortunately is not the case for the much older art of bokator. This art is nearly unknown even in Cambodia.

My driver Sameth took me to the address on the paper I had ripped off of the telephone pole. The bokator school was located on the second story of a parking garage behind the gym.

Only a tiny sign out front confirmed that this was the home of "Boxkator." I later learned that grandmaster San Kim Sean had added the "x" because he hoped to make the sport more accessible to foreigners.

From the dark parking lot building, I made my way up some old cement stairs to the second floor and to a large, open area. The entire floor was dedicated to sports, and during my time there, I'd see hapkido, ping pong, *capoeira* and karate teams. Over the years, the other teams would disappear and give way to increasingly popular bokator. However, on my first visit, bokator occupied less than half the floor.

San Kim Sean sat behind a desk doing whatever grandmasters do when they aren't teaching. He wore the trappings of a grandmaster— gold boxing shorts, a gold *krama* (scarf) around his waist and a smaller gold krama around his head. He was about 60 years old at the time, and despite a large belly, I could see he possessed power. As soon as he saw me, he smiled and placed his hands in a prayer position in front of his chest. He greeted me enthusiastically: "*Jum reap sua*."

I was excited, too, but while I had only been looking for bokator for 18 months, San Kim Sean had been waiting to be found for 40 years.

Later, I found out why he had been so excited to see me: I was the first foreign journalist to visit him. He was pleased about any foreign journalist who might find him and go out and tell the world about bokator.

I would later go on to do an interview with the grandmaster. It was published in *Black Belt* magazine in 2006, while other versions ran in *Farang* magazine in Thailand. The two articles created a tidal wave of interest, and since then, one film crew and many other print journalists have visited the school. San Kim Sean and I would also collaborate on several documentaries together about bokator that appeared on The History Channel. But I'm getting ahead of myself. Let me share what San Kim Sean told me during my first interview with him.

San Kim Sean began training in bokator when he was just 13 years old. According to him, even at that time the art was not very common. "Only a few old men knew the art." It was still practiced in some of the provinces but was largely unknown in the capital. His "uncle," who was a friend of his father's, taught him to fight with his hands. Another "uncle" taught him to use the long staff.

Yet another taught him to use the two traditional Khmer long swords called *dao*.

San Kim Sean was always interested in martial arts, so he practiced Khmer boxing for three years. Later, he earned belts in judo and karate; he became only one of three Khmer to earn a black belt in hapkido.

"I was third *dan*," he told me.

The year he became a hapkido instructor was also the year that Phnom Penh fell to the Khmer Rouge, the political party under the rule of Pol Pot. It was 1975, the city was evacuated and the country was collectivized into an agrarian society. Pol Pot reset the calendar to Year Zero because he wanted to break with the past. Everyone suffered, but groups that were singled out for extreme persecution and extermination included the Cham (Cambodian Muslims), Chinese, Vietnamese, the educated, the literate, artisans, skilled workers, etc. The consequence was that Pol Pot hunted down and killed the masters of all traditional Khmer arts, including singing, dancing and martial arts.

"I don't have to tell you the Pol Pot time was bad," San Kim Sean said.

After two years under the thumb of the Khmer Rouge, San Kim Sean's government-designated work group—generally the size of a village—had dwindled from 10,000 to 500 people. The bokator master had also lost two children at the hands of the Khmer Rouge, and all of his students and training brothers had died. He also held the dubious distinction of being the only hapkido instructor who had survived the Khmer Rouge.

When the regime fell to the Vietnamese in 1979, San Kim Sean went back to Phnom Penh and taught hapkido. But Cambodia had traded one regime for another, and the Vietnamese prohibited the Khmer from practicing martial arts.

"I was teaching in secret, but some Khmer person who was jealous of me, turned me in to the Vietnamese authorities."

The Vietnamese said that San Kim Sean was trying to build an army or had some other subversive goal in mind. He would have been jailed, but he and his wife escaped to a refugee camp in Thailand.

They spent one year in the refugee camp where his wife gave birth to a daughter named Bopa. Eventually, the family was able to relocate to the United States, settling in Houston, Texas in 1980. San Kim Sean found a good job at the airport. He also taught hapkido to Khmer children at the YMCA. Life was good for San Kim Sean and his family, but he missed his culture. On a vacation to the Khmer community in Long Beach, California, he was amazed at the Khmerness of the place.

"The shops had Khmer writing on them. I saw women wearing sarongs. They had Khmer restaurants," San Kim Sean laughed. "I said, 'Hey, this is my country.'"

He quit his job in Houston and moved to Long Beach with his family. Eventually, he found work dubbing Chinese action movies into Khmer, He continued teaching hapkido.

It had been more than decade since the bokator master had left behind the tragedy of his country. He took his American students to competitions, and never once did he hear the word "bokator." He began to realize that no one knew anything about any Khmer martial arts. He began to wonder: Why was he advertising a Korean art?

If the statistic—that each progressive generation learns 10 percent less than the previous—is true, then San Kim Sean couldn't be surprised that the Khmer martial arts were on a downward slide. He began having nightmares about Cambodia.

"Khmer young people don't even know their own history," he said. "They don't know about our greatness in the past, the ancient arts which were taught by the grandfathers' grandfather, which is running in our blood." He believed God was telling him that he needed to go home and help the Khmer people. So he returned to his native land in 1995.

Even then, San Kim Sean didn't teach bokator. He actually helped rebuild the country's national hapkido association. It wasn't until 2001 that he began teaching bokator.

Between 1995 and 2001, San Kim Sean had been busy. He had combed the countryside, looking for any bokator master who may have survived the Khmer Rouge and the Vietnamese. He found a few but they were old. He said, "Many of them were between 60 and 90 years of age." And none of them were teaching. After being repressed by two powerful regimes, they were afraid to start.

"I tried to tell them it was OK. We already had permission from the government, but they wouldn't listen," San Kim Sean said. The old men wanted to stay in the rural provinces, but San Kim Sean insisted, "You have a great gift which was given to you by our ancestors. Do you want to steal it from our children? When you die, the art will die with you."

"Did it work?" I asked.

"Some of them broke down in tears. In April of 2004, we held the first bokator conference in Phnom Penh. Now, there are schools in eight provinces. And, we are preparing for a national championship."

Most martial artists in the West can't be bothered to practice, but here was a man who had risked his life to preserve the arts. More recently, he had given up a well-paying job in the United States to come back to Cambodia to recover a lost martial art.

After the first few days of interviews, I began training in bokator.

In the art, the practitioner's rank is designated through colored scarves called krama. The five white krama animal forms are: king monkey, lion, elephant, *apsara* (traditional Hindu sacred nymph) and crocodile. The green krama forms, which are like kata, include duck, crab, horse, bird and dragon.

I discovered that the art was very complete, containing kicks, punches, knee strikes, elbow strikes and grappling techniques as well as weapon forms and demonstration techniques. (The bokator demonstrations were really something to see. San Kim Sean created extremely elaborate, choreographed sequences in which students flew, leapt and jumped about like movie star Tony Jaa's character in the movie *Ong-bak*.)

Each training session began by paying homage to Jayavarman VII, the patron saint of bokator. After that, San Kim Sean would lead the class through a group workout routine of five of each of the different kicks, elbow strikes, punches and knee strikes on each side of the body. Bokator has nearly 20 knee strikes, countless kicks and almost 30 different elbow strikes. Just doing each of those five times in the air was already a great workout. Once again, similar to my training in Shaolin, I never saw the bokator condition. Their perfect build, strength and athleticism came naturally from practicing the martial art. They also never worked the heavy bag. They developed power and speed from kicking the air, thousands of times before the end of the day.

There was a set routine to training. Once every hour, a signal was given and all of the students—approximately 30 or so—would line up in formation, kneel, pray and bow to the shrine of Brahma, the god of warriors, as well as to King Jayavarman VII.

Then San Kim Sean would take them back through the workout. A half hour later, the class would divide into groups to learn forms, weapons training and sparring. At the beginning of the next hour, the signal would again be heard and the whole process would be repeated. There were students who stayed at the gym for hours, going through the workout ritual several times a day. There were also a number of homeless students who slept on the training mats at

Antonio practices *bokator* with San Kim Sean.

night. These students participated in the workout every hour on the hour, from about 6:00 in the morning to 9:00 at night. Needless to say, these guys had incredible skill in bokator.

Bokator was one of the most interesting martial arts I had seen. It was also the beginning of my appreciation of art for art's sake. I wanted to learn bokator and be part of the team for this historic renaissance of the Khmer martial arts, but I had already bought a ticket back to the United States to go on a speaking tour to promote the release of my book, *Adventures in Formosa*.

I promised the bokator master that I would come back to study with him and be the first foreigner to earn a black krama. However, it would be another two years before I made good on that promise.

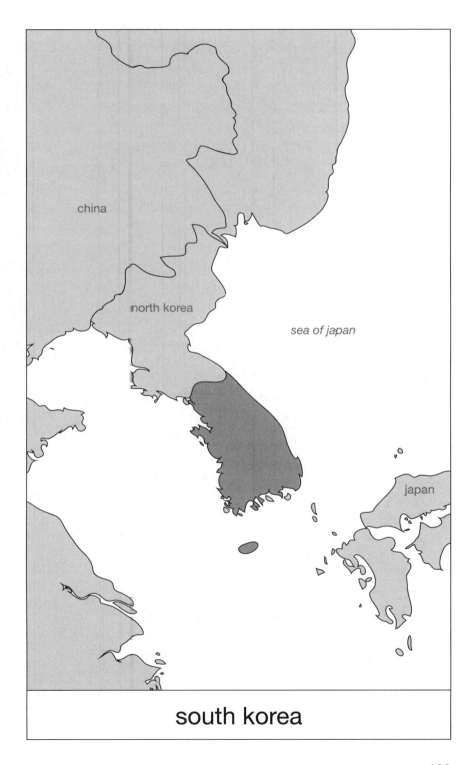

china

north korea

sea of japan

japan

south korea

chapter 6

AFTER CAMBODIA, I SPENT SEVEN MONTHS in the United States doing speaking engagements. I spoke about 70 times on the East Coast between Washington D.C. and New York City. Having absolutely no money to get back to Asia, I went online and found a job teaching in Korea. The company paid for my flight to South Korea, gave me an apartment and a decent salary. The problem was, I hated Korea. It was by far my least favorite country to live in. For me, Korea was impersonal. It was hard to make friends. And even though I studied the language intensively and was offered a scholarship to do my Ph.D., I couldn't stand the thought of spending several years in a country that I didn't enjoy. I left Korea after seven months, even though I signed a one-year contract at my job.

Now, in defense of Korea, I wasn't in the best personal place. After having been in the United States for seven months, I was anxious to get back out into the field—doing stories, studying martial arts and having adventures. To do that, I needed a job, but that job made me feel trapped. It also might have helped if I had been living in Seoul, the capital, rather than Busan, its second largest city. However, the proof of how badly Korea worked out for me is how little I wrote.

In Cambodia, I averaged more than one magazine article a week. In Korea, I wrote less than one per month.

The two redeeming qualities in Korea were the language, which I enjoyed studying, and the martial arts.

China has the Shaolin monks. Japan has the tradition of the samurai, but Korea is the most overlooked Asian country, by foreigners and martial artists alike. It offers the widest variety of martial arts of any country that I have trained in. Within 100 meters of my suburban apartment, I found several kendo schools, called *gom do* in Korean; countless taekwondo, hapkido and *kuk sool* academies and a boxing gym. Expand the radius by about two football fields, and you'd find the historic Korean art of *taekkyon*, Western wrestling, traditional *ssireum* wrestling and muay Thai.

According to official data of the year 2006, Busan boasted over 500 judo clubs. PRIDE championships draw huge audiences on cable television, and Korea runs its own professional MMA and kickboxing league known as Neofight. To me, the best example of how popular martial arts are in Korea was through my university professors at Dong-A University. They were old-school Korean intelligentsia who had attended the all-but-disappeared Korean cultural finishing schools. At the schools, they learned Chinese calligraphy, poetry, abacus calculation and an appreciation for other traditional arts. It just fascinated me that these extremely cultured and educated men had a deep love of Japanese and Korean wrestling, which they constantly debated and discussed over tea.

Training in Korea is also an extremely unique experience. The military, which has compulsory service, has martial arts teams. Universities all have competitive teams for nearly every martial art imaginable. Companies sometimes have teams, and there are numerous community teams and associations, competing at various levels.

Training starts in childhood for many Koreans. It's pretty much expected that Korean children will study a Korean martial art, usually taekwondo or hapkido, at some point in their lives. They are expected to train one hour a day after school, five days a week. They take a belt test once a month so it is pretty much a given that martial arts students will earn a black belt. At this point, many of them quit and never do martial arts again. However, there is a small percentage that does continue to compete in martial arts until they finish university. They train in the evening after work. As a result, world-class Korean fighters are at the top; they're good because they've already been training for 25 years. The Korean martial arts system isn't designed for a 20-, 30- or 40- year old beginner to walk in and become a top martial artist.

There is a darker side to this martial arts intensity, however. The martial arts schools are huge businesses in Korea, which collect money from six to eight groups of kids every day for a period of years. If the children fail a belt test, their mothers pull them out of one martial arts school and enroll them in another. As a result, I have seen young black belts who could barely do a roundhouse kick without falling over. This is why the steps leading to a black belt are like playing Little League for Koreans. Only a handful of Little Leaguers are expected to go on to play in high school teams and even fewer are expected to play in college, and fewer still will go on to play in the majors. But this also means that the top competitors in Korea are some of the top competitors in the world.

I had been in Korea about a month and was feeling pretty depressed. Sure, I was taking Korean lessons at Dong-A University while teaching at a local *hakwan* or cram school—a supplemental educational institute that nearly all Korean children attend daily after school and into the evenings. I also had a few problems. First, in my experience, the Korean language was one of the hardest to learn because the grammar is very complex. Second, I had gained about 22 pounds while I was in the United States. I was hitting the gym every day to get back into shape. Third, I found that, unlike in Taiwan, the Korean school wasn't interested in helping foreign teachers outside of the workplace. This was an issue because without the school's help, I didn't know how to communicate with people and find a martial arts school.

So much of what we learn and don't learn in life depends on our expectations. Most of my life, I couldn't read Korean. So I had just learned, subconsciously, not to even attempt to read signs posted in the Korean language. One night, I walked out of a language lesson very exhausted; I had just finished a three-hour study session. I glanced at a sign across the street, which I had passed twice a day for a month, and for the first time I could read it. It said "Martial Arts School" in Korean. I remember thinking, how do I know this? I can't read Korean but obviously intensive multiple-hour study had helped me learn to read the language. I had just overcome a major mental block to my learning, and as a result, I began reading all of the signs on my street. I found at least 10 martial arts schools within a block of where I worked. I felt like an idiot for not having noticed them earlier. I randomly chose a kuk sool school and walked in.

Kuk sool is extremely similar to hapkido. In fact, I can't tell the difference between the two, and many of my kuk sool instructors were certified in both. The arts specialize in joint locks and manipulations. They are arts that are good for bouncers and police officers because they deal with taking down unruly opponents sans hitting. The arts contain kicks, which seemed similar to taekwondo to me.

The fighting component of kuk sool is point fighting in which the students wear headguards and body protectors. Punching to the face is not allowed, nor is kicking below the belt. Fights are graded on points, and kicks are awarded one point each. Fighters are separated and restart the match after a point is scored, but it was never clear to me if you were allowed to grab and throw your opponent or if you were only allowed to throw your opponent when you caught his kick.

On walking in, I strained to understand the kuk sool teacher because many of the martial arts instructors I met didn't or refused to speak English. I soon realized that all he was saying was a long string of numbers, explaining the various payment options. There were no Shaolin monks here trying to trick you out of your money. Martial arts in Korea is a business.

"We welcome foreign students with open arms," the teacher got across to me.

As long as they have open wallets, I thought back.

In the end, I paid about $130 USD to sign up, which included a single uniform. Each additional month cost $90 USD. To fight in a competition would cost me $30 USD. Belt tests were free. In Taiwan and Thailand, I trained for free. In Cambodia, I paid about $30 USD a month. In China, I paid $200 a month including room and board. Even in Hong Kong, I only paid about $40 a month. So, by Asian standards, Korea was an expensive place to train. In the grand scheme of things, $90 USD a month is not a lot of money. Although I was assigned a certain class at a certain hour, I really could have attended as many times per day as I wanted, and training was five days a week. (I also checked around at other schools that taught mainstream arts like hapkido and taekwondo. They charged similar prices.

By American standards, the training intensity was low. At kuk sool school where I practiced, students arrived on time, but training always started late. The warm-up and stretching session was rushed and nearly useless. As a result, I had to build more time into my schedule to do stretching on my own or arrive early so I could warm up. After our brief warm-up, there was a break. Then we worked on technique. There were days that we did intensive kicking drills, just as I had done when training in taekwondo in other countries. Other days, we did rolls and tumbles.

At the end of a training session, I always felt that while I had invested an hour and a half of my time, I had only received 20 minutes of physical benefit. However, if you do 20 minutes of physical training a day, every day for years, then you become a master. This is just the kind of timeline Asians train on; it works for them. To maintain my fitness and strength, however, I bought a gym membership that cost $80 USD a month. The gyms in Korea are unbelievably clean. Every piece of equipment is well-maintained and in working order. Even small gyms have countless treadmills, stair-masters and bicycles, so there is no waiting. You can find both free weights and machines in Korean gyms. Some gyms also offer martial arts classes. They provide you with workout clothes. When you finish working out, you throw them in a hamper and the staff takes care of the laundry. Many gyms include a sauna and huge Japanese-style public baths with hot and cold tubs.

I also learned that the training in Korean martial arts schools is very focused. It is all about a single art, so they aren't as well-rounded as a professional MMA or kickboxing gym in other parts of Asia. For example, I approached my Korean kendo teacher about cross-training. (Korea was a colony of Japan from 1911 to 1945 so even the Japanese martial arts have taken root here). I suggested that weight lifting would help build up the muscles necessary to maintain a sword in a defensive posture and that running would increase the stamina needed during lightning-fast sword exchanges. He looked at me as if I were insane. He asked, "Why would a kendo competitor need to run and lift weights? This is kendo."

This attitude seemed to extend to other aspects of Korean life. For example, I once used my low-cost health insurance as a teacher to go to an acupuncturist. At this point, my Korean was decent enough that I could talk to the doctor. While I was lying on his table, the doctor said, "You look like a strong man, but you are nearly 40 years old."

"Yes," I said. "I train in martial arts."

This amazed the doctor because he couldn't believe that I could be both an English teacher *and* a martial artist. I told him I was also an author. This understandably astounded him. Many of the guys I trained with would never train again for the rest of their lives the minute they got their first job after university.

"I wish I had your free time," the doctor said, implying that was the only way I could do so many things. "You can't still fight though. Can you?"

"Yes, I fight."

"But how can you win? Your opponent must be very young."

"Yeah," I said. "When I fight, the guys are usually 20 years old. But I have more experience and I have self-confidence. Older guys have more self-confidence, and with that you can often win the fight before it starts."

The doctor didn't believe me. He repeated that there was no way I could win. I should mention here that the reason I was at an acupuncturist was because I had not had a satisfying experience with a medical doctor. When I told the doctor my leg hurt when I kicked, he simply said, "Don't kick."

At my gym, I met a few members of the university sports and martial arts teams. Just like anywhere else, the top competitors were cross-training, but as I mentioned earlier, they represented a small percentage of the total martial artists.

I guess I shouldn't have been so surprised by the culture's rejection of cross-training. Back in the 1970s in the United States, people had a hard time grasping the concept of kickboxing. I remember my father's friends saying, "You can't kick in a boxing match! They will disqualify you."

I also remember a huge debate in the 1970s about whether or not martial artists could lift weights. The general consensus was that they shouldn't because they would lose their flexibility. There was also a silly idea that strength and size didn't matter in martial arts. Although everyone was in agreement on this point, judo, boxing and wrestling had weight classes. Isn't that proof that size and strength matter?

It's also interesting to think that back in the 1970s, Bruce Lee was advocating weight lifting, running and cross-training. He was probably the first person to recognize Western wrestling and boxing as individual martial arts. He used ground fighting and submission grappling mixed in with the traditional arts.

He saw that Western fencers had the fastest and most powerful lunge strike in the world and emulated it. Of course, everyone idealizes Bruce Lee. Most schools had a picture of him hanging up somewhere. But apparently, no one listened to him. They kept doing what they had done for thousands of years. We've come a long way since then, baby!

Back in Korea, I'd flip on the television and see two huge and muscled men in a boxing ring. They'd shin-kick each other in the thighs. They'd use knees, elbows, clinches and takedowns. They'd punch in combinations. Was it K-1? Was it muay Thai? Was it mixed martial arts? Was it *vale tudo*? Does it matter? The truth is that the differences between all modern fighting arts are becoming smaller and smaller.

I'd changed the channel and see guys in starched white uniforms flipped through the air and break boards with their feet. Having been in the ring with champion taekwondo practitioners and other traditional martial artists, I knew that one solid punch to the face would change everything these guys believed about themselves and their art.

This conundrum was one that I would confront again and again, especially in Korea: How can traditional martial arts and reality-based fighting exist in the same world? Why don't the traditional arts adopt newer and better techniques? Why do we still have more than one martial art? I was often reminded of what a commentator said in the early days of the UFC: "To hell with all of these styles! You either punch, kick or seize."

If the goal is to have the most effective fighting system, then it seems that you would just adopt the best techniques from what everyone else is doing. If everyone did this, we would develop into a world with one extremely effective martial art. But somehow, the traditional martial arts just don't do this.

In more than 25 years of training in martial arts, competing in countless challenge matches and participating in many professional fights, I've learned to adapt. For example, when I went back to kickboxing in the 1990s after eight years of doing other martial arts, things had changed. Fighters were using muay Thai kicks instead of taekwondo kicks. When I saw the damage a shin kick could cause, I immediately changed my style and learned the new techniques. When I saw how a kickboxer could wear down a man by thigh-kicking him, I adopted that style. When my boxing coach in Cambodia taught me a better way to hook-punch in a natural position, rather than twist, we undid a style I had been using my whole life. Sure, I'd get the urge to do traditional martial arts every few years. I'd show up to a school and train for a few days, but when I left, I would always run straight back to boxing or muay Thai because I believed that the traditional style required me to unlearn all the fighting skills it'd taken me years to develop.

On my second night of training in kuk sool, my teacher wanted me to fight with one of the other practitioners so they could see what I could do. They were curious about how a boxer/kickboxer fights, and I think I may have been only the second foreigner to ever enter the school; there is always interest in seeing how foreigners do things.

I started looking around for boxing gloves but they told me I wasn't allowed to punch because it wouldn't be fair and someone could get hurt. While I agreed with the safety precautions, I also felt that I wouldn't be able to properly demonstrate what I could do without them. Since I am admittedly the world's worst kicker, this was going to be a one-sided fight.

When the teacher said, "Go," I rushed in and crowded my Korean opponent. I stayed right on top of him, which meant he couldn't use the long high kicks that they all seem to love. From this position, the only kick I could manage was a shin kick to the back of his right thigh, which I threw repeatedly. First, my opponent stopped to complain that I was crowding him. Next, he complained about the shin kicks. A few times, he managed to get a little distance to throw high kicks, but I blocked with my elbows. Finally, one of my elbows landed square on his shin, and he collapsed in pain. The fight was over.

Because I'd fought against traditional martial artists before, I pretty much knew the fight would go like that. I wondered how the teacher and my opponent could ignore what they see on television all the time? K-1, ssireum, kickboxing—they knew what the sports looked like. Why were they surprised by the techniques I used?

The next day when I came to class, the teacher complimented me on my performance the night before. He was really impressed with how I blocked the kicks with my elbows.

"Wow!" he said, or the Korean equivalent. "That is amazing and tough." Then he proceeded to teach me how to block kicks with my open hands.

Antonio throws a kick at a *kuk sool* school in Seoul.

In Korea, I turned 39, and I was still following the same path I began at age 11; I was looking for answers in martial arts. From my first martial arts teacher, H. David Collins, I learned to fight in unconventional ways. He didn't make his students wear uniforms or treat the school as a quiet and temple-like place. He used to have us exercise to music, and at the time, aerobics was a pretty crazy concept. As I grew up, my focus shifted from self-defense and street fighting to challenging and improving myself through martial arts. By the time I was 39, I was learning how martial arts are a gateway to foreign cultures.

In Korea, it happened the same way. I was watching television and came across a martial arts competition that looked intriguing. It was called taekkyon and was one of the strangest martial arts I had ever seen. So I found a school near my house and checked it out.

Taekkyon is an ancient Korean martial art that combines dancing with kicks and throws. During the Japanese occupation, taekkyon was banned and nearly died out. Fortunately, one very old master named Song Duk-Ki survived. He is personally credited with having saved the art, teaching students until his death in 1987 at the age of

96. In recent years, taekkyon has enjoyed a resurgence of popularity with national competitions and demonstrations at festivals. The practitioners I interviewed said that they enjoyed practicing taekkyon because they could enjoy all of the physical and health benefits of martial arts without getting injured. One friend said, "Taekkyon is part of our cultural heritage. By practicing, I am helping to keep our history alive."

The purpose of a taekkyon match is not to injure your opponent but instead to throw him off-balance. For instance, this is what I saw on the television show:

Music plays while the two opponents dance about in a circle in traditional Korean robes. Their movements are fluid and graceful. There is a referee who is dressed in a long robe and high hat, like a government official from centuries past. When the referee gave the signal, they attacked each other. With phenomenal fluidity, the red-dressed opponent threw a long, high kick, just missing the yellow-dressed opponent's face. Yellow moved in and returned a low push kick, which landed just above Red's knee. Red stumbled in his retreat. Yellow brought his knees straight up in a covering gesture before charging in for a final move. But Red caught him behind the head with an open palm strike. Red simultaneously hooked Yellow's legs and tripped him. Yellow fell flat on his face. The referee, who was also wearing an impressive costume, stepped between the two opponents. He waved a collapsible fan, declaring Red the winner.

As much as I was fascinated by the unusual art and its fluid movements, I didn't think it would be a serious martial art. After my first session, I had tremendous respect for the practitioners. They are incredibly skilled athletes and martial artists. Although their outfits seemed somewhat silly—consisting of puffy white pants, wraparound color jackets and ballet-type booties—I couldn't fault their nearly perfect fundamentals, a step that many martial artists skip. The art is not actually designed for combat, but any of the taekkyon team members were poised to become great fighters if they chose to make some slight changes to their techniques.

The taekkyon workout routine concentrated on jumps, breathing, flexibility and, above all, grace and balance. Two of the team members weighed over 200 pounds but had the dexterity and flexibility you would expect from a much leaner athlete.

I was familiar with many of the stretching movements, thanks to my experience at the kuk sool school. We stood in a circle, doing the same exercises while following a leader before breaking into smaller groups and pairs to practice kicking and throwing techniques. But when the taekkyon practitioners began doing knee thrusts, I got lost. This wasn't muay Thai so they weren't throwing knee kicks. Instead, it seemed more like a routine in a Broadway show. We would alternate right and left feet with each step and shift our hips in the most unusual way I kept expecting a choreographer to come out, clap his hands and say, "Step. Step. Cross. Step. Knee and kick. Step. Cross. Step." I wondered if we were going to do jazz hands. Later, I learned that when the upper bodies swayed, the center of gravity remained constant. This meant that the players were almost impossible to knock over, which is key to winning a taekkyon match.

When we lined up to kick, I thought I was back in familiar territory. Taekkyon uses a roundhouse and a push kick, just like in muay Thai. But the kick in taekkyon has to be slow; it does not explode at the last possible second before striking a target. It comes off the hip because the knee is not chambered. The kick makes contact softly, like a push rather than a strike because you're meant to knock your opponent off-balance rather than knock him out.

As a kickboxer, I found it impossible to throw a slow kick to the head. When my teacher saw how much difficulty I was having, he asked my partner to lower the target, and even at waist height, it was all I could do to maintain my balance while throwing a slow kick. Of course, when it landed, my kick had no force at all. The amazing thing about proper taekkyon kicks is that they are incredibly powerful; they knock people straight down despite being slow and seemingly forceless.

When training in Taiwan, my kung fu teacher Wang jiao-lien believed that Westerners, particularly Americans, mistakenly put all their energy into throwing their leg up into the air anyway possible, calling it a "high kick." He said that this was why so many of us had knee injuries by age 30. We used our power to oppose our body's natural limitations, which tears muscles and tendons. He said that practitioners should learn to kick slowly. If you can kick slowly, then you can kick perfectly.

"As high as you can kick slowly is as high as you can kick," he'd say.

The taekkyon crew believed the same thing. My new teacher would have me standing at a ballet bar, throwing painfully slow roundhouse kicks that I could barely get up to my waist. Wang jiao-lien had told me a true master only kicks once a day but that kick takes eight hours to complete. I hoped my taekkyon teacher didn't have a similar philosophy.

Taekkyon contained elements that reminded me of so many other martial arts, but it was also unique; it didn't have any of the grabs, kicks and throws you see in taekwondo, kuk sool and hapkido. Otherwise, the taekkyon leaps and flying kicks reminded me of taekwondo. But in taekwondo the kicks are fast, and there should be an audible pop when they hit the target just right; in taekkyon, the kicks are soft and push the target. There were elements of twe so because the practitioners were constantly looking to use the opponent's balance points; they knew exactly when a head kick would throw a man off-balance. They weren't knocking him out, instead the taekkyon practitioners were just knocking him down. They calculated how a certain amount of force applied at the right time would only take an opponent off-balance. Taekkyon also contained elements of hapkido and kuk sool, such as how practitioners would catch a kick or throw.

I also saw characteristics of muay Thai in taekkyon, especially in regards to the push kick. But in practicing taekkyon, I realized that it was mislabeled in muay Thai. In the kickboxing art, it is executed as a quick stab or strike. In taekkyon, it is a true push, which pushes the opponent back.

Taekkyon impressed me. It is a beautiful art but more than that, the practitioners had phenomenal control over their bodies, placing slow, perfect kicks anywhere they wanted on their opponent's body. While I don't think taekkyon will replace boxing and MMA as big casino sports, you'll see me sitting in the front row at Madison Square Garden, right next to Frank Sinatra, if it ever does.

Being primarily a striker, I have always dreamed of learning grappling. By far the best martial art I found in Korea was ssireum, traditional wrestling. I enjoyed the practice so much that I still fantasize about going back to Korea to practice wrestling full-time. In fact, the wrestling and the language are the only reasons I would ever want to go back there.

Song Mi, my Korean language teacher, arranged for me to train with a high school ssireum team in Busan. I wasn't completely unfamiliar with ssireum at this point in my adventures in Asia. When I lived in Taiwan, I got addicted to watching the matches, and it was an extremely popular sport to watch on television among the elderly.

On the television matches, I would see how huge wrestlers—not quite as large as *sumo* wrestlers—fought in sand-filled circles. The competitors wore spandex briefs, somewhat similar to MMA shorts. They also wore a thick strong belt wrapped around their waist and right thigh called a *satba*. In a match, the fighters start by kneeling on the floor and facing one another. The right hand is gripping the satba tightly at the opponent's waist, the left hand is wrapped in the satba under the opponent's right thigh. When the referee gives the signal, they stand up, left knee first, then the right. They must stand at exactly the same time and without the position changing, or a restart is called and they have to go back down on their knees and do it again. They do this because ssireum is a precision sport; one competitor might be deemed to have an advantage otherwise.

The goal is to throw the opponent. Whichever opponent hits the ground first loses. Throwing an opponent out of the ring only results in a restart. Some matches last seconds; others can last several minutes. Typical winning techniques include lifts, hip throws and trips. Some more spectacular maneuvers, such as a suplex that requires taking the opponent over your head and tossing him behind you, can also be employed. One of the most impressive techniques is a kind of cartwheel, wherein one opponent hooks the other man's leg, then raises his own leg, and the opponent's high in the air until the opponent goes sideways off-balance.

Ssireum is considered to be the oldest Korean sport. According to the Korea Ssireum Research Institute, the oldest record of ssireum was found in a tomb in Manchuria in the 4th century. Other sources claim that ssireum was depicted in artwork dating back to 37 B.C. Regardless of the date, it is clear that ssireum is a very old and important cultural asset of Korea. As a result, the sport is governed by a strict set of rules.

For example, you can't grab the opponent's arm. You can grab a leg but only to throw. You can pull or push the back of the opponent's neck or head, but judges don't want to see you grabbing the back of the neck or head; only a quick push is allowed. The left hand must remain wrapped in the satba under the back of the opponent's thigh. The right hand, however, is free to release the satba. The right hand is often used to grab a leg and trip the opponent. You can't press your head or chin into an opponent's chest. The head is normally expected to rest on the opponent's right shoulder.

Before I actually tried the sport, it looked to me like a close cousin of Japanese sumo. Once I spent a day training with the high school team in Busan, I felt the sport was more reminiscent of Greco-Roman wrestling because the match outcome was so dependent on upper-body strength, lifting technique and balance.

When I walked into the team's practice room and saw the ssireum team for the first time, only one thought filled my mind: Ssireum wrestlers are huge! The smallest guy on the team was 175 pounds while most others were 200 pounds. There was one guy who was 270 pounds. K-1 fans should be interested to know that Hong-Man Choi, the 7- foot tall, 360-pound giant who is knocking people out on Japanese television was a former ssireum champion in Busan. It was a financial decision that made champion Choi Hong-Man switch to K-1. Unlike sumo wrestlers in Japan, Korean ssireum wrestlers earn almost nothing.

The team ranged from age 16 to 18. You can imagine how much bigger they will be when they are in their 20s. It was the first time in Asia that I was not only *not* the biggest guy on the team but my weight was considered average. Just like in the West, they were all taller than me. I never get a break.

If you are picturing smaller versions of sumo wrestlers, think again. The ssireum guys were built more like American football players or pro-wrestlers. They were heavily muscled through the shoulders, back and biceps, with tree-trunk size thighs. Many of the bigger guys were carrying extra fat around the belly in order to maintain mass. Some of them were just as lean as the typical Korean martial artists, with almost no body fat; they just had bigger muscles.

As I am a striker with limited grappling experience, almost everything about ssireum was new to me. I tried to draw from limited experiences with judo and Brazilian jiu-jitsu, but ssireum was its own unique animal. When it came my turn to fight, one of the difficult things I discovered is that you are on the whole time. You must constantly be engaged with your opponent by gripping his belt. In other forms of fighting, wrestling or boxing, you can back off and circle to get a breather, but in ssireum there is no rest.

The constant gripping of the satba becomes extremely painful. Once again, grapplers have no experience with this type of stress. Wrestlers and BJJ practitioners have a phenomenal grip, but they aren't trained to grip a belt, which cuts into their flesh. In this aspect, a guy working on a loading dock would have an advantage.

In ssireum, I learned that I also would have to cope with the cold. You are nearly naked, and of course, the room isn't heated. When I was out of breath in training and huffing and puffing, I felt like the cold air was biting my lungs.

The sand floor was also a problem. When we did our run, the cold sand was tough on our bare feet. When we were fighting, our feet wouldn't glide, as they do in a boxing ring. A boxing ring has a nice clean floor. The sandy floor dragged at my feet, impeding me from moving them where I wanted them to go and tripping me up.

I lost nearly all of my bouts because of the sand, but I will say that if you're going to get slammed by some huge wrestlers 70 times on a cold winter's day, then the sand is not a bad place to land. Of course, you also had to deal with sand in drawers for subsequent bouts, but the ssireum team members didn't seem to worry about sand or the other frustrations I faced in trying to learn their art.

The coach told me that four months out of the year, during the semester holidays, the team lived at the school and trained eight hours a day. Although they spent much of their time running to build stamina through cardio, they didn't lift weights. So their strength was built naturally through wrestling. Because the team was made up of young boys, the coach assured me they did a lot of cross-training by playing soccer, baseball and American football.

There used to be professional ssireum teams in Korea, but now the highest level of ssireum is considered semi-pro in that the money wrestlers earn is small or nonexistent. Big corporations like Samsung, which own all kinds of sports teams, are also pulling back on their ssireum sponsorships. Like in Taiwan and Hong Kong, traditional ssireum has trouble attracting new members. Parents expect their children to study 24/7. Often, Korean children start school early in the morning and attend until 4 p.m. Then they attend hakwans until 11 p.m. While I was there, the government passed a law that hakwans could no longer be open 24 hours because there were stories about students sitting in class past midnight. It blew my mind that the team members' parents let them wrestle full-time in place of studying.

The team also maintains a hefty competition schedule. During the ssireum season, from May to October, they compete once a month. There are seven competitions, leading to the national championships. Outside of Korea, there is almost no ssireum, but the team is often invited abroad to do exhibitions at large-scale traditional wrestling events. Some of the countries they exhibited in include the United States, Japan and Spain. Spain, of all countries, has a form of traditional wrestling that, according to the ssireum coach, is similar enough that they can compete with the Korean team.

Aside from just loving martial arts and wanting to see and experience all that Asia has to offer, I am always on the lookout for some formerly overlooked martial art that can be used in MMA competition. Right off the bat, the fact that the ssireum players could lift and control the upper body was a good sign that at least some of their skills would transfer over to reality fighting. Of course, they were huge and unbelievably powerful, which were two more pluses. They were also interested in other martial arts. As soon as I mentioned fighting in Cambodia and Thailand, they all crowded around me, wanting to learn knee kicks and elbow strikes. We went several rounds of free wrestling, but I still managed to maintain my losing streak. The ssireum fighters also all had unbelievable balance. One of their typical exercises is lifting their partner in the air and then bending 60-70 degrees to either side, with one leg in the air. One of the guys lifted me in this fashion and leaned to the side until my head was almost touching the ground, and still maintained his balance.

Ssireum is an incredible sport to practice or just to watch. Of all the traditional martial arts in Korea, the ssireum seemed to me to be the most honest. It didn't claim to be for kung fu supermen like so many other arts claim to be. Ssireum is a sport and not an infallible super martial art, and the Koreans play it better than anyone.

Characteristic of *ssireum*, the fighters wrestle over sand.

✦

Although I wasn't completely done with Korea, I knew it was time to leave. After years of living in Southeast Asia, I just couldn't take the Korean winters. Also the training and fighting in Thailand and Cambodia were calling me. Because I was getting older and out of shape, I had a fear in the back of my mind that if I didn't get back in the ring immediately, I might never be able to fight again.

With the seven months I was home in United States plus the seven months I was in Korea, it had been more than a year since I had trained in muay Thai or Khmer boxing. I gave notice at work, relinquished my end-of-contract bonus, bought a ticket and prepared to go back to Thailand for training.

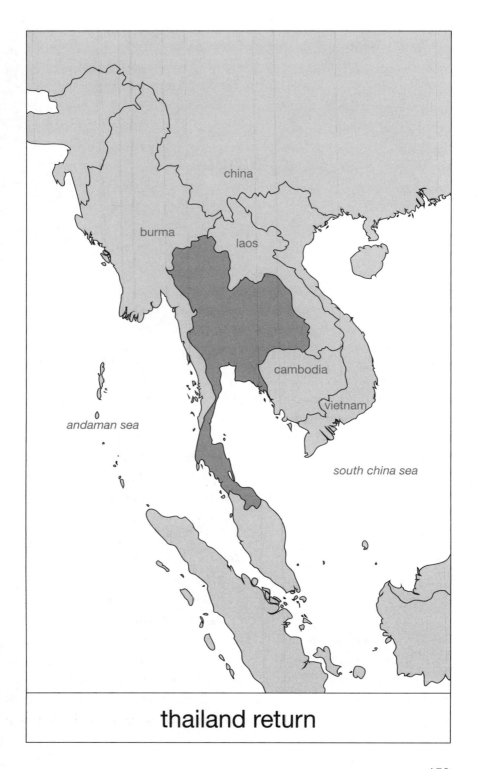

china

burma

laos

cambodia

vietnam

andaman sea

south china sea

thailand return

chapter 7

WHEN I LIVED IN CHIANG MAI in 2004, I'd heard about a Spanish ex-monk and muay Thai champion who was living in the city and teaching a more spiritual and religious form of muay Thai known as muay Thai *Sangha*. I filed the information away in my brain, knowing that someday I would seek out the instructor and train with him. So, upon my return to Thailand, he was the first person I looked up. My plan at the time was to train with him and film a documentary called *Brooklyn Monk in Asia: Muay Thai Sangha*. (I eventually posted it on the Internet.)

Kru Pedro Villalobos came from Madrid, Spain, but he had moved to the United States and later to Thailand to pursue a career as a professional fighter. At one point, he was a top-ranked Lumpini fighter. Somewhere along the way, he became a Buddhist monk. He spent long hours studying, meditating and praying. As much as he loved the monkhood he had to leave because he knew that his destiny included muay Thai. Monks are not allowed to practice martial arts. (Pra Kru Ba, my old teacher, is an anomaly. He may be the only monk in Thailand who teaches muay Thai.) After leaving the monkhood, he began teaching a religious form of muay Thai. Muay Thai Sangha combines the techniques of ancient muay Thai known as muay Thai *boran* with spirituality, philosophy and *krabi krabong* (stick fighting and sword fighting).

Muay Thai boran literally translates to "ancient muay Thai," but it includes a lot more flying elbow strikes and knee strikes. In every Tony Jaa movie, he uses a lot of the very cool muay Thai boran techniques, such as running up his opponent's body and dropping an elbow on the opponent's head.

Krabi krabong is the Thai art of long-stick fighting and double-sword fighting. The stick is about the same length as the height of a man and is very heavy because it was meant to be used against swords, which is very different from the light and flexible long stick that I used at the Shaolin Temple.

Because muay Thai boran and krabi krabong aren't ring sports, meaning there is no way to earn money with them through fights, they are disappearing. Kru Pedro's teacher Kru Lek openly taught a muay Thai boran style known as muay Thai Chaiya in Bangkok, but Kru Pedro had to comb the countryside to study with other teachers. Each teacher gave him small pieces of muay Thai boran and krabi krabong, which allowed him to create his own variation of muay Thai Sangha. He coined "muay Thai Sangha" to mean a religious form of muay Thai that paid constant devotion to religion and spirituality. (The Sangha are people who wish to live a religious and disciplined life but who cannot follow all of the rules of monkhood. Monks have 227 prohibitions to observe. Sangha can pick and choose which rules to follow.)

The spirituality of the Sangha, of course, was Theravada Buddhism.

When I met him, Kru Pedro was in his late 30s and incredibly fit and strong. He always wore traditional Thai clothes—loose-fitting wraparound trousers and a loose, pullover shirt. He lived in a small house outside of Chiang Mai. He spoke Thai exceptionally well and knew more about Buddhism and muay Thai than most Thai did. I knew that I would have to become Kru Pedro's student in order to make a documentary film about training with him. Training in muay Thai Sangha is an all-or-nothing deal; Kru Pedro's students trained six days a week and were not permitted to have jobs or do any activities outside of training. If I were accepted as a student, even for a short while, I would have to follow the rules: participate in prayers, meditate, abstain from alcohol and meat. I would live more or less as a Sangha. So on the first day that I visited him, we did a mutual interview. He was evaluating me to see if he would permit me to come back the next day for training and filming.

Like many traditional teachers, including Pra Kru Ba, Kru Pedro believed in spirit teachers. Spirit teachers are the ghosts of long dead muay Thai masters who come and teach the worthy when they are meditating. In the case of devout Buddhist students or Sangha like Kru Pedro, they tried to live the most pious lives they could so that spirit teachers would be pleased and would teach them more. If a Sangha went off his path, the spirit teachers would stop visiting him, and his learning and growth would stop.

If a devout Buddhist or Sangha were also a teacher, he would invite the spirits to dwell in his school or muay Thai camp. He would especially welcome them to dwell in his shrine. In this way, the training camp became a holy place that should not be defiled or upset by earthly intrusions. This is why smoking or drinking alcohol would never be allowed on the premises. This is also why Kru Pedro had to interview me; he needed to ask his spirit teachers if it was OK that I and my cameras came into the camp to train and film. Every major decision and each new student had to be approved in this way.

On the first day that I visited Pedro, the day of our mutual interview, Pedro led me through his small teak house to the top floor where he had his Buddhist shrine. I had expected bags swinging, people jumping rope and pounding the focus mitts. What I found was a glimpse into ancient Thailand, made all the more unusual by the fact that the teacher was a farang, a foreigner. He spent the next hour explaining each of the fascinating objects on his massive shrine of the Buddhist, Brahman and Hindu religion. This was where he came to meditate and pray each morning and each evening. Among his prayers, Kru Pedro said he sent thanks up to his spirit teachers, asking them to open his mind so that he might be a better teacher of the Thai martial arts.

"This one is Hanuman," Kru Pedro said, pointing out the white monkey god from the Hindu epic *The Ramayana*. He pointed to another photograph and said, "This represents the five Buddhist elements: earth, water, wind, fire and ether."

I was about to snap a photo of one of the small statues on the shrine, but Kru Pedro cautioned me, "Please no photos. This statue has a spirit inside."

Other images included Lord Ganesha, the elephant God of the Hindu religion. Kru Pedro pointed to a photograph of a fierce warrior and told me, "This is the Tiger King, Pra Chao Sua. He went in disguise to the town and fought in competitions."

Kru Pedro explained about one very ancient looking statue: "This was given to me by the father of one of my students. In his family, they had been muay Thai fighters for generations. Before they fought, they always prayed before this statue." Kru Pedro held the statue in his hands with great reverence because of the generations of merit and spiritual energy it contained. He said, "This one has a fighting spirit inside."

To the side of the shrine was a beautiful sword. "I put bone and hair from a famous monk inside of the handle and sealed it with pure silver. Now there is a spirit inside of the sword."

Through the interview, Kru Pedro and I alternated between English and Spanish. He also spoke excellent Thai, but there was no reason for us to speak it together unless we needed a clearly Thai concept or word, like "pra" or "kru" or "muay."

One of the photos on his shrine was Kru Lek, Pedro's teacher for muay Thai Chaiya. I didn't know it then, but several years later, Kru Lek would become my teacher as well.

In demonstrating the effectiveness of his Sangha, Kru Pedro expertly kicked me with the ball of his foot, pinpointing nerve endings in my thighs, abdomen and chest. While he wasn't executing the techniques with speed or power, they still caused me pain because Kru Pedro performed them with precision. If he had executed his strikes with speed and power, then I would have been nearly dead by the end of the interview.

I couldn't imagine him hitting me at full force. The strike with the ball of his foot to the front of my thigh almost knocked me over.

"I teach when I can and I follow when I can," he said in absolute humility. Throughout the interview, Kru Pedro dropped sayings like that. I would later learn that they were his own form of philosophical wisdom that he taught to students; I came to refer to them as Pedroisms.

"I like people who walk, not people who talk," he'd say, meaning he preferred monks who helped people rather than monks who talked about helping people. When he said this in regard to the fighting arena, he meant that he preferred fighters to people who only talked about fighting.

"If we are muay Thai fighters, we must run. But if we only run, we will be runners, not fighters." To Kru Pedro, this implied that great fighters need to be fighters first and runners second. They must actively do what they practice.

Another Pedroism I would come to like was, "practicing wrong made you wrong."

When the interview was over, Pedro said the spirits would allow me to train and film with him for the week.

❁

Early the next morning, I was to report to him with the following items: five white lotus blossoms, five white candles, five jasmine flowers and nine incense sticks. Together, we would make an offering to Kru Pedro's shrine that would make me an official student.

While Kru Pedro taught me the delicate art of folding the flowers to make them appropriate for the offering, we talked.

"I only want to teach good people. I believe that if a teacher teaches a bad student, and that student hurts someone, the teacher gets some of the bad karma," he said.

I also was surprised when Kru Pedro expressed his belief that muay Thai wasn't a sport.

"We don't fight for the ring," he said. "I think two people fighting is not a sport. I don't like it, but if they want to, my students can go to the ring to learn to defend themselves."

When we were done with the offerings, Kru Pedro and I waited for his student to arrive. Training took place entirely at the Spanish master's house. While it was small, the entire first floor was a wide and open room in which students—12 students who were all foreigners and ranged in age from their early to late 20s—could gather and pray in the morning. Training took place in the front yard where Kru Pedro had a number of heavy bags. His living quarters and shrine were located in the floors above.

When the students arrived, Kru Pedro led us in Buddhist chanting. The chant was done in Thai, but Kru Pedro had printed out copies written phonetically in Roman script so that foreign students could read and chant along.

Next we skipped rope and did a structured workout until 11:00 a.m. The structured workout consisted of 15 basic exercises that are the foundation of muay Thai Sangha. Students learn these exercises and in doing them they build up the muscle balance needed for successfully performing the art.

The workout routine was one of the best I had ever witnessed for laying down a solid foundation of movement. When you are in a ring fighting, you don't run, do push-ups, do sit ups or skip rope. But lots of people do these things when they are training. The muay Thai Sangha exercises were specifically designed to mirror movements and techniques required for fighting in the ring. They included a lot of stance changing—hopping from one stance to the next, hopping into kicks and strikes, transitioning, sliding, avoiding and countering. They were at once teaching actual techniques while developing the specific muscles and conditioning necessary for the foundation of the entire art.

Many schools have students pounding away on a bag on their first day. Some never teach movement and angles. "People try to build house from the roof down," said Kru Pedro. For this reason, the muay

Thai Sangha students were building from a solid foundation up.

When this exhausting exercise was finished, the students practiced krabi krabong, muay Thai or sparring until noon, depending on what Kru Pedro believed we needed to focus on that given day.

After lunch and a good siesta, which is typical in Thailand, we returned for afternoon training and bag work.

Our bag work was timed into rounds of three minutes with a minute break, which is what would happen in a real fight. During the break, however, we did push-ups. At the beginning of each round, the lead student—usually a student who had lived with Kru Pedro for a year and was training to be a teacher in muay Thai Sangha—would call out the specific techniques to be worked on during that round. For example, one round might be the push kick, another might be elbow strikes or roundhouse kicks.

One of the two unique things about Kru Pedro's bag work, as compared to other muay Thai schools, was that he required us to train barehanded. This meant that our hands and elbows would bleed for the first few months of training with him. Kru Pedro said that it was because he wanted his students to learn power and how to endure pain. It was obvious who the new students were because our hands would be bleeding from the knuckles after a few rounds of barehanded bag work. The seasoned students, on the other hand, had knuckles carved from stone. When those hands were later wrapped in a real fight, the opponent would feel them, like two daggers piercing the padding.

The other unique aspect was that the timed rounds were purposeful in that we were expected to work on specific combinations. In a normal muay Thai gym, the teacher might say: "OK, go work the bag for three rounds," but he wouldn't necessarily tell you what to do during those rounds. The advantage of Kru Pedro's way was that you were constantly learning new techniques and combinations. If you were doing this on your own, in another gym, you would only practice moves that you already knew. Here, you were being forced to practice everything—new techniques, new moves, old moves, old techniques. In Kru Pedro's system, you practiced the gamut of muay

Thai Sangha movements and strikes just on the bags.

Bag work was followed by pad work, where Pedro dictated the pace of the training by calling out what he wanted us to do. He would call out the techniques fast or slow. He might call out an eight-punch combination or worse—an eight-kick combination that would wipe you out. Some students would get too aggressive or pushy, burning up their air and energy on the pads. To remind them to slow down, Kru Pedro would kick them in the thighs or slap them with the pads.

"*Calmate,*" he'd yell in Spanish.

The rest of the session consisted of sparring, running, and ground fighting. The training day ended at 7:00 p.m. in the evening with chanting and meditation.

Of course throughout the training day, Kru Pedro would drop his Pedroisms.

"We must be hard on the outside and soft on the inside."

"Without self-respect, you cannot learn. Without compassion, you cannot teach."

"If people do wrong, no problem—as long as they want to improve."

"Those who follow the religion and practice inside can teach, but he must have understanding. If not, he could never be a great teacher."

"A student doesn't have to tell me he wants to improve. I can see it."

"My teachers taught me never tell people what to do. You teach by example."

"We train mind, body, spirit and heart," Kru Pedro said. "The mind is trained through meditation and chanting. The heart is made better by surrounding yourself with flowers, candles, incense and water. Helping people, sharing, talking and giving are all from the heart. Muay Thai trains the body. We help the spirit by studying the Dharma and the teachings of Buddha."

Although no longer a monk, Kru Pedro followed the Brahman precept of love for all people regardless of race, rank or sex; the precepts of compassion and self-respect; and the precept of thinking before you take action. In addition to the Brahman precepts, Kru

Pedro followed the five precepts of Buddhism: Don't kill. Don't lie. Don't steal. Don't take intoxicants. Don't commit adultery.

But Kru Pedro realized we students lived complicated lives in a modern world. He didn't expect us to shave our heads and go cold turkey on all of our indulgences. For the most part, we weren't professional fighters and had little or no interest in becoming professional fighters. Many of them were university graduates in their late 20s and 30s who worked professional jobs in their home countries, saving their money to come and train with Kru Pedro.

Pedro explained to me that first his students learned martial arts for self-defense, health and self-respect.

"Later if he wants to fight pro," he said, "I can train him. Fight and win OK. Fight and lose OK. No problem, just do your best. I don't care if a student's muay Thai is good or bad. I only care when he comes back to me and says, 'Kru, you changed my life.' "

He put me in the ring with a student he called Titan, who was about 6'4". When I left Korea I was about 22 pounds overweight. Training with Kru Pedro only made me more tired and sore. Now, he wanted to put me in the ring against a man who was at least 10 years younger and twice as tall as me. Oh yeah, and he had been training with Kru Pedro for months while I had been training at the taekkyon school.

The behemoth, Titan, followed the precept of compassion and never hit me hard, although he could have killed me. It seemed to me that after only a few months of training, Kru Pedro's students achieved a level of fitness and technique that many fighters will never achieve, thanks to Pedro's simple, good fundamentals. When I closed on Titan, he was all knees and elbows. When I tried to make distance, he was all kicks and leaps.

Round one didn't go well for me, and rounds two and three were worse. When the bell rang, I came out and threw jabs, but Titan was so much taller than me that I couldn't even get close to him. When I got frustrated and saw no other option, I rushed in, grabbed one of his legs, and threw him to the ground. It wasn't a strictly legal move in muay Thai, but that's how we roll in Brooklyn.

As Titan got to his feet, he glanced over to Kru Pedro as if to ask, did you see this guy foul me like that? Pedro gave a look that reminded me of the court judge in a movie who says, "I'm going to allow this."

I tried again to get in close and throw punches and kicks, but Titan tied me up and kicked me easily. So, I grabbed his leg and threw him again.

At the end of the fight, I just collapsed in the corner. I was bleeding a little over my eye where I had caught an elbow on one of my mad dashes inside of Titan's guard.

"Do you want another round?" asked Pedro, joking.

"Oh, yes," I said. "I've got him exactly where I want him. Now that he thinks he's winning, he will make a mistake."

"Are you serious?" asked Kru Pedro.

"No. In fact, I can't even stand up."

Pedro, Titan and I laughed. I thought the fight was funny enough to put it on the Internet but on some level I was really worried. What if I never got it back? What if this time around, I didn't lose the weight, I didn't get back in shape and I didn't fight anymore?

Kru Pedro, however, seemed please with my pathetic showing.

"I didn't know you could fight," he said, after my fight with Titan.

"I got beaten," I said.

"Yes, but I didn't know you could fight at all. I thought you were only about the cameras and the writing." Somehow, getting creamed by the massive Titan had endeared me to Pedro.

He took me over to a quiet corner of his garden where we sat down on two chairs and he opened up for a lengthy interview. We didn't know it at the time but right after I left the spirit teachers would tell him not to do any more interviews. So what followed was a rare and candid look into a man who had devoted himself so fully to martial arts.

"The reason your Western boxing doesn't hold up well against muay Thai is because when you come within your punching range, Titan can hit you with elbows, which are much more effective," Kru

Pedro said, analyzing my sparring with Titan.

I steered the questioning away from training for awhile by asking what he thought of my hero, the movie star and muay Thai martial artist Tony Jaa. Kru Pedro thought his movies were good. I then asked what he thought about martial artists who use their skills to make movies. It shouldn't have surprised me that his answer was classically him.

"I think it depends what Tony and his teacher do with the money they earn. Maybe they will help many people."

I asked how Pedro felt about trainers who had never fought. He responded: "What you can do, what you can teach, and what you can apply may all be at different levels. Some people can be great at training and terrible in the ring.

"People have a gift at birth, karma, and they can develop it," he continued. "Their good deeds earn them merit and help to determine their rebirth. Some people, very special people, are born with an ability to teach without ever having been a fighter, but these are very rare."

We discussed how Thailand is one of the few countries in the world where the national sport is fighting and the Thai people in general are some of the best fighters, pound for pound, in the world. Thailand is one of the few countries in the world where an 18-year-old boy who is 150 pounds might be matched against a heavyweight pro from Europe and win. The obvious question was, Why?

"A unique gift which the Thai people possess is a tremendous respect for the teacher," Kru Pedro said. "Spirit teachers, angel teachers, help to open the mind and help to develop their respect for the teachers and they learn more."

"Why are there so many martial arts in China, Korea and Japan but really only one in Thailand?" I asked.

"In Thailand, the art was used for fighting in wars and in the ring. So, it basically had a straight-line development, over a period of hundreds of years, focused on succeeding at these two goals," Pedro said. He also explained why he thought that no grappling arts appeared to exist in Thailand or most of Indochina: "The Thai arts were developed for soldiers to use on the battlefield. Soldiers don't want to go to the ground because they can only fight one opponent at a time and going to the ground would expose their back."

Kru Pedro said that much of what is taught in traditional martial arts, such as Shaolin kung fu, karate or hapkido, wouldn't actually work in a real fight or in the contemporary ring because the arts weren't designed for that arena. These traditional arts were probably viable martial arts at some time in the past. If everyone used hapkido strikes and kicks, for example, then hapkido blocks would work, but if we use modern techniques such as muay Thai, Brazilian jiu-jitsu, Western wrestling or boxing, the traditional arts are less effective.

This brought me to my favorite subject of mixed martial arts, The Ultimate Fighting Championship. Kru Pedro had a lot to say on the subject.

"MMA took the best of everything and combined it," he said. "If your goal is fighting, then MMA is the best thing. So far, there is nothing better. Then combined with some wrestling and it is the most effective way to fight. But that only helps you achieve the goal of fighting nothing else._

"UFC is not art," Kru Pedro continued. "Because there is no spirit. When you get old, what then? I can practice 'til I am 100 because I am concerned about improving and doing the best that I can. So, when I am 70, I will do the best I can at 70, and that will be good enough." Kru explained that sport martial artists, such as in MMA or K-1, would reach a peak and then be in a state of steady decline for the rest of their lives.

"Also, with MMA, who are their students? Maybe they are bad people. I am very careful about who I will teach. If the student is not a good person, I give him his money back and send him away. But if you are a professional trainer, you care only about winning. So you will take the strongest student, even if he is not the best person."

Kru Pedro was quick to point out that he didn't dislike the MMA or K-1. "Some people have found their way," he said. "Others are looking for the way. This is the same for teachers. If there are teachers looking for the way, I don't interfere. I was a fighter once. I hadn't found the way yet. It is OK. We will search and search until we find it. If they are teaching MMA or they are teaching everyone, including bad people, but they don't know any better yet, how can we say they are bad? How can we blame them? We have to allow them to search."

The sparring match with Titan was a wakeup call. I needed to learn to fight again and go beyond where I had been before. I needed to lose weight. So, I decided to go back to Bangkok and sign up for a proper muay Thai school.

Kru Pedro demonstrates some boxing to Antonio in Chiang Mai.

Back in Bangkok, I signed up for an experimental Thai language Automatic Language Growth program, taught at AUA. While I had learned a lot of Thai from Pra Kru Ba, I had never officially taken lessons.

It was through one of my teachers that I learned of a muay Thai gym called Chakrit. I was really interested in visiting the gym because I had only ever studied with Pra Kru Ba and Kru Pedro. Now, I was finally going to see how the rest of the world learned muay Thai.

Chakrit consisted of a single room, the size of a large studio apartment, with glass windows from ceiling to floor and a quarter-size practice ring in the corner. The head trainer was Adjarn Chakrit, and because he behaved more like a sports coach than a mystical martial arts master, I always thought of him as Coach Adjarn. There were two young muay Thai fighters who worked as assistant coaches, and an older guy—a year or two older than me—who may or may not have been a co-owner. Sometimes he would do pad work for foreign students.

While Chakrit was the first "typical" muay Thai place I trained at, I later discovered it was more like a boutique school. The fees were ridiculously high compared to the fighting camps, costing 600 to 800 baht or $18 to 24 USD. The bulk of the students were made up of foreigners. In fact, the only Thai students I ever saw were a small group of young boys who were taught by a separate trainer in the early afternoon.

The young boys were fighting professionally for the gym, as were the two assistant trainers. Occasionally, richer Chinese-Thai students would come to train for the same reasons that American students practice martial arts. They didn't last long; school is extremely demanding in Asia, and students are really expected not to do much else.

Among the foreigners, many were just tourists passing through Bangkok who wanted an "authentic" muay Thai training experience. Others were people living in Bangkok who just wanted to keep fit. There were, however, a good number of professional Japanese and Western fighters who would come to Chakrit for their tune-up before a fight. Some Western and especially Japanese fighters would use Chakrit as their tune-up gym while they were getting used to the foreign climate and preparing for an upcoming fight at Lumpini Stadium or even preparing for *kyokushin* karate fights back in Japan. Apparently in Japan, there is a well-developed kyokushin karate circuit and some submission-grappling circuits that allow kicking. A lot of these professional Japanese fighters would come to Thailand to improve their low kicks. My best friend at Chakrit was a Japanese guy named Ryuki, who hung around to box mostly for fun and to prepare for his first professional fight.

The most intense fight training I had had at this point of my martial arts career was the year and a half I had spent with Paddy Carson in Cambodia, where I trained nearly full-time and had a couple of fights. One or two hours of fight training is harder than a whole day of other kinds of training, bar none.

Paddy stressed Western boxing skills because he believed that the biggest weakness of most muay Thai and Khmer boxing fighters was their hands. He required all his students to become fully qualified Western boxers before he trained us in muay Thai kicks, knees and elbows, and when I left Cambodia, we had just begun to start kicking.

In practice, muay Thai is basically Thai kickboxing. You hit with punches, kicks, knee strikes and elbow strikes. The kicks are very special because they hit with the shins, not the feet. The elbows and shin strikes are very hard and can cut you wide open; fighters often need stitches after a fight.

When someone tries to kick you with their shin, you can't use your hand or your arm to block because you will get hurt. You block using your shin bone. You raise your leg up and take the impact shin to shin.

You can imagine how much that hurts. As a result, a lot of the muay Thai training deals with toughening the shins, deadening the nerves, and building up scar tissue. This process is called "hardening" the shins.

In provincial training camps, poorer Thai often see boxing as a way to earn money for their families. They go live in a camp and become part of a stable of fighters. The camp arranges fights for them and takes a percentage of the purse. In return, the fighters get free room, board and training. In these camps, you will see people doing all manner of crazy exercises to harden their shins quickly. They kick trees, kick bamboo or kick metal poles. At night, they sit around hitting their shins with sticks or with bottles. They also use coke bottles as rolling pins, rolling them up and down the shin bones. They smear all sorts of traditional medicines, potions and lotions on the skin to quicken this hardening process, and this type of training does work. The fighters can go from zero to totally hardened shins in about 90 days, but it is a terrible experience, and the shins will be all cut, open, bleeding, and infected the whole time.

When I trained with Pra Kru Ba, I didn't intentionally harden my shins. When you first start out, just kicking the bag is already painful enough. After the first day of training at the monastery, my shins looked sunburned and my elbows and hands were bleeding, but I had to train again the next day. Many modern coaches, such as Paddy, believed that the shins should be allowed to harden naturally from kicking the pads and bag over time. But this is only in muay Thai or in Khmer boxing. Western boxers don't use elbow strikes, and they don't harden their hands or other body parts aside from their shins. Doing bradal serey, my hands and elbows got completely torn open just in the course of normal training and bag work. The normal training was brutal enough, and there really wasn't the need to kick trees.

It is normal for beginners to be cut or "sunburned." If you're new to training, you shouldn't even consider doing any hardening until a few weeks or a month into your training. A rule of thumb could be, don't think about doing any hardening until kicking the bag doesn't hurt anymore. Start on the bag, then move up to harder surfaces if you want. Because it had been about two years since I trained with Pra Kru Ba and Paddy Carson, I had to start all over from zero. Fortunately, I think that the two years I trained with Paddy probably conditioned my hands permanently because while my knuckles became red, they never bled.

In hardcore gyms, the bags are hard to help you toughen up. In some of the foreigner gyms, the bags are softer and the coaches will do things like fall down or act like you have hurt them to pump you up and make you feel good. Take it with a grain of salt. Remember, you're paying them a lot of money for that praise.

Provincial Thai people are very welcoming and will probably invite you to train with them. They may not charge you anything and just ask that you contribute for food. A provincial camp could be a great cultural experience, but if you are serious about learning to fight, Bangkok, Chiang Mai, Pattaya, or one of the more developed areas may be better for you. In a provincial camp, if you don't know how to box already, you may not learn anything. Your training will consist of a lot of running and bouncing on tiers or jumping rope. You will be told to kick the bag but probably won't be taught HOW to kick the bag. You may or may not get face time with the coach in the ring, working the pads. You won't get a lot of instruction. Also, if you don't speak Thai, they probably won't be able to communicate with you.

If you train in Bangkok, the average cost seems to be about 7,000 to 8,000 baht per month (although this is creeping upward now, with many gyms charging 10,000 baht). That is just for your training. Food and lodging are extra. The advantage is that a coach is assigned to you, and you get a lot of one-on-one instruction. At Muay Thai Chakrit, I could have as many rounds with my coach on the pads as I wanted. In fact, I could have as many rounds of pads, sparring and anything else I wanted. So, it was more expensive but I was literally never alone. The coaches followed me around, even watching me work the bag and stepping in to improve my kicking technique.

In the end, that was great because I was free to write, train, eat and sleep.

Antonio poses for a picture with some fighters at the Chakrit gym in Bangkok.

I spent my days at Thai language school and my evenings at Chakrit practicing Muay Thai. At school, I became friends with a missionary couple from the United States, who offered to take me to Surin City in the northeast Isan region of Thailand. Isan is a relatively poor region that borders Laos and Cambodia. The dialect is very close to the Laotian language but in Surin City, the predominant language, aside from Thai, is an older form of Khmer. I had long wanted to visit Isan because of this fossilized form of Khmer in order to compare it to the Khmer I spoke in Phnom Penh.

Because writing is my bread and butter, any traveling means an opportunity to write an article or book or do a movie or video or all of the above. From a martial artist's standpoint, Isan is also the region that produces the largest percentage of great fighters in Thailand. Of course, it probably has something to do with the poverty; the poor are willing to get into the boxing ring to support their families.

Surin City is also the birthplace of movie star, and my personal hero, Tony Jaa, who Westerners might know from the movie *Ong-bak* (2003). The movie was the first to depict muay Thai as a cinematic martial art rather than the Hong Kong cinematic kung fu that dominated movies like *Charlie's Angels* (2000) and *The Matrix* (1999).

The missionary couple drove me to Surin City and dropped me off at a monastery near the city's center, where I met up with my friend Sameth. Since I had met him in Phnom Penh, Sameth had returned to the monkhood and was studying at a religious university in Surin City. He had actually been a monk before we had met. In fact, the five months that he worked for me was the only time in his adult life that he hadn't been a monk.

Five months in the secular world drove Sameth right back to the monkhood, but this time he went with a goal: He wanted to get out of Cambodia and secure a foreign education. He worked hard to gain acceptance into the university in Surin City. His tuition was $50 USD a year, and since I had seen him, he was now halfway through his B.A. in Public Administration. (Helping my friend, I felt, was one of the best things I ever spent $100 USD on.) Sameth greeted me at the monastery gate, all decked out in his monk's robes. The smile on his face was tremendous. We were so happy to see each other again.

Sameth had spoken nearly perfect English when we worked together in Cambodia but now his Thai was at native speaker level. When we went around the town, asking questions and conducting interviews, people reacted well to Sameth because he was Khmer, like many of our interviewees, and he could speak to them in their own language. Also, having a monk with you in Thailand tends to open a lot of doors.

Sameth and I hired a *songthaew* driver for the day to take us to the family residence of Tony Jaa. A songthaew is a bus that is more like a pickup truck with a covered bed for passengers to sit in; they go anywhere you want and are quite cheap. Sameth and my driver took us, and a fellow monk, the 20 minutes outside of Bangkok to a huge mansion surrounded by a high wall. We got out and rang the bell at the gate but were completely ignored by the occupants. Eventually, a man from across the street came over to ask what we wanted, mostly because I was with two monks. A very long discussion followed, that mostly involved Sameth and the man from across the street switching in and out of Thai and Khmer. Sameth explained that I was a journalist who wanted to conduct an interview with Jaa's parents. It turned out that the man we were talking to was Tony Jaa's brother. He called his parents on the phone, and they let us in.

Mr. and Mrs. Jaa were a diminutive, happy and normal-looking couple; you probably would have missed them on the street, not knowing that they were the parents of the most famous movie star in the country.

They invited Sameth and our fellow monk to sit on a raised bamboo dais with a sunshade on top. For wealthier rural people, this serves as a kind of porch where they can entertain guests outdoors.

Mr. and Mrs. Jaa and I sat barefooted and cross-legged on a throw rug on the floor, drinking iced tea, which is the Thai custom. The two monks sat on the bamboo platform above us. Being taller than most Thais, I always have to be careful that my head does not go higher than the monks'. I was extremely nervous about protocol, not wanting to offend the Jaas, who were known to be very religious. (Mr. and Mrs. Jaa had said that they had stopped granting interviews to journalists but made an exception for me because I arrived with two monks.) When seated, it is very important that your feet never point at anyone. This is considered a huge insult. To achieve this often means contorting your body into an uncomfortable position, so your feet point in a neutral direction.

When he was ready, the father signaled that I should begin my interview.

I complimented them on the beauty of their house. It was strange to see a mansion beside all of the other village houses, which were tiny two-room affairs.

"After he became famous, Tony bought this house for us," Mrs. Jaa said. She was obviously very proud of her son. "It cost 10 million baht."

"Where did you live before?" I asked.

"In that house," she said, pointing.

As we had entered the compound, I had noticed an old, ugly, dilapidated wooden house and wondered why they kept it on the grounds. Now I understood.

"Every day, we look out the window and we know where we came from," she said.

Tony Jaa was born with the name Panom Yeerum, which he later changed to Jaa Panom for professional reasons. But today, even his parents generally refer to him as "Tony."

"Tony was always playing sports," Mr. Jaa said. "He liked all sports, including basketball, but he especially loved any kind of martial art.

"When he was five years old, he fell in love with martial arts. He watched Bruce Lee movies and copied the moves. He already said that when he grew up, he would be very famous. We never doubted him."

We talked about how their son actually learned muay Thai at

a young age from Mr. Jaa, a boxer himself. Then as a teenager, he studied taekwondo and other martial arts while winning competitions. When he was older, the still-unknown star wanted to study with Thai martial arts actor Panna Rittikrai, but Rittikrai wanted the young man to finish school first. So Tony Jaa earned a scholarship to study at one of the national sports universities.

Then he came back and studied with Rittikrai, who helped Jaa get his first work in the movies.

His parents were proud.

"He is 175 centimeters (5'9") tall and just over 60 kilograms (136 pounds)," his father said.

"He is tall and strong and good looking, with big muscles. And women go crazy for him," his mother said.

"Even foreigner ladies want to date him," Mr. Jaa added with a naughty grin.

We then talked about one of the more contentious topics about their son. Because Surin Province was actually part of Cambodia until about 250 years ago, approximately 70 percent of the people have Khmer blood and speak the Khmer language. Therefore, many Cambodians say that Tony Jaa is a Khmer and that the martial art he uses in his films is Khmer bokator.

We had been speaking Thai, but now, the conversation switched to the Khmer language, which Mr. and Mrs. Jaa spoke perfectly. Hoping to settle the argument once and for all, I asked if they were Khmer or Thai. The answer surprised me.

"We are Kuy," Mr. Jaa said.

The Kuy, called Suoy in Thai language, are an ethnic minority and tribe from India who migrated through Cambodia and arrived in Thailand about 400 years ago. They brought elephants with them, which the Thai king quickly realized had excellent military applications. He gave the Kuy Thai citizenship and made them the official royal elephant handlers. Today, no matter where you go in Thailand, the handlers are probably Kuy.

As if to prove his ethnicity, Mr. Jaa noted that he was born in the famous elephant village of Ban Taklang. He also noted that the Jaa family still keep elephants to this day. Suddenly, Tony Jaa's second movie *Tum Yum Goong* (2005) made sense because the whole plot revolved around the theft of an elephant from Thailand.

After my interview with the Jaas, we went to Ban Taklang elephant village, which was about 12 miles away from Surin City. At the village, we met a Kuy man named Kun Da who knew Tony Jaa and his family when they lived in the village.

"I was born in this village. My grandparents and all my ancestors were born here too. I started living with elephants when I was a boy. Now I am 60 or 70 years old, I don't know for sure, and I live with the elephants. There are some elephants who are older than me," Kun Da said. "I know Jaa Panom.

"He lived here before. His parents were born here. Then he was born here. Then they went to live near the mountain."

Kun Da also talked to us about elephants. He told Sameth and I that there aren't any wild elephants in the forest in Thailand anymore. Instead, the Kuy catch them in Cambodia. He explained how there were about 50 or 60 elephants there in the village. Some families have one and some families have two or three.

In Kuy tradition, a boy is given an elephant when he is about one or two years old; the boy and the elephant grow up together. Elephants have a life cycle similar to humans and live to be 60 years old or older. The respect that is given to the elephant is the same as a person of the same age. An elephant of five is treated like a child of five. When they get older, the elephants are consulted on family decisions. If the Kuy want to get married, build a new house or move to a new location, they have to ask permission from the elephants. When an elephant dies, it is like losing a member of the family.

Behind the village, Kun Da showed us the elephant graveyard where the remains are kept in reverence. When an elephant dies, the village has a special religious ceremony in which the animal's bones are cleansed and set in the ground in concrete crypts that are glass-topped so that people may look inside and pay homage to the dead elephant.

Beside the graveyard, a number of young monks were crowded

around a statute of the Hindu god of the elephant handlers. A small boy said he was becoming a novice today because the king of Thailand was sick. When a family member is sick, a boy may become a monk to bring a blessing of healing to that person. In this case, the boy's family loved the king so much that the boy was becoming a monk to give strength to his king. The child monks were all very excited because on the next Buddhist holiday of that year, Tony Jaa was planning to preside over the festival.

When Sameth and I were finished talking to Kun Da, we entered a nearby forest monastery where Tony Jaa's father had once been a monk. The entire temple was dedicated to the elephants. There were altars with elephant bones and the entire skeleton of a baby elephant. Set into stone and covered in natural vines were massive statues of the Buddha but also of the elephant god, Ganesha, and the monkey god, Hanuman. (Hanuman is highly respected in Thailand because he is considered to be the most intelligent of the animal gods. A lot of moves in muay Thai boran are also based on the deity. For example, Tony Jaa does a double-handed uppercut in movies, which is called Hanuman Present the Ring.)

From left to right: Mrs. Jaa, Sameth, Mr. Jaa and Antonio

Tony Jaa's parents had told us the name and approximate whereabouts of Tony Jaa's first teacher, Adjarn Sok Chai, so Sameth and I planned to visit the teacher the following day. The next morning, Sameth and I got up early and went to the center of Surin City where we asked every motorcycle taxi driver if he knew where we could find the Adjarn. It only took a few minutes until we found a man who would take us for a dollar.

In my years of studying martial arts in Asia, I found that the art, religion and language may change from country to country, but one thing remains true: Masters always live in visually distinctive dwellings. In this way, Adjarn Sok Chai did not disappoint. ("Adjarn" is a Thai word that means "teacher of teachers.") His front walk was flanked by tremendous shrines of Vishnu and Shiva. The wall around his yard was decorated with hand-painted panels. The first panel depicted an image of Adjarn Sak Chai in his signature tiger-striped pajama-looking pants, which he always wore. To the right of this was the image of a spirit teacher, wearing a many-headed serpent about his shoulders. Next was a panel depicting a series of figures in positions of suffering. In the Brahman religion, life is considered suffering and the Brahmans believe they need to be liberated from life.

This liberation could occur through meditation and later death, but you have to make sure that you live a pious life to ensure a good rebirth or you will be reborn back into suffering. The last panel was a mix of Hindu, Brahman and Buddhist gods, which clearly illustrated the mixed religions of Indochina. Most prominent of the Hindu gods was Ganesha.

The Adjarn came out to greet us. He looked like some wild spectacle; his hair, which had to be at least six feet long, was wrapped in dreadlocks and tied up behind his back. He had a long mustache and sparse beard, composed of a small number of exceptionally long hairs. Just as in the mural, he was wearing his striped pajama pants with no shirt. His upper body was extremely lean and muscular.

Although he was 47 years old, the Adjarn possessed one of the most incredible strength-to-body-weight ratios I had ever seen. Within minutes of meeting me, he was performing circus tricks, which he used in many movies he had made with Tony Jaa.

He dove onto his hands and pressed up into a frog stand, then into a handstand.

"I can walk 100 meters (about 110 yards) on my hands," he said. "Do you want to see?"

"Well, I did drive all the way out here," I said uncertainly.

The Adjarn took off at a dead run on his hands, all the way up his street. It was all I could do to keep up with him, shooting photos. Back at his house, he walked down a flight of wooden stairs on his hands. Next, he did the splits between two chairs. Then he began to juggle. It started with plates, followed by bowls, which he juggled on his feet, then kicked in the air and caught on his head.

"This is a good exercise because it teaches us balance and concentration," the Adjarn said. "It will make you a better fighter."

For his next trick, the Adjarn balanced a 65-pound concrete barbell on his nose. The only way to top that off was to juggle real swords, which I photographed from under a table. The juggling done, he balanced a 45-pound head-chopper's sword on his nose.

"This all relates to meditation. If you don't meditate, you cannot protect yourself," he said. "If we do the sword balancing wrong, we can get injured or blind. In a muay Thai ring, if we lose concentration, we can get injured."

The Adjarn showed me a permanent hole in the end of his nose from 30 years of balancing things on it. As far as occupational hazards went, that really put carpal-tunnel syndrome into perspective.

To strengthen his jaw, the Adjarn bit into a rope and raised a 45-pound can full of cement with his neck muscles.

"This protects us from getting knocked out."

Next, he balanced a chair, a bicycle and a refrigerator on his nose. OK, there was no refrigerator, but it wouldn't have surprised me.

After I dove out of the way to avoid the falling bicycle,

I finally spoke.

"My name is Antonio," I said, thinking the meeting had been a little out of sequence.

The Adjarn laughed and welcomed us inside of his house. The interior was a crazy clutter of animal bones, rusty old weapons and myriad religious amulets dangling in every corner. Several swords were stuck in the wall at various haphazard locations. The centerpiece of the room was a massive shrine, which featured the bones of dead monks.

The Adjarn's wife brought us water, and we sat down to talk. While we chatted, he was making religious amulets by hand.

"After they have dried," he said, "I will do a ritual to bless them." The Adjarn explained he was doing this because he was a Brahman holy man.

The Buddhists would refer to people like the Adjarn as an ascetic. These are men who follow the direct teachings of the Gautama Buddha. The ascetics—like the Sangha Kru Pedro—are not monks but laypersons who follow a strict set of precepts and abstain from most earthly pleasures. They are strict vegetarians and only eat one meal per day. They are celibate, and fill their days with reading the scriptures, chanting and meditation. Much of their focus is on suffering and hardening their bodies.

Ascetics often have the role of healer in their village. The Adjarn told Sameth and me that he was often called on to bless new buildings and enterprises. When movies are made, he is called to bless the set before filming can begin. He showed us a picture of him in an underground concrete crypt full of the bones of more than 200 dead bodies. He sat in wild-eyed prayer among countless skulls.

"This is in Bangkok," he said. "All of these people died without families. The bodies were burned and the bones stored in this vault. They asked me to come in and do a ritual to make the bad spirits go away."

The Adjarn and his wife were engaged in observing the last two days of the Chinese Thai vegetarian food festival. During this period, they are not allowed to kill anything and, of course, don't eat meat.

"In the past, there was a disease that was killing people and no doctor could cure it. An old man told the people, 'Stop eating meat.' And suddenly, the disease went away."

As a matter of health, Chinese Thai abstain from eating meat for the length of the festival each year. However, the Adjarn is not Chinese. Although he is a Brahman priest, he identified his religion as Theravada Buddhism like everyone else in Thailand and China.

"Chinese and Thai Buddhists are the same religion. We believe the same things, only our practice is different," he explained.

As if something very important had just occurred to him, the Adjarn set aside the amulet he was working on and asked Sameth how long before noon. Because monks don't eat past noon, the Adjarn was being very considerate. (Kru Pedro observed this when he was a monk. Pra Kru Ba didn't observe it because he was a forest or working monk.)

"It is five minutes to 12," he answered.

Barking an order like a sergeant, the Adjarn ordered his family to provide food to the monks before the clock struck noon. No sooner had the words left his mouth than a silver platter of rice, vegetables and broiled fish appeared.

The family prostrated while my friend ate. Afterward, Adjarn Sok Chai told us about his history.

He had made a lot of martial arts movies, including several with his former student Tony Jaa. Right now was preparing for the film Ong-bak 2 (2008). I found it interesting that anytime he told us about something in the past, he used the Buddhist year, rather than the international date. (The Thai Buddhist calendar begins at the Thai New Year, which can occur as late as April.)

"Tony learned his basics here. Then he went to learn other styles. He had many teachers. At the sport university, he learned taekwondo and also learned gymnastics. Eventually he made up his own style."

When the Adjarn smiled, you could see his teeth were dyed completely black from a lifetime of chewing betel nut, which is a commonly chewed nut in Southeast Asia.

"Tony didn't make it on physical strength. He made it because he is respectful and helps his teachers and the students and his family.

Jaa meditates a lot in the forest and with monks at the temple. Monks taught him special meditation for universal strength and power of earth, water, air and fire. It was this spiritual power that allowed him to make *Ong-bak*.

"Every time Tony comes here he gives me money to help train the kids. The gymnastic mats were paid for by Jaa," the Adjarn said. He lives in a poor neighborhood and is worried about local children getting addicted to yaba, a methamphetamine.

"I invite [the children] all to my house, and I train them for free," he explained. "I teach them self-defense. I want them to learn so they will be good people, not so they can fight professionally. However, if they choose to go fight professionally, I support that, too. I also don't train them specifically to be actors, but the top four students went to Bangkok to live with Jaa and be in the movies.

"We train long staff, sword, gymnastics, contortion, and muay Thai boran, mixed with krabi krabong." Gymnastics was the modern component of what the Adjarn was teaching the kids, but he was solidly rooted in the tradition of muay Thai boran.

After training with a number of teachers in Thailand, I have come to the conclusion that muay Thai boran is a fighting system encompassing hundreds of different movements, high and low stances, and various angles of attack. If you watch muay Thai in professional bouts, you will probably notice that 90 percent of fighters use less than 20 different techniques, even though there is no requirement limiting them to this small number of techniques. Most muay Thai boran moves would be permitted in sport muay Thai, but it's rare to see modern fighters use them. Sometimes you do see the occasional flying knee strike or double-drop-elbow-to-the-top-of-the-head strike. I have even seen spinning back kicks and side kicks. So while it is safe to say that many modern fighters know some of the ancient techniques, very, very few base their entire fighting style on them. The ones who do win, like the boxer Parinya Charoenphol, are well-respected.

The Adjarn felt strongly about the superiority of the old ways.

"Muay Thai and muay Thai boran practice striking, breaking,

throwing and wrestling. But muay Thai boran has more wrestling. One more difference between the two arts is that muay Thai boran includes the spirit. Nowadays the teachers don't teach the principles of muay Thai. They teach only as a business. They lack meditation and concentration."

I asked the Adjarn about the long-raging debate between Thailand and Cambodia about who invented muay Thai.

"I don't believe that all martial arts originated from a single martial art," the Adjarn told me, "The martial arts originated first from animal styles, but different countries formed their own martial art based on their culture and imagination. We took the basics from nature to protect ourselves. Since all countries started at the same place—nature—this would explain why there are some similarities between the arts. But we developed separate beautiful styles according to our culture."

The Adjarn's idea also fit well with the development of contemporary muay Thai. Unlike karate and judo, there is no governing body that unifies all systems of muay Thai together. There are no specific series of moves for each muay Thai student to learn or to master before moving to a new level of expertise. Instead, muay Thai styles depend on the region a student comes from and with whom he studies. Every teacher has his own variations, and some vary dramatically. Consider how different my experience was training with Pra Kru Ba as compared to Kru Pedro.

"Throughout Thailand," he said, "some teachers become famous because their students win fights. In the old days, when two people fought, you could see by the style where he came from. Today, however, when you watch the fights it is not as evident where they come from because the modern style is becoming more universal.

"When I was learning, we put sand in the bag and kicked with our shins. Then when we got tough enough, we added cement. After that, we kicked banana trees. In the final phase, the students stood in water up to their necks and kicked a banana tree, under water, until the tree broke. After you finished the last step, you could open a sports club.

"It took about 20 years. Today, no one trains like that anymore."

The Adjarn then closed the interview by saying: "You come back tomorrow, and I will teach you the basics. After that, it is up to you to develop your own style."

I asked how much he wanted me to pay.

"Teaching is a form of conservation," he said. "It is good that a foreigner wants to learn our art. So the pay is up to you."

❂

The next day I arrived at the training field, which was located in an empty lot beside the Adjarn's house. The otherwise empty field was filled with broken glass and debris. I found the Adjarn walking on a tightrope.

"Balance," he said simply.

Next, he did a routine for me by spinning a long staff, twirling it around his body and tossing it up in the air. He repeated the routine with a flag tied to a long pole, which spun like a red propeller.

"Tony Jaa is so good because he has good fundamentals: a good mind and good spirit. You must also have a strong physical body, balance and focus. Use the gym to make your body strong. Meditate to strengthen your mind and spirit," he told me.

The Adjarn teaches muay Thai and muay Thai boran mixed with krabi krabong with a heavy emphasis on gymnastics. It's important to note that no instructor teaches pure muay Thai boran anymore; instead, teachers teach a muay Thai boran that is heavily influenced by the sport of muay Thai.

We began my lessons with muay Thai boran kicks, which went beyond the fundamental two muay Thai kicks—the roundhouse and push kick. He started with a series of stomping kicks executed with the ball of foot. The Adjarn used this stomp kick to strike what he called the dangerous parts: just above the knee, inside of the thigh, where the leg meets the pelvis, the solar plexus, the throat and the chin.

"The best way to build power on this kick is to practice on banana trees," he said. "But to be strong you must use all parts of body and mind, strength, meditation and fighting. No one can do this today because they don't learn anymore, but the boran style was the best."

In the next sequence, we worked on knees. The Adjarn's assistants had wrangled a heavy bag from somewhere and hung it on a tree to help me practice.

"When you throw a knee strike, your knee must always go higher than the target," the Adjarn said. "When you strike, you must come in with your full body weight and focus the power on the knee."

We went through a number of exercises where we just practiced bringing up the knee as high and as fast as possible. Since muay Thai boran uses knee strikes at all manner of angles, we practiced coming up on the side, in the front, in the center, across the body, outside, and inside.

Next up, we addressed punches. Modern muay Thai uses punches similar to Western boxing, but muay Thai boran expands on this by using big overhand lefts and rights as well as big uppercuts and a huge hook, which my first teacher, H. David Collins, referred to as the "behind K-Mart" parking-lot punch. The Adjarn demonstrated one for me, winding up and swinging his whole body into the punch. In boxing, my hooks and uppercuts travel only about three inches.

I found the change to be too difficult. While I wasn't sure if winding up for power and swinging wide was the better way to go, I listened to the Adjarn with curiosity.

The Adjarn still had some tricky moves. He caught one of my punches between his two hands and pulled me into a knee strike. I kicked at his head, but he wrapped his leg around my leg and took me down for a submission.

"Some styles of muay Thai are very low. Others fight with their hands open, like in other martial arts. Some can grapple well. Some don't grapple at all. When they catch your leg, they hit you with an elbow instead of wrestling."

To illustrate the extra dimensions of muay Thai boran, the Adjarn then taught me some grappling.

In muay Thai, grappling occurs when opponents lock up at the head, grabbing each other around the back of the neck while raining knee strikes in on each other. These are short, fast knee strikes that don't do a terrible amount of damage but which earn points. Muay Thai boran is not about points. It is about winning a fight and taking out your opponent. To do this you have to first get distance. The Adjarn and I locked up, and he showed me how to leverage off my forearms to push away from an opponent. Then I was to step back with one leg, gain distance and come in with a full swinging knee strike. At the same time, I was to use my arms and body weight to throw myself into the strike.

Combining the clinch with the knee strike wasn't without its perils because you can't see what your opponent is doing. You have to feel it. If his shoulder suddenly drops, or his weight shifts to one side, be aware that he is about to throw a big knee strike. This is a good time to twist, turn, jump, pull or push to force your opponent to redistribute his weight in order to avoid falling down. Once he shifts his weight back to center, the danger of the big knee strike is past. To avoid it, first you have to FEEL it.

Because of clinching, most muay Thai grappling consists of grabbing the neck and head. The Adjarn also grappled from the waist. When I went to grab his head, he ducked under my arms and grabbed me around the middle. He was careful to set his head off to the side with his face against my hip where it was out of range of knee strikes. In an impressive display of flexibility, he brought his knee up over his head and smashed me in the face. A variation of this knee strike involves bending at the waist and grabbing the back of the opponent's leg, then bringing your knee high up over your head and striking him in the face.

The Adjarn also demonstrated a number of techniques where he caught my leg and threw me down. In some cases, he scooped or pushed my base leg. In other instances, he used my kicking leg for leverage and tossed me to the ground. Sometimes, he pushed with his shoulder and sent me tumbling to the ground. In one very cool technique, he ducked under my kick and came up just as it was passing over his head. He stood up, trapping the leg on his shoulder.

When he stood up, the power and strength of his entire body was pitted against my extended leg, and I had no choice but to fall. This is also the technique that Tony Jaa uses at the beginning of *Ong-bak* to defeat a huge bare-knuckled champion.

We finished the day with some more muay Thai boran. Because muay Thai boran teaches you to destroy your opponent's weapons, it's more common to attack thighs rather than legs or biceps. For example, the Adjarn asked me to punch him. He used his elbow to push the punch down so it wouldn't hit him. Then he rotated his elbow across my forearm, gained control of my arm and pushed me to the ground. It was very similar to a hapkido technique, but it was all done using the elbow for leverage instead of grabbing the wrist or forearm of the opponent with your hand. Certain martial arts have a theory that when you grab a man's wrist, you have committed yourself, but at the same time, you've tied up one of your hands. By using the elbow to gain control—without grabbing—you are still free to fight with both hands.

The next day, we talked about movie fighting.

The children arrived for their training, carrying mats donated by Tony Jaa all the way from the Adjarn's house to the practice field. They lined up on the field and at the edges of their mats. One by one, the Adjarn and one of his assistants stretched out each child, twisting them up like pretzels. With one small boy, the Adjarn and assistant lifted him bodily by the head and feet and pulled at him, as if he were on a medieval rack. The child's flexibility was incredible. A 14-year-old boy also showed me how he could put one leg behind his head and hop with the other. It was as if the Adjarn commanded a legion of boneless children.

The Adjarn said that the children needed to use acrobatics for fake fighting in the movies. The kids practiced back bends, walkovers and hand springs. The kids lined up, and one by one, the Adjarn kicked them in the chin with a fake movie kick designed to look deadly from the right camera angle. The kids would flip way up in the air and land on their backs as if dead.

"When Tony was training with me we didn't have any mats or

safety," he told me. "That is one reason he is so good and so strong today because he trained on the hard ground."

At one point, the kids lined their mats out under a cement wall. They then scaled the wall and jumped off of it, executing a flip on the way down. I have to admit it was a bit frightening watching children as young as eight take a dive off a high wall. But the Adjarn explained: "This is one of the first things you have to learn to be a stuntman. But the children decide what they want to do. I don't push them.

"Being a stuntman and doing good movie fighting is a matter of training. Even if you are fat, you can do it," the Adjarn continued. He called his son up to demonstrate. The young man could easily play a thug in action movies because he weighed about 260 pounds. On command, he did a back flip, landed on his back in a near perfect breakfall position, then sprung back to his feet without using his hands.

It was time for me to learn to fight in the movies, which involved using weapons. In my career as a martial artist, the only weapon I have ever used are arnis sticks. So, picking up a weapon felt extremely foreign to me. (This was also different from my cinematic fighting experience in Cambodia. There, I had a difficult time learning to do exactly what the script asked whereas here, I had no idea how to use the weapon.)

The Adjarn taught me some techniques from krabi krabong, the Thai art of double sword and stick fighting. He practiced by attacking a tire mounted on a wooden pole, which served as a wooden man. The long stick he used is similar to the bo staff used in other martial arts, but it is very heavy and not flexible like the ones I saw at the Shaolin Temple. Often, the Adjarn took the long staff by the end and swung it like a baseball bat.

The short sticks were heavier and longer than Arnis sticks, but the important thing I had to remember was that they really weren't "sticks" but swords. If you were a master of Arnis you probably couldn't apply your skills to these longer, heavier weapons. The Adjarn taught me a basic pattern: strike to the left shoulder, strike to the right shoulder, strike to the top of the head. When you swing a sword in krabi krabong, you have to get a real wind-up swing, twisting your body and reaching far back behind you. Then you let it fly and the weapon cuts your opponent in half.

After doing the basic three-strike combo on a tire for a while, I was permitted to practice with a live partner. I attacked, stepping forward with each strike. The opponent defended, stepping back at a 45-degree angle and blocking as he went. Then he attacked, and I retreated and blocked. We practiced again and again until we could do the pattern at speed.

We then practiced these same movements but this time as if we were fighting in a film. We did the same basic power, but on film you have to use a lot more energy and add in a great deal of shouting and snarling. It looks really mean in the cinema, and it looks like two men beating the crap out of each other.

During unarmed fake fighting, the Adjarn showed me how he uses his deadliest kicks in a fashion so as not to injure his opponent. The opponent swings. The Adjarn ducks the punch and comes up behind the man and kicks him in the back with a loud, resounding "thud!" The trick here is that the Adjarn hit the man with the whole bottom of his foot, instead of stabbing his back with the heel or ball of the foot. Instead of striking the base of the spine, which could be lethal, his foot lands across the man's shoulder blades, missing the vital areas, but making an impressive sound. He uses a similar technique in the front, hitting an opponent across the chest, rather than driving into the solar plexus.

Practice over, the Adjarn took me back to his house. At the top of a flight of wooden stairs was his prayer room, which featured a massive shrine covered in magical objects. There were photos of famous dead monks in prominent positions around the altar. The Adjarn opened a canister and showed me its grizzly content.

"These are bones from a dead monk. They were very small when I first got them. But I have been praying every day and they grew bigger."

In one corner was a huge pile of religious medallions on beaded chains. The Adjarn explained that when he does his work as an ascetic holy man, he wears up to over 100 pounds of religious amulets.

"After training, I bring all the children up here to pray and meditate, so they don't get hooked on drugs or drink alcohol," he told me. His religious beliefs also influenced how he thought about his martial art.

"There are four powers in the universe: earth, wind, fire and water. Martial art is just one of them. People talk about ghosts, but there are no ghosts. When we die, we leave a dead body, and in the next life, our powers don't disappear. They are just reborn. I have three spirit teachers who come to teach me when I meditate. One of them is my older brother. They mostly teach me about meditation, not as much about martial arts.

"My teachers taught me that muay Thai and martial art are only one part of the process of attaining enlightenment," the Adjarn explained. He continued to illustrate his thoughts. "It is most important that we purify the mind. Tony Jaa meditates and prays regularly. That is why he is a good martial artist. He always shows gratitude to the spirits, teachers and parents. Every holiday, he comes to the temple to make offerings. Training the body is only one step. We have to train the spirit and all the parts will become strong."

Just as I was leaving, I noticed that one of the amulets the Adjarn wore bore an image of King Jayavarman VII, the ruler of the Cambodian empire of Angkor and the patron saint of bokator. Once again, I asked the Adjarn if he believed that Cambodian martial art could have been the origin of Thai martial art. The Adjarn answered: "There were a lot of martial arts styles in the past. Some have similarities because they all originated from nature. But we developed these styles out from their natural base until they became unique and beautiful arts. The transformation occurred according to our imaginations and according to the culture of the country, which created them."

Then the Adjarn closed the interview with a line that summed up my six-year quest in Asia.

"If we want to know about a culture, we can go learn their martial art. And that will tell us who the people are and what they are about."

✪

After this trip to Isan, Bangkok would wind up being my home base for the next several years. I would still travel and do my martial arts adventures in other countries, but I would call Bangkok home. But even when I was in Bangkok, I was more away than home. I would average one or two months a year in Thailand and the rest of the time I would be abroad, traveling and doing martial arts.

My next stop would be the Philippines.

Adjarn Sok Chai

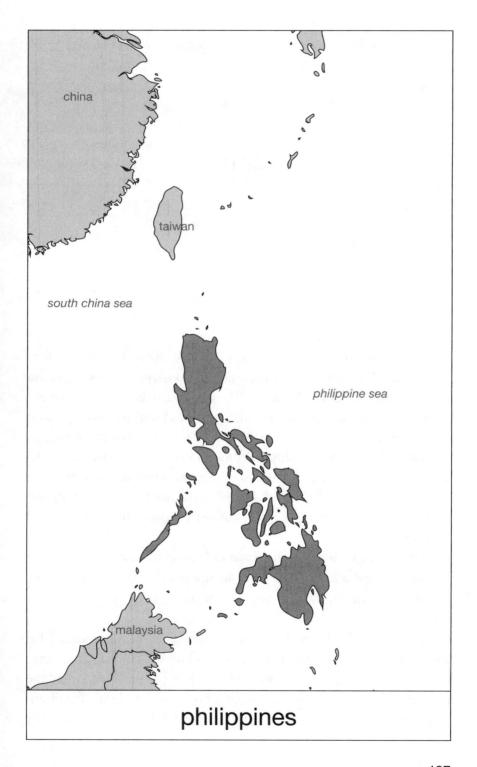

china

taiwan

south china sea

philippine sea

malaysia

philippines

chapter 8

WHILE I WAS STILL IN THAILAND, I received an e-mail from a film journalist who worked with the mayor of Puerto Princesa City on the Philippine island of Palawan. The film journalist was a fan of my books (I had published four at this point) and told the mayor about me. The mayor liked what he heard about my martial arts adventures and offered me a sponsorship to come to his city and write about its adventure tourism. I took the assignment as much out of interest as necessity; I'd been living off of the savings of my Korean teaching job in Thailand, but that money was gone. I needed a place to live and food to eat.

I paid for a one-way plane ticket to Manila from Bangkok. When I landed, I had about $100 USD in my pocket. (I also wasn't due to get any more money for weeks until some magazines I had been writing for paid me.)

I went to the Puerto Princesa mayor's office in Manila, and his secretary handed me a free plane ticket to Puerto Princesa City. Once in Puerto Princesa, the mayor had a police car pick me up at the airport and take me to the second best hotel on the island. Television journalists usually got to stay at the best hotel, but for me, even the second best place was pure luxury. I had a huge room with a balcony and a view. The hotel had a swimming pool, and the staff wouldn't let me carry my own bags or open the door for myself. The mayor didn't give me any cash but he said I could charge anything I wanted to the room. So I ate at the fancy restaurant at the hotel three times per day and billed my meals to my room. I also billed my laundry and anything else I could think of.

The island of Palawan is tropical and exotic. Most of the island is now protected forest so you can find animals and plants that don't exist anywhere else in the world. Palawan is also home to two UNESCO World Heritage sites—an underground cave network and a reef marine park. The city of Puerto Princesa is like a Philippine version of Mayberry, Alabama. There is one main street with shops along either side. The street ends at in a public park where free concerts and other community programs take place. The city itself, in terms of zoning, covers a huge geographical area and it takes about 45 minutes to drive across; the main development is on the main street. The university and the sports stadium are outside of town. The main means of transportation is the small converted motorcycles, which people referred to as tricycles. It was nice riding out to the stadium because I would pass the beautiful tropical landscape as well as scenes of rural Philippine life.

For the two months I was in Puerto Princesa, I banged out a bunch of tourism stories and sent them to a list of online magazines I worked with so the mayor could see right away that I was working. He was a man who loved publicity, and he told the hotel to let me stay as long as I wanted. When I didn't have any money to leave because my payments had been delayed, the mayor simply sent over a police car to take me to the visa office to give them a note that read: *Visitante del mayor.* My visa was instantly extended another 30 days, as were my free food and cable TV at the hotel.

In between tourism stories about remote tribes, fishing, mountain climbing and hiking, I joined a weight-lifting gym to keep up my strength training; it cost less than $1 USD per day. Of course, I asked every person I met, interviewed or worked with if they knew where I could find a martial arts master.

No one seemed to know of any martial arts on the island. They all kept telling me I would have to wait till I got back to Manila. The one thing I knew for certain was that there was an amateur boxing team in Puerto Princesa, and I figured I could at least start training with them until I found a martial art. In the Philippines, it sometimes seems as if you always need a personal introduction or a friendly politician to pave the way for you. Since I had all of the mayor's resources at my disposal, I had someone from the tourism department arrange for me to meet the city boxing commissioner. I was told that I could see him during an open session of the city hall.

The open session took place in a tremendous hall, sort of like a bigger version of what a television courtroom looks like. Rows and rows of people sat on wooden chairs while, on a stage in front, the important people sat on a bench much like a judge's. Unlike a television courtroom, people were jumping up and down on their seats and crowding the stage. As I didn't know what the boxing commissioner looked like or who to apply to for help, I didn't know whether to push my way inside or what.

At the beginning of any official event in the Philippines, you will usually see a live band playing the national anthem. People were constantly going in and out of the chamber, and as the doors swung open, I heard the music playing. When I went inside, I saw that there was a band on the stage beside the commissioners. My heart jumped when I recognized the lead singer. There are Philippine bands playing in bars all over Asia and no matter what country I am living in, I tend to find Filipino friends. I had seen Ryan, the singer, perform in a bar on a separate adventure. Before coming to the Philippines I had loaded a ton of phone numbers in my phone of Filipinos I had met all over Asia who'd said, "Call me if you are in my country."

As Ryan was on the other side of the sea of applicants, I called him from my cell phone during a lull in the music and reintroduced myself.

"Antonio!" Ryan said into his cell. "Are you coming to Puerto Princesa?"

"Actually, I'm here," I said. "I need to see the boxing commissioner. I'm a 'visitante del mayor.' "

Thanks to Ryan, a uniformed guard came and escorted me to the private office of the boxing commissioner who left the open session to see me—after all, I was a guest of the mayor's. He ordered us some sandwiches and coffee.

The commissioner was an extremely likeable man who just wanted to take boxing in Puerto Princesa to a world level to help promote the city. This seemed to be the goal of everyone in Puerto Princesa from the street sweepers to the school teachers. I could understand their desire, especially considering that Puerto Princesa has some of the highest quality of life to offer its citizens compared to much of the rest of the country. In fact, the mayor is part of the reason behind the area's good fortune; he is personally credited with raising the standard of living for many of the city's citizens.

The commissioner called his assistant who took me to the stadium to start my boxing adventure.

Despite Puerto Princesa's prosperity, it was still terribly poor. Thus, the Puerto Princesa boxing team had nothing, but the fighters managed to stay cool while training in the intense Philippine sun. They had no gym, no ring, no weights and no jumping ropes. They only had one heavy bag, no medium bags, no speed bag, and no floor-to-ceiling bag. Most fighters didn't have boxing shoes. The team owned several pairs of smelly, decrepit boxing gloves, which were coming apart. The two coaches had to share a single pair of coach's gloves. The teams they fought from bigger cities had all of that, and more. Yet, in spite of all of the things they were lacking, the Puerto Princesa boxing team is one of the hardest working teams I have ever trained with. More than anything, their energy and enthusiasm put a smile on my face every day when we turned out for training. Sometimes I lost my smile when we were running six laps or the coach was slapping me, to teach me defense, but for the most part, they were a happy bunch.

The training was also free to all, sponsored by the city government.

The fighters met every day at 5:00 p.m. at the sport stadium to train on the running track. While doing our shadow boxing, we sometimes had to step out of the lanes to make room for the track team coming through. The team's single heavy bag was stored in a tool shed on the other side of the stadium and was toted by two or more boxers several hundred meters to a makeshift iron frame at the start of each training session. At the end of each session, the bag had to be taken down and returned to the shed.

At the beginning of each session, we stood at attention before the coaches: 42-year-old Romeo Zligan and 21-year-old Lelord Bautista. Romeo was a retired professional fighter while Lelord, in addition to coaching and studying at Palawan State University, continued to fight as an amateur.

There are two things you will notice when you train in the Philippines: One, they switch constantly between English and one of the Filipino languages. Often, even when they are speaking their native tongue, you can follow what they are saying because all of the keywords are English or Spanish. The second, interesting phenomenon is that sports organizations, and sometimes even companies and schools, are modeled after the U.S. military. So standing at attention, saluting or being declared Away Without Leave (Filipinos use the whole term) are common to civilian life.

The lead boxer, 18-year-old Ryan, stood before the coaches, saluted, and announced, "Coaches, all boxers are ready for training." The coaches returned the salute, and Coach Lelord explained the rounds and laps expected for the day's training.

The workout always started with a run on the track. When running, Coach Romeo sang cadence, like in the U.S. army. My favorite song while training with them was this Romeo-led-special: "I am just a lonesome boxer, far away from home. I climb the boxing ring, for I use it to come home. Darling if I die, you can marry again. Use my pension for your next honeymoon." Of course, because we were in the Philippines, we had to mix Tagalog—the common language of the Philippines—with English. At the end of each verse, we shouted.

"*Pangkat naming maganda* Puerto Princesa Boxing Team!" I didn't understand the meaning, but I always felt elated saying it.

After the run, we would do several rounds of shadowboxing, an important part of any fighting regimen. Shadowboxing gives fighters the opportunity to practice punching combinations. It is done in rounds, just like a real fight, so it also reinforces the fighter's ability to pace himself for an actual round. Additionally, shadowboxing gives the coaches a chance to walk among the boxers and make on-the-spot corrections to their form.

Romeo and Lelord followed shadowboxing up with several rounds of exercises, like jumping, skipping or hopping. The coaches had to be creative because of the lack of equipment. In my experience, I find that a boxer's workout should concentrate on three areas: cardiovascular fitness, strength and technique. To their credit, Romeo and Lelord found a way to cover all three, even with their lack of funds.

We would also do abdominal exercises with a twist. The fighters would lie in the dirt because we lacked mats, and each team member would run across the abs of those on the ground. When it came to my turn, all my teammates just started laughing hysterically.

The guys always asked me about my experiences fighting in other countries, and I told them how fighters don't earn much in Thailand.

"We don't get a lot here either," one fighter said. "If we win, we get $3 USD. In a big fight, we can get $6 USD."

Ouch! That is a lot of training and punishment to go through for so little money. Despite that, the 20 or so boxers on the team are polite, hardworking, bright and happy. I have never seen smiles and heard laughter like I have in Puerto Princesa. From the pleasant disposition of the people, you would guess they didn't have a care in the world. The reality is, economic problems color every aspect of Philippine life.

While several of my teammates were attending university, many actually had to give up their educations after high school to support their families. Unable to find work, boxing is the only activity they have to look forward to all day. For me, this is the saddest of circumstances: Talented young people who would be on their way to becoming skilled professionals in other countries are left with few options in their homeland. As such, at least a quarter of the country's people are working abroad.

One evening during training, we did some light sparring. Because I outweigh the biggest fighter by about 70 pounds, I opted to work on the heavy bag alone. Romeo then took me on the coach's mitts for several rounds. He was a good trainer with a good eye, but I could see from the expression on his face he wasn't used to having a clumsy 200-pound American swing at him. When he called out combinations, I could tell he was more than a little nervous that I would zig instead of zag, thus hitting him. Of course, I was nervous, too. Romeo held the gloves differently than my coaches in Cambodia and Thailand. The fact that he used different words, sometimes confused me. He often had to leap out of the way if I accidentally threw the wrong punch at him, like a driver in the wrong lane.

At the end of every training session, we would line up at attention again in front of Romeo and Lelord. Ryan would salute the coaches.

"Coaches, all boxers have finished training."

"Congratulations, boxers," replied the coach.

"Are all the boxers happy?" Romeo always yelled.

"Yes, coach!" we'd always yell back. When we filed out of the stadium, each boxer would run past Romeo and Lelord to give them a high five. Then we'd do the same thing the next day.

Through the boxing coaches, I was introduced to Dennis Santos, a trainer for modern arnis who taught lessons on the other side of the stadium track. So after boxing, I would train with the arnis team.

The Philippine martial art of modern arnis is composed of stick fighting techniques developed by the Muslim Sultans of the Tausug tribe on the island of Mindanao. Earlier versions of the art were called *kali* or escrima, names still used in Mindanao today. The student

The boxing team practices at the Puerto Princesa sports stadium.

begins training with a single stick; later he will train with two sticks and two blades, and then he will learn how to defend himself with his bare hands.

Arnis has forms, like other martial arts, but every single movement in the arnis form is a viable fighting technique. As you practice forms, so shall you fight in combat. One of the most unique aspects of arnis is that the movements are the same with sticks, blades or hands. A practitioner needs only to master one set of movements and then practice it with each of his weapons.

A distinctive aspect of arnis is in how you wield the sticks. Unlike in krabi krabong, the practitioner doesn't swing the sticks like in a double-bladed attack—one high and the other low. Instead, he moves the sticks independently of each other; when one stick blocks, the other strikes, etc. At the same time, the practitioner uses every part of the sticks as a weapon. The tips can be used for stabbing, slashing and knocking an opponent off-balance. The butts can be used for strikes to the face, collarbone or solar plexus. The practitioner can back up a punch with the hardness of the wooden stick. In grappling situations, the practitioner can use his sticks as levers to take down a bigger opponent, which is what Dennis would do with me; he would wedge his stick under my armpit and trap my head in a lock.

The first thing you will notice when you pick up an arnis stick is that it is much smaller than a baseball bat and not nearly as heavy as a tire iron. In fact, no matter where you are from, this delicate piece of wood, which is 22 inches long and the thickness of about two fingers, will appear to be anything but a deadly weapon. Before you write off this unassuming killing machine, talk to a master.

Kyud (brother) Dennis Santos—it's important to call people by their title in arnis—was a man of about my age, or slightly younger. He was large, weighing at least as much as me. He had a big belly, but he could really make the two sticks sing.

On the first day of training, he had me watch two of his students go through a sparring routine. There was a flash of brown, an image blurred by speed, the end of the deadly stick sliced through the air. A strike to the head … CRACK! The weapon was deflected by the opponent's stick. A strike to the knee smashed directly into a blocking stick. Two opponents, sticks in both hands, four sticks striking in succession, left right, head, shin, head, shin. Each strike was expertly blocked with perfect timing.

We next observed Israel, Kyud Dennis's number-one student, demonstrate the figure-eight pattern with his sticks. He circled, crissed and crossed his sticks while picking up speed.

"The striking patterns in arnis come from the weaving patterns used to weave the walls of traditional Philippine house," Kyud Dennis told me. Then he asked, "Could you box him?"

I watched Israel's skillful practice and saw his sticks move like the rotary blade on a propeller. I wanted to throw a carrot at him just to see if it would come out diced on the other side.

"Not unless I want my hands pureed," I said.

To reinforce the effectiveness of close-quarters combat, arnis practitioners learn to fight with a *dulo-dulo*, which is a small wooden cylinder about the size of a roll of quarters. They wrap a hand around the dulo-dulo to add more wallop to their punches. The dulo-dulo also has a one-and-half-inch projection that sticks out on either side of the hand. This projection can be used for locking and trapping techniques. It can also be used for the nerve and pressure-point strikes.

Because arnis is such a fierce fighting system, it has often been limited by colonial powers. Under Spanish rule (1521-1898), arnis was completely banned. In order to maintain their art, practitioners developed a type of dance which incorporated traditional music with the martial arts and knives. This allowed them to continue practicing martial arts. The art was also banned under Japanese occupation (1941-1945), but resistance fighters used the art to plague Japanese soldiers until the end of the war.

"Arnis is the best martial arts," I was told by my first arnis teacher Ricky, who I met in Hong Kong. "When we have a riot or a protest, all we have to do is grab a stick and we are ready to go."

This readiness and toughness seems characteristic of the culture. Because of the mix of Spanish and Asian ideals, things like saving face and preserving honor are important. (Although, Kyud Dennis had two daughters who practiced the art, and I wouldn't have wanted to face them.) For example, Kyud Dennis told me about a fight venue on Luzon island, where Manila is located. He said that fighters sign wavers before a fight so that no one will be sued or arrested. Then the competitors fight with unpadded sticks; they are able to hit knees, elbows and biceps to wear down their opponent's defenses.

"We also have open invitational fights," he told me, "where you can use hands and feet. You can grapple and fight on the ground. Hooking and sweeping are also allowed. We wear fighting gloves, not boxing gloves. We also don't kick with the shins. We use the heel, knife-edge or ball of the foot. Our motto is, take an opponent's balance and take his head."

"The best thing to do is run away," Kyud Dennis said. "But if you are attacked, give them a lesson. You have to fight to win."

Much of the arnis training deals with striking drills, like those I had witnessed when I first arrived. First, Dennis taught me the five basic strikes. Next, I learned the 12 strikes. After that, I began working with a partner, striking and blocking in set patterns at a faster and faster pace. We also practiced striking, blocking, and disarming or striking, blocking and grappling. Each time we mastered a pattern, Kyud Dennis introduced a new pattern, then another and another.

Getting off beat or out of rhythm resulted in getting hit with a stick. Each time I became frustrated, he just reminded me, "Go with the flow."

After just a few weeks of training I was surprised at how natural the drills became.

"If you learn the forms and drills, then your movements will be instinctive in a fight," explained Kyud Dennis, summing up the entire training routine. "But, it makes no sense to study the form but lack the practice fighting." Kyud Dennis said they generally only promoted black belts who had mastered fighting as well as the art. He believed the best place to test a black belt's skills is on the street. "When people in the Philippines hear you are studying martial arts, they will attack you to test you out. And they may be my former students or black belts."

I had visions of a gang of toughs waiting for me outside my hotel. In horribly dubbed English they would shout, "Your boxing style is no good. I will use my sticks to teach you respect. Now you must die!"

"Ah, but can your dragon beat my praying mantis?" I would counter.

Knife practice is the second step in the evolution of Philippine martial arts training. The first step is learning the double sticks. Next come the knives, and finally, open hand. The unique aspect of Philippine martial art is that the techniques and the drills learned in stick fighting are the same for knife fighting and the same for empty hand fighting. Stick fighting is practiced with a partner, drilling patterns, over and over again, until the patterns become second nature. Strike to the head, block, counter, reverse, strike to the leg, block, counter, reverse, etc. The rhythm is the key to stick fighting, and the motto is, "Go with the flow." You must always move with the force, reacting in the right way, increasing your speed as you go, maintaining expert timing. Any slip up and you could severely injure yourself or your training partner.

The patterns a student learns at the beginning may have as few as two or three moves. Eventually, the patterns will increase in complexity, adding attacks at all manner of angles. Attacks to the head, the legs, slash upward, downward, wrap around your head and hit the opponent, change hands with your stick. Disarm the opponent and strike him with his own stick. The patterns will build up to as many as 10 movements, which each partner must perform with perfect timing. Then the drill begins again. After the patterns are mastered, they are further complicated by adding movement. The patterns are done moving forward, moving backward, side-to-side and circling.

Some patterns are done with the classic block, strike, return. Others involve disarming. In these patterns, you block your opponent's stick, and then take it away from him, usually by using some type of joint manipulation or grappling. These patterns can look very much like wrestling, as they are done at extremely close range and may include sweeps and throws, as well as locks and traps.

"Our two main goals in Philippine fighting are take away your opponent's eyes and take away his balance," Kyud Dennis said during a knife-sparring session. Kyud Dennis set his knife aside and demonstrated a finger strike to the eyes. A finger strike to the throat will instantly paralyze an opponent, for a split second. But a split second is all you need in a knife fight. As painful as it is to get hit in the throat with a finger, I imagine it would be much worse to get hit in the throat with a stick or a knife.

We square off in fighting position, each armed with a five-inch blade. Kyud Dennis, casually lays his knee against the side of my knee, then twists and leans in. The pain is excruciating. It is clear that if he put his full weight into it, my knee would have been ripped right out of its socket. Apparently, the first rule of knife fighting is, fight dirty.

"We can destroy the knee with this technique, but we can also turn it into an economical sweep." Dennis repeated his lean and twist on my left knee, but this time, he hooked his foot behind my heel and pulled forward. Now, instead of ripping the left knee he attacked, I felt a tear in my right knee, my base knee. Either way, I would have wound up on the ground and possibly never fought again.

Knowing that I also study muay Thai (Thai kickboxing), Kyud

Dennis clinches with me. He sets his leg between my legs and begins striking the inside of both my knee with his knee. The technique is painful, but what he is actually doing is trying to change my balance. The second he feels my weight shift, he executes a sweep and takes me down.

Many of the disarming techniques for the stick feel a lot like hapkido. You begin by blocking, stick to stick, then, with your free hand, you twist the opponent's wrist outward or upward, attacking the joint. Once the joint is stressed, you push your opponent's stick, toward his fingers, rather than toward his palm. The hand opens, and the stick comes free. The push can be done with your knee, your forearm, your hand or your stick. You can also disarm by grabbing the thumb—which is, of course, a joint— and bending it back toward the wrist. Then, you follow up by pushing the stick out of his hand. In some of the more complicated techniques, you wrap your arm around your opponent's arm, like a snake, and your arm or shoulder winds up removing the stick as you tighten your grip on him. If you continue to apply pressure, the opponent's arm will break at the elbow. Even in these advanced techniques, the basic premise is the same: attack the joint, then push the stick out of the hand by applying pressure towards the fingers, not the palm.

With the knife, the techniques are the same. The important thing to remember with the knife is that you must always push the dull side of the blade with your hand, forearm or knife. Obviously you don't want to disarm someone by pressing your forearm against the sharp edge of the blade. A typical knife set works like this: The opponent stabs. You block his strike with your hand placed on top of or under his wrist or forearm. The opponent's hand will be immobilized for a split second, which is enough time for you to slash him. The beauty of the slash is that when the opponent sees what you are doing, he will jerk his arm back, which of course will mean he is dragging it along the blade of the knife. His own instincts betray him at that point, and he does your work for you.

In some of the more Steven Seagal-like techniques, you block the knife, twist the wrist, do a twist-and-flip and force the opponent to stab himself. Kyud Dennis calls this one, "return to sender."

When blocking the knife hand, it is important not to grab the hand or wrist. The second the opponent feels you grabbing him, he will break loose. Your natural reaction would be to hold on. This could be bad for you. He could be pulling you off-balance, or at least pulling you out of your stance and into a compromised position. If you just block by putting your hand in the way of his forearm or wrist, he won't notice for a split second, and that gives you time to slash. If he moves his hand away before you slash, it is no problem because you still have your balance and you are still in position. Remember, every slash is followed by a stab. In this way, if the opponent moves his arm and avoids getting slashed, there is a high probability he is not ready to parry your thrust, and you could stab him, ending the fight.

Oh, yeah, and most importantly: Kids, don't try this at home. Someone could lose an eye.

Antonio practices knife techniques with Kyud Dennis.

✪

My checks finally came in and I finally had money to return to Thailand for some other adventures and studies. But less than a month went by before the mayor of Puerto Princesa invited me back to cover the city's big festival for some magazines. This time, he bought me a plane ticket from Bangkok to Puerto Princesa and put me back up at my hotel. I half expected the reception to hit me with a bill of refuted charges from my last stay, but the mayor was just as generous this time. I wound up staying for another month on Palawan, writing stories and training with the modern arnis and boxing team.

After my month at Puerto Princesa, Kyud Dennis actually arranged for me to go study kuntaw with his master, Frank Aycocho. For about a month, I lived in Master Frank's house, training every day. We also spent a lot of our down time watching UFC videos in which Master Frank would teach me his fighting philosophies. It was a lot of fun to do this because Master Frank was in his 60s and had a lifetime of martial arts behind him. He loved martial arts and martial combat. He loved to practice it, study it and talk about it in all its forms. This was very refreshing, especially considering so many of my previous masters were solely focused on one style.

So what brought Master Frank to kuntaw?

Most martial artists are familiar with the Philippine arts of kali, escrima and modern arnis, but these are weapon styles. Kuntaw is the ancient Philippine art of hand and foot combat. It is an all-inclusive art that includes stick and knife fighting as well as striking and grappling. A kuntaw black belt is probably well-versed in some arnis training but isn't necessarily an expert, but a kuntaw practitioner would know how to lock, grapple, kick and punch barehanded. It does not contain forms, but it is a fierce art. Master Frank demonstrated this to me during one of our first sessions. Picture two fighters facing each other. Both have their left legs as the lead and are standing in fighting stance. Fighter A lifts his left leg and smashes the ball of his foot into the inside of the calf muscle of Fighter B's left leg. Fighter A's foot continues past Fighter B's leg and then in the air it switches direction, comes back and smashes the outside of B's thigh.

Despite the effectiveness of the art, the simple truth is that kuntaw is overshadowed by foreign arts, especially taekwondo. In fact, taekwondo is the most popular art in the Philippines. Karate is next, and the Philippine arts bring up the rear. The government has actually made taekwondo the official martial art to teach in schools.

"People want the things from the other countries," Master Frank said, "and I really wanted to join the national karate competition. I went to the YMCA and studied karate 'til someone told me about kuntaw. I changed to Kuntaw because I was interested in promoting the ancient Filipino art."

One reason for the popularity of martial arts in the Philippines is as a defense against the high crime rate. Because of its reality, Master Frank often talked to his students about defending themselves.

"If you are standing on the corner and someone grabs your cell phone, or they stick a knife in your side and say 'give it to me,' " Master Frank said, "just give it to them. Don't fight, because you might get injured. At least if you have a little knowledge of martial arts, you can fight to save your life. You can delay the bad guy and hopefully a Good Samaritan or policeman can come and help you."

Good Samaritans in the Philippines aren't always officials.

"Sometimes the police are in on it or they just don't care," Master Frank explained to me. "One time, a guy tried to rob me on the street when I was in the army. I subdued him and dragged him to a police officer. The officer pretended not to see me. I said, 'Hey, you have to take this guy to jail.' The officer said, 'Sorry. I only work traffic.' I wrote down the officer's name and dragged the criminal to jail myself."

Kuntaw teaches students to move away from force in a circular motion when attacked. If you do meet force with force, you can double the impact of your strike when attacking. For example, when the opponent punches, duck under his strike and punch him with your extended knuckle under the arm, under the bicep, or in the armpit. Or, you can hook to the floating ribs. Move in closer while you are striking. This kind of force and thinking leads to a quick win, and Master Frank felt that many professional fighters didn't consider how a single and powerful blow would end a fight.

"Look at pro boxing," he said. "They hit each other in the face for 12 rounds and the guy still doesn't go down. That shouldn't be. If they wanted to win, they should concentrate and throw a single powerful punch." He also felt that fighters should target the body rather than the head because the floating ribs and solar plexus were such soft targets.

Master Frank showed me how to duck under a punch, then drop my hand to my waist and turn my entire body into the punch from my waist to shatter the opponent's floating ribs.

"Even if your target is the upper body or face, you can get more power punching from the hip and by twisting your whole body into the punch."

We practiced punching a candle flame.

"Throw the punch like you are throwing a baseball and the candle will go out," he explained.

Sometimes, Master Frank would move all his furniture from the kitchen so we would have room to grapple. I was always surprised at how strong he was, given his age, but then again, the master had a past. He once told me about how he used to go "suicide hunting" as a youth.

"When I was young and living in the provinces, we hunted for wild pigs with a sharpened bamboo pole. This was called suicide hunting. You put your back against the tree and held the pole in front of you and waited. Eventually, the pig will come to hunt you. When he charges you, you impale him on the pole."

He also had fought in the army, competed in kickboxing and been a medic for most of his adult life.

During our grappling sessions, Master Frank taught me how the best defense against a grappler is to hit him.

"You should hit him with a perfect hook under the armpit or in the side of the head or the ribs," he'd say. "You can also punch the tricep and disable his arm. Or take a step back and hit him in the face with the knee. You have to anticipate his movement. You punch just as he is shooting in. If you think he will shoot, instead of moving back and away, move forward with a knee to the face."

Kuntaw uses kicks below the knee to disable the opponent. They also use sweeps. Master Frank had developed some techniques kicking the side of the knee, which would disable the opponent. He used a stomping kick, instead of a push kick.

"If you know the real striking power, you can dislocate the knee," Master Frank said. "Do not use any techniques whose outcome is not defense of your position. If you punch at me with a straight punch I can break your arm. If you do a hook elbow, I can snap your arm."

He demonstrated how he could slap the upper and lower side of my arm simultaneously, breaking the elbow. In another scenario, I punched at his head, but Master Frank came up with a knee strike to my floating ribs, then stomped my foot. He then reached down to grab my heel, which gave him the opportunity to also hit me in the solar plexus with his shoulder. This knocked me down. Master Frank wasn't finished yet; he took my knee across his chest and did a knee bar and heel hook simultaneously.

"I am the guy that when I watch UFC, I bang on the table and shout, why did you do that? I never see these moves in UFC," he said.

Kuntaw teaches a quick delivery and a quick retraction. When you deliver a punch or kick with quick retraction you are ready for another punch.

"In UFC or boxing, they use prolonged strikes and punches— too many strikes. They hit too much without knocking the man out because the delivery is not right. If you punch in this manner it doesn't have enough force, but if you punch in the concentrated manner, you can put anyone down," Master Frank explained to me.

Part of having good delivery is maintaining strength without losing flexibility. Lifting heavy weights will destroy the flexibility in your body, so it is better to use isometric tension and resistance to build punching strength. Practice punching in the air with light weights. You call a wrestler and he turns like an 18-wheeler. He has to turn his whole body around to see you. You call Tony Jaa, and he whips around, ready to fight. So instead of heavy lifting, Master Frank practiced with elastic bands hooked anywhere in his house. He'd sit in a chair, holding the bands, and practice punching in the air.

To me, Master Frank was a piece of living history. He'd had an interesting past—growing up as a small boy in the provinces, fighting in free-fighting competitions at fairs and festivals, fighting as a soldier and working as a medic. He knew Dan Inosanto before Inosanto went to the United States and trained with Bruce Lee. Now he was training and sharing it all with me.

Antonio spars with Master Frank in Manila.

A magazine had called me while I was in Puerto Princesa and asked me if they could buy one of the articles I had written. I agreed, and they were supposed to meet me at Master Frank's house to hand over a check. Instead of taking the payment, I decided to do a trade with them instead.

For years, I had been planning a TV show called *Martial Arts Odyssey*. The concept was basically to get cameras to follow me around Asia, training with my different masters. The show would be about martial arts, as well as culture—basically all of the things I wrote about in my magazine articles and books.

I had done a lot of consulting work for various TV networks when they were working on martial arts shows, and each time I would pitch them my show. However, no one seemed interested in producing it. Finally, I had the idea to take advantage of the Internet and put it online to see if that led anywhere. Because this particular magazine had a small film production company, I asked them to shoot and edit the pilot of my TV series in lieu of payment. They agreed and the show was born.

Master Frank and the Philippine martial arts were the subject of my pilot episode. We shot it a park near his house in metro Manila. I'll admit that that first episode had its problems, but that's mainly because I didn't know exactly what each episode should look like. In the end, I didn't care that it wasn't perfect. *Martial Arts Odyssey* (2008) had finally happened. I would actually go on to develop more than 100 episodes over the years. As for Master Frank, the popularity of the show online reestablished him in martial arts circuits. He received more than a few "we didn't know you were still alive" notes.

Even better, Master Frank was recognized by the Philippine government for being a master and repository of Philippine martial arts. Because of his newfound influence, he was able to convince officials to change school policies so that Philippine martial arts were the official arts taught in schools.

Back in the then-present, I wrapped up that episode in two days. I was on a tight schedule because an American TV network wanted me to scout out masters and locations for them to shoot an episode of a TV series in Cambodia. So, three weeks after we finished filming, I left Master Frank, stopped off in Bangkok to collect a few things and then went to Cambodia.

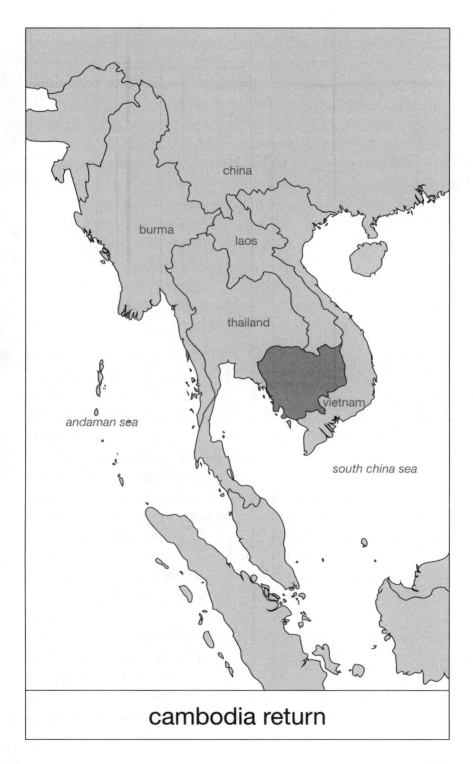

china

burma

laos

thailand

andaman sea

vietnam

south china sea

cambodia return

chapter 9

OVER THE LAST SEVERAL YEARS, I had been involved with several different production companies. For the most part, production companies called to discuss the possibility of shooting shows in Southeast Asia, such as one for bokator in Cambodia and another on Pra Kru Ba in Thailand. Neither of these shows ever made it into production, however, because of the logistics of shooting.

What I'd come to learn about reality television was that it was unrealistic. Showrunners wanted things to look dangerous and exotic when they weren't actually dangerous or exotic. Or, production companies just weren't adaptable in dealing with other cultures. For example, I often received complaints about how I never included phone numbers, mailing addresses or Web site information for many of the martial arts masters. But guess what? Many of these masters don't have telephones or Web sites, and nearly no one in countries like Cambodia and Burma have mailing addresses.

Sometimes, shows just got it. The History Channel had flown me in to consult for an episode of *Digging for the Truth*. Because of my experience in the country, my part was eventually expanded into translator. I even gave an on-camera lesson to the show's host about bokator. In spite of the fact that Cambodia is a very complicated place to live, the cast and crew were very interested in learning about the culture. They often asked me about possible cultural faux pas, and when they left, all the Cambodian people involved only had nice things to say about them.

In fact, one of my funniest moments occurred with The History Channel cast and crew. We were filming my "hero walk," wherein I walk while a voiceover narrates who I am, in front of a random temple near Angkor Wat. While we were filming, a little boy walked through the shot with a herd of water buffalo. At first, the crew was annoyed—we had to wait for these slow-moving animals to get out of the way? But then, the producer got an idea. She "rented" the buffalo from the boy for $5 USD to use as background props for my shot.

When the producer asked me to translate: "How much to rent your buffalo?" into Khmer, I laughed hard. It wasn't a phrase I learned in school. The boy was just as perplexed. His face said, "I hear what you are saying but that is so crazy I must be hearing wrong." Instead he answered very politely, "Yes, older brother."

In Cambodia, you often have to provide a lot of context to make sure you're on the same page with the person you want to bargain with. So here's what happened:

First, I complimented him on his herd of buffalo. The boy looked back at his herd, as if seeing them for the first time. He agreed they were nice.

"Do you know we don't have buffalo in America?" I asked. Now he thought I was really crazy.

"America is a rich country. You have everything. Why don't you have buffalo?" he asked.

"We don't," I said. "That's why we want to film your beautiful buffalo. Would that be OK with you?"

He understood and named his price. Maybe he had understood the whole time.

"Ask him to sign a receipt," the producer told me, handing me money.

"I'm pretty sure he wouldn't know how to do that," I explained. Somewhere, $5 USD must have been added to a column in accounts labeled "miscellaneous expenses associated with Antonio."

With the buffalo rented, the humor continued because we then had to move the buffalo back and forth for reshoots and make sure they stayed in the shot. I think the little boy definitely left with a story that day. I wound up with about 10 minutes of quality screentime. In my opinion, it was the best thing I had ever done up to that point for the Khmer people. It was a major victory.

Now I had a new contract with another show and was headed back to Cambodia. Once I arrived in Cambodia, my mission was to travel around the country and find surviving bokator masters. I also had to decide which masters and students would be good for the show. The experience of working on this show was incredible up to this point. I was on my own, traveling around Cambodia with a decent budget and doing what I love to do.

Unfortunately, this production was riddled with cultural and linguistic difficulties. The cast and crew couldn't believe how difficult it was to operate in the country. When doors slammed in our faces, the producers didn't understand how their status didn't impress the Khmers.

"Tell them the name of our network," they would say.

"They don't have cable," I would try to explain.

"Tell them that this will be good advertising for them," they would say.

What they didn't get was that the Khmer masters and students weren't concerned with being famous or getting free advertising. They were concerned about getting rice today to feed their families. They were concerned about bare feet and the lack of plumbing and electricity in their homes.

It's a common Western assumption that money can solve all poverty. The Khmer hate their poverty, but they aren't motivated by money. They have lived in poverty for years; they're good at it. You aren't going to jerk them out of their ways by offering them a few bucks. An amount of $50 USD won't change a Khmer's life. Instead, he will pay his rent, go to karaoke, buy some food and then be poor again three days later.

Things got worse when the hosts showed up. They had no interest in learning anything about the culture. They didn't learn the names of any of the Khmer martial artist nor did they even ask me one question about Angkor Wat, which we had the privilege of having to ourselves to film. Worst of all, one of the hosts appeared to intentionally injure a Khmer martial artist, which obviously angered Khmer onlookers. If a Khmer crew member hadn't pacified the crowd, I'm pretty sure the Western crew and I would have been mobbed. When I later confronted the host, he said, "This is my show and I do what I want."

Suffice it to say, I was glad when the final day of shooting happened. I'm still not sure if the experience was worth whatever the financial benefits were afterward.

When the cast and crew finally left, I couldn't have been happier. Originally, I had envied those hosts. I wanted to have my own show. After I saw how sour their attitudes were, I never wanted to work with their like again. I kept imagining what it would be like to travel around the world only to be disrespectful of any culture you were documenting. It was a blessing in disguise, and I was glad to get back to writing, which is what I believe God put me on the planet to do.

I remained in Cambodia for about three more months, studying bokator and training to receive my black krama (belt) in the art with San Kim Sean. During that time, I stayed with an American named Derek Morris. A year earlier, Derek had been in Iraq as a U.S. soldier. He had read my first article on bokator and had traveled to Cambodia to study it after being released from the Army. In the beginning, he lived on the floor of the bokator school, training all day, every day. By the time I arrived in Phnom Penh, he had taken an apartment and was kind enough to lend me his spare room. I stayed for free and chipped in for the electric bill, and it was just fun to hang around an American again. We spent a lot of time talking about martial arts and fighting. We bought a DVD player and watched lots of movies. We had the same schedule: wake up at 5 a.m., go to wrestling practice, eat breakfast, nap, train in bokator and go to the gym. After the gym, I would go to Paddy's and Derek would continue to train in bokator.

Because bokator is an all-inclusive art, every bokator teacher and black belt had to be proficient in the entire art in the old days, which meant they had to learn boxing, wrestling, animal styles and weapons. Today, it is nearly impossible to demand that type of commitment from anyone. So, there are two basic paths. There is the bokator animal-style path, which is what Derek did. This meant that he had to learn all the animal forms and the thousands of techniques in the forms to earn a black belt. Second, there is the fighting path, and that is what I did. On this path, I had to study three components: Khmer wrestling, Khmer boxing and bokator. The main reason I had to learn Khmer kickboxing and wrestling was because ancient bokator masters were expected to kickbox and wrestle at the same level as a professional kickboxer and wrestler. Then, San Kim Sean would teach me how to combine my boxing and wrestling skills with the unique bokator techniques. The bokator grandmaster would also teach me additional techniques that are not present in modern Khmer boxing and wrestling. For example, I had to learn submissions and chokes for wrestling. I had to learn about 20 elbow strikes and about 20 knee strikes in contrast to the two basic knee strikes in modern Khmer kickboxing. I had to learn all these additional punches. My point is that Khmer boxing and Khmer wrestling represent a very small percentage of the total techniques in bokator. Even within bokator, Khmer boxing and wrestling are still a fraction of the art.

I trained for boxing and wrestling outside of San Kim Sean's class. I learned wrestling with a Mr. Kim, who officiates at Khmer wrestling matches and is part of the Bokator Federation. I learned Khmer boxing from Paddy, my old kickboxing coach. However, I had to practice every day with San Kim Sean. So throughout the three months of training for my black belt, I would train for wrestling in the morning, followed by bokator until lunch and then boxing with

Paddy in the evening.

❀

In the several years since I had written the first magazine article about him, grandmaster San Kim Sean had been recognized as the man who revived bokator from near extinction. He was pleased.

"Bokator was sleeping for nearly a thousand years," he told me. "Now we will make it live again in Cambodia."

Since I'd last been there, bokator had really grown. The first time I walked into the club, San Kim Sean had about 200 students, but outside of the training room, no one had heard of him. When I came back in 2007 to train, he was well known in Cambodia, frequently appearing on Cambodia TV and in the press. The French language newspapers in Cambodia ran stories about him. Foreign journalists had interviewed him, and his story was spreading slowly around the world. I even found out one of my bokator stories had been translated into Japanese and was running in a sports magazine in Tokyo. I was pleased with the growth that had happened. Because I was constantly being approached by people who wanted to document bokator or train in bokator, I had managed to stay in contact with San Kim Sean, even though I hadn't trained with him in years.

Every day after wrestling practice, I would eat a late breakfast and head to the bokator school for my private lessons with San Kim Sean. In the beginning, he taught me about bokator history and techniques. In those lessons, I learned that, unlike the sport of Khmer boxing, bokator is an art form like traditional apsara dancing or singing. Unlike dancing and singing, it encompasses fighting arts like wrestling and weapon styles. Students make a lifetime commitment to the art. Several of them live in the school and train from waking until sleeping. Many of the techniques, particularly those using the stick or sword, are flamboyant and showy.

"The instructors have to learn to do demonstrations," San Kim Sean explained. "When people say, 'Show me your art,' they must have something to show."

And show they can. Advanced students can spin a fighting staff so fast that it can barely be seen. They continue the spin, leaping into the air, with the deadly weapon orbiting their bodies. This is only for show. The real fighting is different.

Although students are taught to fight from any distance, the real power of bokator is at extremely close range. The punches and elbow strikes are designed and practiced from a distance of only three inches. The practitioner keeps his arms completely relaxed, hanging loosely at his side, while he dances around a punching bag. Suddenly, his hand snaps out, and his fist strikes like a whip. You'll probably hear a loud "POP!" but you'll only see the bag swing violently.

San Kim Sean and I talked a lot about how bokator was different from boxing and wrestling, especially because I was learning those two components from outside instructors. He believed that I needed to learn the modern ways first, in order to appreciate the differences of the ancient ways. For example, let's return to the idea of how the bokator fighter is completely relaxed, which is very different from what fighters want in boxing.

"When you box," San Kim Sean told me, "your muscles are tense and this reduces your power. In bokator, you relax, and the power comes naturally. The power comes from the speed."

The kickboxer, like in other arts, has a very powerful-looking stance, which drains energy from their bodies, he continued to explain. In bokator, the point of being relaxed is to conserve energy. According to San Kim Sean, the bokator fighter can fight all day without getting tired.

The power in bokator also comes from air. You breathe in before you hit, and when you hit, you release the air. The power comes. If you are holding your breath when you hit, you will lose power and you could damage your lungs.

To illustrate how important speed is in combination with relaxation, the grandmaster told me the story of the *srongai* (young rice.) When the big wind comes, the mighty oak stands rigid to defeat it. The young rice (or willow in other stories) just lays down to let the wind pass over it. When the hurricane comes, the mighty oak snaps in half. The young rice survives because it has learned to bend.

"Boxers get their power from big muscles," San Kim Sean told me. "We call this 'muscle power.' We have muscle power in bokator, too, but we also have 'speed power' and 'spirit power.' This is why we are so strong. In the old days, the masters also had 'medicine power.' "

Legend says that past bokator masters used combinations of natural roots and plants to make themselves impervious to harm so that even a knife could not cut them. San Kim Sean believed that the medicinal component of bokator probably died out before he began studying. He did mention that his teacher drank cooking oil every day. "When he was fighting, he sweated oil. The opponents couldn't grab him or wrestle him. They had no way to hold on." (I don't think I should have to say that you shouldn't try this at home.)

Today, he still taught his bokator students how to use spirit power.

"God made us with two hands," he said. "The left hand comes from Buddha. The right hand comes from Brahma. Buddhism teaches us not to fight. So when someone strikes you, you block with your left hand and say, 'Please stop.' If he strikes again, you block with the left hand and say, 'Please stop.' If he does it again, you block with the left hand and strike with the right. The right hand comes from [the Hindu god] Brahma. So, the right hand can fight."

Of course, this is only the conceptual and religious basis of bokator. In actual practice, practitioners can block and strike with either hand. To me, this illustrated the interesting cultural blending in Cambodia of Hinduism and Buddhism. Brahma, or as he is known in Cambodia, Bret Brom, is one of the three gods in the Hindu trinity. He is also the god of bokator.

Buddhism comes from the Theravada Buddhism practiced in the country. If we look to Angkor Wat, it's interesting to note how carvings and statues go through an evolution. The earliest depict Hindu gods. The latest depict Theravada ideals but with Hindu and animist elements remaining in the religion and culture. In fact, the king's religious advisors today include a grand patriarch of Theravada Buddhism and several Brahman priests. (There is also a grand patriarch for the other style of Buddhism, known as Mahayana.)

Before practicing bokator, San Kim Sean's students would kneel on the ground to say prayers before images on an altar. The main images were of Brahma and Jayavarman VII, the builder of Angkor Wat and the obvious patron saint of bokator. He is also depicted on the official bokator logo in a seated lotus position on a cushion while holding a special sword. When regular people sit in a lotus position, they sit with both legs folded under them. The king has one leg folded under him and the other hanging down from his cushion. This is so he is always ready to stand up and fight. Again, the cultural blending comes into play. Or as San Kim Sean explained it, "The Buddhist can sit and say, 'Please stop.' But only Jayavarman VII will get up and fight if you don't stop."

The students recite prayers first with their hands over the left shoulder and then over the right. They even hold their hands in front of their chests and behind their backs. Many of the prayers deal with the concept of spirit teachers, long dead masters who would come to impart their knowledge to the students.

"In front of your body is where we say the prayers for the god Bret Brom," San Kim Sean explained to me early on. "Behind the body is where we say prayers for the ancestors. The gods live in front, so the ancestors (blood relations and spirit teachers) cannot live there. They live behind, and we honor them and ask their help."

This deeply religious moral code was another thing that differentiated bokator from Khmer boxing and wrestling. There were more technical aspects as well.

For example, bokator contains more than 20 elbow strikes. Bradal serey contains less than 10. The bokator students practices knee strikes, which come at all manner of angles, including a downward knee strike designed to jam a kick or break an opponent's leg. The best students have as much dexterity with their knees as the best karate masters do with their feet. Bradal serey has essentially two kicks, a roundhouse executed with the shin, and a push kick executed with the ball of the foot. Other techniques do exist in bradal serey, but because of rules, very few are used in professional fighting. Bokator, in addition to the roundhouse and push kick, also includes heel kicks, spin kicks, hook kicks, and up-kicks done from the ground. In a close-quarters combat situation, a bokator student has the option of hook kicking the back of his opponent's calves, thighs, kidneys or head.

In comparing the two arts, I could see how they came from a single origin but how time had brought them to different paths. Bradal serey became a sport, so it had to be watered down in order to conform to sporting rules. Profiteers have also diluted it, teaching students only the easiest of moves so it doesn't take as long to learn how to use it effectively. Bokator takes years of constant practice to master.

During my training, I concentrated on separating out the excellent fighting techniques in bokator. For instance, kicks are the longest-range weapon in many martial artists' arsenals. Punches are medium range and elbow strikes are close range. In bokator, punches and elbow strikes are designed to travel a distance of only three inches for maximum power. However, a skilled bokator fighter can also kick, punch or elbow strike from any range at maximum power, too. This is another reason it is important to keep the body relaxed before striking. Your body is soft during the movement, but right before your hit, you use power. To demonstrate this, San Kim Sean asked me to feel his arm muscles before and after he executed an elbow strike. Both times, they were completely relaxed. I found that my size was actually a disadvantage in training for my bokator black belt because so much depended on whip-like speed. San Kim Sean often pointed out that I held too much tension in my shoulders, which reduced the power of my strikes.

During my time with San Kim Sean, my goal was to learn the bokator way of fighting, as opposed to the most effective way to overcome an adversary. Afterward, I would find ways to incorporate his teachings and techniques into my own style—something that I did with every new master and the addition of every new technique.

✲

It was late summer when I was in Cambodia, and the whole country was gearing up for the Khmer wrestling (*jap bap* boran Khmer) championships that take place each August in Phnom Penh's main stadium. The championships happen on the same day as the modern freestyle wrestling championships, which determine which Khmer athletes go to the modern Olympics. The two sports differ dramatically in both execution and outcome. Olympic wrestling is a sport, played by modern athletes wearing singlets made of spandex. The national team, based in Phnom Penh, is composed of 16 members—10 men and six women. Naturally, they lead the nation in the number of medals won. Both of the team's coaches were trained abroad; my teacher Mr. Kim trained in Russian while the other coach Vath Chamreun trained in North Korea. In addition to having proper equipment and twice-daily training sessions, the members of the national freestyle wrestling team receive a monthly cash stipend of 30 dollars, which is slightly higher than the average monthly income in Cambodia. With so many advantages, it's nearly impossible for any provincial team to compete against them.

Khmer wrestling, on the other hand, has a more level playing field and is dominated by teams from the provinces. Freestyle competitors aren't allowed to compete in the traditional wrestling competition because their purposes are different. The goal of the freestyle competitors is to win in the most effective way possible. The goal of the Khmer wrestlers is to keep the art alive.

The continued existence of Khmer wrestling is greatly dependent upon the provincial people. Unfortunately, resurrecting any cultural asset in the provinces is problematic. Most provincial families are subsistence farmers, concerned more with earning a living and having enough to eat than they are with playing sports. The poverty also robs them of strength, making it impossible to train. Even for the national sport, Khmer boxing, it is difficult to keep the tradition alive. Most provincial boxing coaches say that their students only train in the dry season because the roads are impassable in the rainy season and because the boys need to be back at their family farms at that time. At least with boxing, there is the chance of someday turning pro and earning an income. Most provincial families see wrestling and other sports as a dead end.

As a result, traditional wrestling teams don't have regular practices. Most only prepare for a few days before the competitions. For many villages, the only competition they participate in is the national championships. For some Khmer, preserving wrestling is a matter of national pride.

"Before the Khmer Rouge, nearly every village wrestled," Vath Chamreun told me in an interview. "They wrestled at festivals and on holidays, such as Khmer New Year or Pchum Ben. But the art was banned during the Khmer Rouge time and many of the top wrestlers and coaches were killed. [In the 1980s, under the Vietnamese, wrestling was still banned.] In 1985, Prusat was the first province to have wrestling again. It wasn't official, they just started doing it."

Vath Chamreun laughed, making it seem like some village men, drunk on rice wine, just started having a go at each other. This was the rebirth of Khmer traditional wrestling. After the end of the Vietnamese domination of Cambodia, some villages resumed wrestling, although most did not. The first official championships were not held until 2001.

"In some provinces, the wrestling has started up again," Vath said, "but it has been incorporated into bokator and other traditional Khmer martial arts. So, it is no longer pure wrestling."

Because he was working on a book about Khmer fighting sports, Vath was often able to talk about them in context. He once told me how there were many martial arts in Cambodia that dated back to during or before the Angkor period. Khmer wrestling was just one part of a vast body of arts.

"[Ancient officials] used wrestling to choose the strongest men to be the military leaders. They also incorporated wrestling into military training. First, the soldiers trained in wrestling. Later, they trained with swords, sticks and other weapons," Vath liked to explain.

Vath also told me how ancient Khmer would wrestle in three

rounds for tournaments, meaning the first person to win three rounds won. If an opponent quit before then, he lost. Also, if he was thrown to the ground, he would lose.

"Each year, the king's representatives called all the people from the provinces and organized a wrestling tournament. Anyone could fight. There were no weight divisions. One person would enter the circle and the official would say, 'Who will fight him?' Volunteers came. They used incense sticks, cut in half, to time the rounds. If you lost a round they would ask you, 'Are you strong or do you want to quit?'

"There were no technical rules, just throw the man down," Vath Chamreun laughed.

In that interview, I think Vath landed on an apt description of the difference between wrestling and kickboxing: "When a wrestler and a martial artist fight, the wrestler must get very low so he can't be hit." To demonstrate this, Vath ducked under my punch and grabbed the nerve beneath my lat muscle. Then he twisted his body and grabbed my leg, lifting me up and throwing me on my back.

"When wrestler is against boxer, the wrestler has to be willing to sacrifice. He will get hit several times, but then he can throw the boxer."

On a Saturday morning, Mr. Kim, the head wrestling teacher, took me to a remote village to wrestle in the dirt. We were accompanied by another wrestler, Jap Leun, and a Khmer journalist named Kay Kimsong who worked for the English language newspaper *Phnom Penh Post*. As far as I was aware, Kimsong had never practiced Khmer martial arts, but he loved them and was a leading expert in the country. He had written his master's thesis on Khmer wrestling and was working on a comprehensive book on Khmer martial arts. He wasn't on assignment for this trip, but since he liked to go on my adventures and I liked to have him along, he came to help out.

On that day, rain poured, turning the dirt road into a sea of mud, and we swerved to avoid hitting a young boy riding a water buffalo. Our car skidded to a halt in Vihear Sour village in the Kandal province. In spite of the heavy rain, the villagers came out in droves to welcome the hero, Jap Leun, home.

As a native of the village, Jap Leun explained that the traditional Khmer wrestling championships held in the capital are a sterile affair. To see the real event, practiced as it once was, you need to visit the village during Pchum Ben.

On this religious holiday, the village inhabitants wake up at 5:00 a.m. and walk to the local temple. There, they toss small food offerings on the ground in honor of their ancestors. Then they go to the shrine, which is next to the temple and holds the statue of a great general, to receive a blessing from the monks. The first event of the day is buffalo racing in which buffalo and their riders race in pairs over a distance of one-quarter to one-half of a mile, beginning at the temple. The winner normally receives a small cash prize of about 10,000 riel ($2.50 USD), which is provided by the local government. After the races, it's time for the wrestlers. They light incense sticks at the temple and then insert the sticks in the ground along the racing course in a circle, forming the wrestling ring.

The villagers gave us a demonstration of Khmer wrestling as it was practiced thousands of years ago. It was held outside on the ground, with no mats. Musicians in traditional Khmer clothing beat two drums and plucked string instruments. Jap Leun served as the referee of the event. Before the wrestlers came into the wrestling arena, he performed a dance in a loin cloth and frightful mask of a mythical creature. At times, he danced gracefully and at other times he lunged aggressively at the band. Whenever he "attacked," the musicians would increase their tempo and volume to compliment Jap Leun's movements. When the dancing and music had worked the crowd into a frenzy, the wrestlers entered. Jap Leun removed his mask to officiate.

There were several pairs ready, but only one pair of wrestlers fights at a time. All the men in the village were wearing similar attire—a colored loincloth. Half wore red and half wore blue, like in kickboxing. When Jap Leun gave the signal, the first two wrestlers began to dance. They took on animal forms that I recognized from bokator—the monkey, the crocodile or the dragon. The dancing, which lasted several minutes, served the dual purpose of warming up the wrestlers' muscles and paying respect to their trainers. Then a signal was given by Jap Leun. The fighters turned on each other, tearing at each other like two crocodiles locked up in a battle to the death. Seeing that neither was willing to give the advantage, the opponents split up and went back to their dance. This is how it went: the bout resumed with men alternately wrestling and dancing. The rules were simple. Place your opponent's back on the ground and you get a point. Three points is a win. So, when the score reaches two to zero, the fight is over. Fights were quick and furious. One wrestler would shoot in but in the muddy, dirty ground, it was hard to do a controlled slide. The fighters would look up, toss and roll. Jap Leun, when he stepped in to compete, was exceptionally skilled from his years of experience training in Phnom Penh. He did some complicated maneuvers, such as lifting and flipping his opponents.

I found it hard not to fight on my back. In mixed martial arts, in fact, it's considered advantageous to fight from your back. Wrestling on a clean mat in Phnom Penh was one thing, but wrestling barefoot in the dirt, as it was traditionally done, was something else. The rain and sweat made it hard to grab my opponent. The mud was gritty and seeped into every kind of crevice of my body. It grated roughly against my skin and ran into my mouth. I suddenly knew how an oyster felt and thought I probably could have made a pearl the size of an orange.

My fights had a bit of panache, but I lost all four of my bouts. This was particularly pathetic since I outweighed most of my opponents by about 80 pounds. Of course this was allowed since there are no weight divisions in Khmer traditional wrestling.

Seeing how badly I did, one very old woman said. "Please come back for Pchum Ben." I think she was planning to match me with the smallest guy in the village and bet against me.

Jap Leun introduced me to the village wrestling coach, The Thain, who explained that they didn't practice regularly, like the team at the national freestyle wrestling team. According to him, every man, woman and child in the village could wrestle. Even the women compete in traditional wrestling.

"They don't need to train," Thain said. "When they bring the buffalo to the rice fields, they wrestle amongst themselves. Particularly, one month before Pchum Ben, they wrestle in the fields to prepare for the big day." Thain explained that wrestling was a kind of play for the village boys who were bored with their farm work. "Some only train three days or one night before Pchum Ben."

My wrestling ordeal behind me, all the wrestlers and I took a shower, Khmer village style. Normally, people in these kinds of villages don't even have running water, so they stand outside their house and dump buckets over their head, wearing a sarong. In this village, however, one man had a compressor pump. He fired it up, attached a fire hose to it, and we all got hosed off.

After we had changed clothes, Jap Leun took me to the village temple where he showed me the statue of the village patron saint, General Meun Ek. He was the military commander who defended Cambodia from Thailand centuries ago.

Before boys from the village go to the army, they first pray before the statue. They take a small piece of dirt from behind the statue and carry it with them for protection. (Generally, military service is only done by desperate people because the salary is only $8 to $10 USD a month.)

"Every wrestling club prays before they wrestle," Jap Leun told me. "They have small Hindu statues and give thanks to the ancestors for creating martial arts. We pray, 'please stay in my heart and make me strong.' "

Inside the temple, there was yet another live band, playing music.

"If they play music the spirit will welcome you," Kimsong explained. "After that, he will recognize you and protect you wherever you go. In our mind we can say, 'Buddha, please protect us from enemies and give us success and prosperity.' "

Perhaps playing music at traditional wrestling, boxing, stick fighting and other events is a way of asking the gods to preserve the Khmer culture.

While in Vihear Sour, Antonio wrestles with a Jap Leun.

Paddy Carson was still my main coach for fighting. He was the man who had done more for my fighting ability than anyone else in the world. While I was preparing for my bokator black belt test, I still spent evenings training with Paddy.

Listening to the wisdom of these two great masters—San Kim Sean and Paddy Carson—was an exceptional education for me.

"We have to remember why we are in that ring. We are there to hurt the other guy; we aren't in there to make love to him. So, the quicker we can hurt him, the better. You want him to think, 'I don't want to get hit like that again,' " Paddy said. You should remember not only are you here to knock your opponent out, but he is too.

"It's all technique. You have to get the technique right first, then you will get the explosion on your punches and kicks in the fight," he would say during training. Those words would really help you make the pads "POP!" with a series of perfect roundhouse kicks.

The reason Paddy has always impressed me as a teacher is that he's trained on both sides of the Cambodian border and around the globe. Because he worked as a coach in Thailand for more than a decade, he understood the strengths and weaknesses of Thai boxers.

He'd say, "We are all built differently in this world. Some people can do double flying spin kicks or whatever, but some people can't. If you aren't a high kicker, then what do you want to do high kicks for? You do what you were built to do. If you can't do high kicks, then do low kicks. In Thailand, I told my foreign fighters, don't train and fight like the Thai."

The fourth component of my black belt training was to put all the pieces together. Because Khmer wrestling wasn't as high a priority to learn as Khmer boxing or bokator, I stopped training with Mr. Kim a few weeks before my test. The main reason San Kim Sean wanted me to learn Khmer wrestling was for a few good takedowns that would mix well with bokator sparring techniques. Other essential wrestling techniques like chokes, submissions and locks were all from bokator and were taught to me by San Kim Sean. In essence, I had to use bokator submissions rather than a ground and pound.

When I was at the bokator school, I would sometimes train with my friends Serey and Sovanara, who were two of the top four bokator fighters in the school. Sovanara had incredible toughness. Serey's big advantage was his intelligence. He also had a black belt in hapkido, which augmented his martial art foundation. Sovanara's story was interesting. He and his best friend Win, the school's number-two bokator guy, had been living on the streets of Phnom Penh. Win had no family while Sovanara had come to the city to earn money for his family back in the village. San Kim Sean allowed them to live at the bokator school where they had nothing to do all day but train. Some Christian missionaries later gave Sovanara a scholarship, but when he refused to convert to Christianity, they revoked it. Sovanara went back to the bokator school and full-time training. Eventually, San Kim Sean formally adopted Win. Sovanara won the first overall national championship in bokator. He hit one of his opponents with a bare fist so hard that officials told me that they were afraid he had fractured his opponent's skull. They rushed the competitor to the emergency room; he survived.

I would practice shooting in to take them down with bokator submissions rather than the MMA ground and pound. Even after months of training with Mr. Kim, San Kim Sean and Paddy, I still couldn't kick as well as either of them, but they couldn't punch as well as I could, and that's mostly thanks to Paddy Carson.

(I just want to point out that bokator is not mixed martial arts. I believe an MMA fighter would easily best a bokator fighter but only because the art is still developing, after the Khmer Rouge. Bokator fighters are pretty tough though. They can walk into a training session or sparring match anywhere and make a good showing.)

By the end of three months, Derek and I wrapped up our preparations to take our separate bokator black belt tests. When his day came, Derek needed an entire day to complete his exam. It was one of the most grueling affairs I had ever witnessed. He had to memorize and literally perform thousands of techniques. He earned his black krama in bokator—the complete system except fighting. He also earned his instructor's certificate.

My test was easy in comparison. It only lasted half a day. I had to demonstrate various knee and elbow strikes as well as kicks and punches. I had to do defensive and offensive grappling techniques. For example, if an opponent kicked me and I caught the kick, what would I do? I had to spar with Sovanara, who was one of San Kim Sean's best bokator fighters. The point of the sparring wasn't to compete but to show whether I could apply various techniques to a moving target that was hitting me back. I also had to do some ground fighting, and by the end of the day, I was tired, mostly from nerves.

After the tests, many people hoped that Derek would go back to the United States and be the first foreigner to open a bokator school. But Derek found his own path, which was actually my path. He asked me to arrange for him to go to Thailand to study with Kru Pedro, and that's where he remained for several months. After that, Derek decided to go to China and learn sanda.

Derek and I, along with an Australian bokator student named Matthew, pooled our resources to provide Win and Sovanara professional training in Thailand. We bribed officials to get Sovanara a Cambodian passport, which would help him go through normal channels to get a Thai visa. Because Win was a "stateless person," he couldn't get a Cambodian passport and had to enter Thailand illegally. This meant that Win had to make his way across Thailand to Chiang Mai, which is hundreds of miles from the Cambodian border entry point.

When he arrived, he called me for help; he had been on the streets for days and hadn't eaten or slept. I immediately took him to my hotel, fed him all I could and let him rest. Then I took him to Kru Pedro. Win and Sovanara improved tremendously under Kru Pedro, but eventually they had to return to Cambodia because of potential problems with Win's status in Thailand and because Derek and I could no longer afford to sponsor them. As of 2010, Win is a professional Khmer kickboxer for the official Cambodia army team, which mostly fights in Thailand. Sovanara is married with a baby he loves dearly. He drives a *tuk tuk* to support them, and while he wishes to fight, he doesn't because he doesn't want to risk an injury that might impair his ability to support his family. He teaches bokator to foreigners in front of the royal palace in Phnom Penh.

As for me, the TV network from the beginning of this chapter finally decided to pay me. I had enough money to last for several months of adventures. So I paid off my landlord, said goodbye to my friends and headed north to Vietnam.

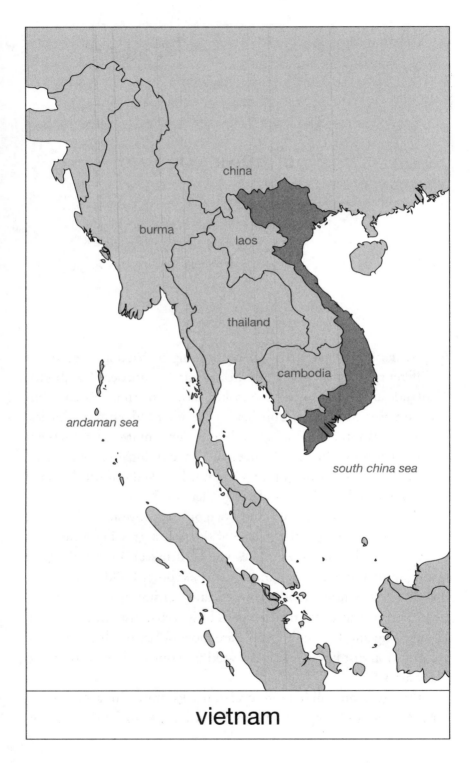

china

burma

laos

thailand

cambodia

andaman sea

south china sea

vietnam

chapter 10

FOR YEARS I HAD BEEN DREAMING of going to Vietnam because it is different from the other Southeast Asian countries. Cambodia, Thailand and Laos used a Sanskrit-based writing system, but Vietnam used the Roman alphabet. In the other Indochina countries, kickboxing was the national sport, but in Vietnam it wasn't. Vietnam is also the most Chinese-influenced of all the Indochina countries.

The first time I woke up in Vietnam, I walked out on the hotel balcony and yelled: "Good morning, Vietnam!"

Ho Chi Minh City (formerly Saigon) was awesome. It is one of the fastest growing cities in one of the fastest growing economies in the world. In the time it takes you to drink an incredibly good tasting, potent cup of Vietnamese coffee, another building has gone up. The city is huge, loud, crowded and constantly on the move. I have never seen a city that looks so busy. Obviously in New York, Hong Kong and Bangkok, people are moving fast but here, they are rushing. You just know that every waking moment is spent trying to make a buck.

The streets are full of motorcycles, trucks from China and luxury cars. Bumper to bumper traffic moves at a brisk 40 km/hr and you risk a fatal collision about once every 30 seconds. (Your experience may vary.) Space is so limited on the streets that you better not let your knees and elbows stick out or they will get sheared off.

Vietnam has a written history of universities, languages, learning and studies dating back about 2,000 years. The first university opened there a thousand years ago. Until the second half of the 20th century and the rise of communism, there were country-wide exams in martial arts. The best students were sent to a martial arts and military tactics university. Only recently was the Vietnamese government started to encourage the promotion of Vietnamese martial arts.

Vietnam's military knowledge is extreme. It is the only country in the world to have fought and defeated China, Mongolia, Cambodia, Champa (ancient kingdom of the Cham people) and France. It also called a tie in a war with the United States and had a no-contest rematch with China. To the Vietnamese, this coupled with an economy that is predicted to be number one in Southeast Asia is why the Vietnamese have every reason to be proud of their history.

People always ask me whether Cambodia is fun. I say Cambodia is interesting because there is always something to learn and write about. However, Vietnam has as many layers or more, but with the advantages of an upwardly mobile state in the process of modernizing. In theory, it could pass all its neighbors, including China.

While for many Americans, the country of Vietnam is synonymous with the conflict we fought there in the 1960s and 1970s, I thought that I could live, study and write there for hundreds of years.

If you check The Lonely Planet guide book to Vietnam, most of the attractions listed are temples, and the city certainly has a lot of them. Religion was suppressed during much of the communist rule of Vietnam, beginning in 1975. In 1986, a new administration began a program called Doi Moi—an openness policy similar to perestroika in the U.S.S.R.—and the country began to open up. By 1991, there was private ownership of businesses as the country moved to a free capital business model. Restrictions on religion began to loosen up, and today, a number of religions are practiced openly in Vietnam. In fact, communist party membership is down to 200,000 while membership in organized religion is in the millions.

The predominant religion in Vietnam is Mahayana Buddhism, the same branch of Buddhism practiced in China, Japan and Korea. This makes Vietnam unique in Indochina because the other Indochinese countries—Laos, Cambodia, Thailand, and Burma—all practice Theravada Buddhism. Vietnam was a colony of China, until winning its independence more than a thousand years ago. As a result, every aspect of the culture, from religion to language and martial arts, bears a distinct Chinese influence, but the Vietnamese have created their own unique and fascinating culture. The Vietnamese Buddhist temples are distinct because of their color—yellowish cream—and architecture.

The vibe in Ho Chi Minh City is very positive. The people are educated. Young people can find well-paying jobs and can participate in the new economy. I also noticed that there didn't seem to be as much "economic apartheid" or separation between Westerners and Vietnamese. What I mean is that in Cambodia, Khmer are welcome in any restaurant but because they can't afford to patronize them, you won't see them in restaurants. Foreigners and Khmer are effectively segregated because of money. In Ho Chi Minh, there are many nice cafés and expensive restaurants, and most everyone in them is Vietnamese.

What I also found in Vietnam was similar to Taiwan and other developed countries I had trained in. The main focus in the society was economic development and advancement. Parents push their kids to excel in school, study English and make money. Martial arts were low on the priority scale.

Most Vietnamese said to me, "Why do you want to waste time on martial arts? You could teach English and make a lot of money."

In spite of this attitude, sports programs are extremely well-developed in the city. In Chinatown, there is a huge martial arts training center with a gym downstairs. I saw that the city offered all manner of martial art, both Vietnamese and foreign, and most were available for about 60,000 dong ($4 USD) per month. A gym membership at a private gym only cost about 180,000 dong ($10

USD) per month. So, even if you were in the city for a week or two, just pay for the month and you are only out six dollars. (Like in other parts of Asia, people practice tai chi in the parks in the morning and evenings.)

In addition, research had taught me that the Vietnamese have a number of traditional martial arts. I discovered a traditional form of wrestling called *vat*, which seemed to have disappeared or may only have existed in the remote provinces. I learned that the Vietnamese also have a kickboxing art, but this art appears to have died out.

The two main arts I was able to find were *thieu lam*, or Vietnamese kung fu, which was brought into the country by the Chinese. The second was *vovinam*, which is the quintessential Vietnamese art. It is a hybrid martial art that was invented in Vietnam in the 1920s. The art is also referred to as *viet vo dao*, or "the way of Vietnamese fighting."

The cost of all this development, coupled with the fact that Vietnam is a communist country and forbids professional fighting, is that the local martial arts are dying out.

In Saigon's Chinatown, I found a massive sports center. In the basement, there was a full weight-lifting gym. The other five floors of the building were dedicated to martial arts. Walking up the stairs, I felt like Bruce Lee's character climbing the tower in *Game of Death* (1978). On the first floor, there were about a hundred people doing karate. On the next floor, there was thieu lam. Up a level, I saw kendo and aikido. On the next floor, there were more karate practitioners and taekwondo practitioners. On the top floor, I found my home: boxing.

As I was in Vietnam to learn something new, I had found a place to study vovinam. Because traditional martial arts rarely include a comprehensive strength, cardio and conditioning component, I wanted to supplement my vovinam training. With my new find, I was able to do weights in the morning before vovinam and then do some boxing at night. The boxing really made my training day complete.

In Ho Chi Minh City, people go out late, study late and train late. Boxing training started at 7:30 a.m., which is amazing. In Cambodia, no one would ever consider going out that late. Even more amazing, people were coming in for their martial arts lessons even as I was leaving my two-hour workout.

When you walk into a new martial arts school in Asia, you always need to be respectful and show it because you are constantly being sized up by the instructors and students. You don't want to look weak, but you don't want to look like a challenger either. If they think you have only come to fight, they may not train you, or they may hurt you. Or, if they think you are showing disrespect, they won't deal with you at all.

In boxing, there is none of this. The minute I walked into the boxing gym, the coach Mr. Ahn welcomed me with open arms. He was all smiles, asking me a million questions about my training and experiences in other countries. He called the boxers around to listen to my stories and ask me questions. Because Mr. Ahn spoke excellent English, he translated his students' questions and my answers into Vietnamese. (Later, I would learn the language.)

Whereas I usually need to build up a rapport with teammates before I can take out my camera, Mr. Ahn immediately asked me if his students could take some pictures with their new American friend.

Since there is no professional boxing in Vietnam, all the students were amateurs and were in their early 20s. They generally attended university full-time and boxed part-time. According to Mr. Ahn, there were only four boxers registered in Vietnam at the highest weight division.

"At national championships they give one gold, one silver and two bronze medals. So, everyone wins," he said.

He went on to say how the Philippine and Thai boxers were the best in the lower weight divisions. He felt his students could learn a lot from them. In fact, Philippine champ Manny "Pac Man" Pacquaio was almost as much of a hero to the Vietnamese boxers as he was to his fellow countrymen.

I'm always amazed by the steps that coaches take to improve their training. Mr. Ahn's openness to other fighters was one such example. Another was that one of his current team's coaches had trained in Thailand with Vietnam's national boxing team.

The good thing about training in a socialist country is that the government supports sports and education programs. Sports are made available to nearly everyone, regardless of how poor they are. The downside, of course, is that while top athletes have state-of-the-art training and equipment, the average gym is not as good as what citizens can pay for in a rich country. Boxing training at the sports complex was free, but the boxing team had absolutely nothing. They had half a heavy bag and some rotting, smelly gloves.

The bag was hung too high and wasn't heavy enough for me to do body punches or low kicks. There were no coach's mitts for pad work. Mr. Ahn showed me where there had once been a floor to ceiling bag, but it was broken. One very cool piece of equipment they did have was a *makiwara* board that hung on the wall. This padded board is normally used in karate and other martial arts to practice focus punching. The boxers used it for speed and power drills. One guy would stand at the board and one-two, one-two as fast and hard as he could for 30 seconds while his partner shadowboxed. Then they would switch off. Thirty seconds board and thirty seconds shadowboxing while alternating for three minutes … . It was brutal! By my third rotation on the board, I was completely beat. My arms would barely stay up.

Usually when I train with amateurs, the coaches leave me alone and let me train the way I want, which is nice if I am there for a short time. If I am going to be there for a year, it is a problem because then I am not learning anything new. Mr. Ahn offered just the right balance. He was involved enough to teach me without being overbearing.

During the drill, Mr. Ahn stood by, and made sure my hands were coming back to a proper guard position between punches, so I was punching off my face, straight through.

Because the gym had an inadequate heavy bag, I got the impression that they didn't work the heavy bag the way pros do. Instead, they did most of their training through shadowboxing and mock sparring. It's something that I notice a lot of other amateurs do in Asian countries I've trained in, and maybe it's something that could be beneficial, too.

After board work, Mr. Ahn had me spar with two of his guys, one round each. Our goal wasn't to hit each other but just to work. Because there was no ring, we sparred on the floor. This meant my normal strategy of shepherding my opponent onto the ropes or into a corner to pound him wasn't going to work. It was much harder to box in an open fighting situation. The speed and stamina of the smaller amateur opponent is a bigger advantage.

The second boy I sparred with had one hand on his waist and punched off his hip. He did all right with it, but it still looked dangerous. When you leave your hand on your waist, you open your face and upper body to attacks. In pro boxing you are always looking for that knockout or a win by attrition. You lead with the left, but you are constantly trying to set the man up for the big right hand. In amateur boxing, you are trying to win by points. Throwing a flurry of punches, whether they are hard or not, will win you points. As a result, amateur fighters don't need to work on strength as much as pros do. At the same time, they are less afraid of getting hit because the hits are less injurious. So, the boy holding his hands on his hips is an example of a chance that an amateur could take and that a pro couldn't. A cool thing he kept doing was switching off, left- and right-hand lead. He didn't actually change his lead leg but would twist his body about 50 percent and lead with a right-hand jab. It was tricky and kept giving me a new picture to look at.

While I learned a lot with the boxing team, I was only able to train with them for a few days. The other days, I practiced vovinam and later thieu lam during the two weeks I was in the country.

Two Vietnamese boxers spar at Mr. Ahn's gym.

Vovinam is taught everywhere in Ho Chi Minh City. The practitioners see it as a matter of national pride, similar to the way Koreans view taekwondo. Vovinam is a very complete martial art with elements taken from many styles. There are kicks from taekwondo. There are grappling techniques from hapkido and throws from judo. There are also a limited number of elbow strikes. Vovinam practitioners also train with an array of weapons taken from China, Vietnam, Korea and Japan.

A Vietnamese friend helped me find a school where I could learn vovinam. Vovinam is a synthetic martial art, founded by Nguyen Loc in 1938. The practitioners wear blue karate gi and earn belts just as in many traditional martial arts. "Vo" means fight. "Vinam" means Vietnam. So vovinam means "Vietnamese fighting."

Apparently in the past, the Vietnamese martial arts were as developed as those of China. A martial arts university was founded nearly a thousand years ago where students studied all forms of combat and also read the classics, such as Sun Tzu's *The Art of War*. National exams were held regularly until sometime during the French occupation. Even under the French, martial arts continued to develop with Vietnamese students competing in French competitions of foreign martial arts from Korea, Japan and China.

Today, students of vovinam seem very proud to be studying their national art, but like in many parts of the developing world, society pushes young people to excel in their studies, particularly English and IT, and to make money. If you ask a person on the street about vovinam, they've heard of it and like it, but they generally haven't practiced it nor can they recommend a teacher to you, especially one that will teach a foreigner.

Given the difficulty I had in finding teachers and teams, I would say that martial arts are on the decline in Vietnam but still infinitely more alive than in Cambodia or Laos. Taekwondo seems to be extremely popular and was being taught at many high schools and universities. Most parents feel that letting their kids study taekwondo is a good compromise since they probably won't get injured. Now that it is in the SEA Games and the Olympics, taekwondo has become a matter of national pride, the same as gymnastics or any other Asian-dominated sports. The sad thing about the rise of taekwondo and economic prosperity is that it means the demise of traditional martial arts.

The other sad thing about traditional arts is that sometimes their practitioners don't seem to want to help save them. During my first class with Master Hai, he admonished me for taking photos. As a result, I was never able to sell a story about vovinam to foreign magazines; they wanted visuals.

Hai agreed to train me, and the price was very low—a few dollars per month. He required me to wear a blue gi, which is the typical uniform for vovinam. Almost all of the students were black belts, but I would find out that red was the highest belt. Changing the order of belt colors I suppose is a way for the practitioners to make vovinam unique. After all, one style I had studied in the Philippines had a belt hierarchy that went red, white and blue.

For the most part, vovinam was one of those typical traditional martial arts that I have trouble practicing. I hate wearing a gi because Southeast Asia is hot. As students, we also had to stand in rows military style, according to rank, and do our exercises in unison. There was also a lot of standing and static throwing punches, chops and elbow strikes. Your knees had to be straight during these drills. Hai even yelled at me for dropping into a fighter's crouch.

The vovinam team was located in a tremendous indoor sports hall located inside the grounds of a high school. It was mostly empty but for a few chairs for parents and training equipment—kick pads and things. It reminded me of the high-school gym basketball court back home.

I don't know the exact arrangement of ownership, but in Asia, public schools are considered public grounds, so many evening and weekend activities and sports for the public are held there. The vovinam team members were a mix of high school and college students; the oldest were in their early to mid-20s. Like in other Asian countries, Master Hai ran the team as a private enterprise. He collected fees from the students and gave a percentage back to the school. He agreed to train me and my translator if we paid monthly membership dues.

When I first started training with the vovinam team at a local high school, I thought the art looked too much like taekwondo—similar roundhouse, similar kicking-pad drills, similar multiple-target leaps and kicks. The vovinam forms also looked like taekwondo kata. But when I started grappling with an instructor, I found out there was a lot more to the art than high kicks and leaps.

Vovinam contains a lot of impressive joint locks and locking throws, similar to what you find in hapkido. I learned a few cool hip throws wherein Master Hai would lock his arms under mine or grab my head to throw me. There were also throws that seemed to have come right out of a judo textbook, but there was one difference.

"In judo, they grab the clothes," Master Hai explained. "But if you try and grab someone by the T-shirt, it will rip, and what if he isn't wearing a shirt? So, we only practice throws that can be done from body-lock positions."

So when I did a throw in vovinam, I would do a lock or follow up with a punch. In vovinam, I didn't see practitioners use any common submissions, chokes or finishing moves.

The striking side of vovinam reveals influence from neighbor

Cambodia and bradal serey. It contains low kicks that strike down into an opponent's calf but that hit with the top of the foot. Vovinam includes some knee strikes. The most obvious connection to me was how vovinam included five different elbow strikes. Three of these five—uppercut elbow, hook elbow and spin elbow—are techniques that are pretty unique to Cambodia and Thailand.

The elbows appeared in training when I learned about vovinam combinations, of which there are several. If your opponent kicks a certain way, you counter with, say, a combination three. If the opponent strikes another way, then you counter with a combination seven. From what I understood, if you started a combination, you had to finish it. Also, these strikes could only be done within the context of those combinations. To a boxer like me, such rules always seem very restrictive and not conducive to actual fighting.

It's not at all uncommon for me to clash with instructors over traditional martial arts.

For instance, Master Hai wanted to teach me a hook, but he wanted me to execute it from a traditional stance—hands on hips and my knees straight. If I moved, he'd yell at me. Now, boxers generally know how to throw hooks. To get power into this punch, you need to stand in a fighting stance, one foot in front of the other, and then push off your back foot to rotate your hips and shoulder. Standing square is definitely not going to put any power into your swing and you're likely to hurt yourself.

Another argument we had was over how to hold my fist in a hook. This is an argument that I've had repeatedly all over Asia. I originally learned that you always turn your fist on a straight punch but never on a hook. Many traditional martial artists insist that you have to turn your fist on a hook. Maybe it's because they're only punching air? While they train for several hours a day, none of them trains on a bag like a fighter would. I guess none of them are actually fighting so they can throw their hooks however they want.

Master Hai always talked about fighting as if it were always theoretical.

"If someone strikes you …" he'd say.

I'd even had one of his instructors try to explain how vovinam was more lethal than muay Thai because kickboxers "kick once and stop," but in vovinam, practitioners "kick and punch at the same time."

One thing they did right in vovinam was the warm-up. It was composed of useful martial arts techniques. When you do taekwondo in other countries, they often rush through the exercises. They count the exercises out very fast, sometimes finishing them all in less than 10 seconds. Generally, the students only do 10 push-ups and 10 sit-ups. In vovinam, we did push-ups for about three or four minutes. Then we did ab work for about 20 minutes. We also did kicking and punching drills, which looked as if they were taken from taekwondo. One guy held up the TKD-style kick pad while his partner kicked it as many times as he could in a certain time limit. Fighters who are training for matches or competitions don't do this drill because it doesn't really test your ability to throw good kicks. It tests your ability to do the drill. The first kick is real, but after that, students tend to only bring their leg back halfway before kicking again. This is the wrong way to practice. Sure, the vovinam students could do the drill fast, but it had zero impact on whether they could kick in a fight or not. Also, partners would do this kick drill with the pad held high at the head or shoulders. This is also something I rarely practice. In muay Thai, kicks are generally aimed at the floating ribs on down.

Traditional martial arts like vovinam can be excellent for your health because they will increase the range and variety of your movements. As we age, we reduce the types of movements we do. We stand up, walk, sit at a desk and open the refrigerator every day. When you were a child, you climbed, slid, jumped, belly-flopped, went under the couch … you moved your body in every way possible. As an adult, even in your exercise, you are limited in what you are doing. If you lift weights, how much are you actually moving? How many different kinds of motion do you do in a day?

Even I was limited in my boxing and kickboxing movements compared to traditional martial artists. In doing the same motions every day, muscles and joints begin to function only within the scope of that very limited range of motion. Basically, if I do something that feels like boxing or muay Thai, I am pretty good at it. But as soon as I leave that kinetic comfort zone, I'm lost.

I could tell that my vovinam training partners were stronger than me in this regard. Sure, my hook was stronger than theirs. However, if I learned to throw a hook the vovinam way, I would probably develop muscles that I wouldn't normally use, like in swimming or cross-training. Even then, traditional martial arts need to be coupled with other exercises. Arts like vovinam still rarely require enough cardio or strength work to be beneficial. For instance, we would run around the gym for cardio. That is just silly. You need at least 20 minutes of cardio to get a workout, and running in tight circles will just be bad for your knees.

On the plus side, vovinam has more grappling than most traditional martial arts. As with taekwondo practitioners, I noticed that vovinam students had a lot of dexterity in their feet. They can effectively plant a kick down, up or sideways—anywhere they want. That is impressive, but the flip side is that they've most likely never kicked a real bag.

I was not in Vietnam to disprove the effectiveness of vovinam. In the context of what its practitioners were doing, vovinam was very good. The pride I saw that the Vietnamese had for their art was also a good thing. They love their country, and they should be proud of Vietnam's progress.

❂

The last martial art I looked into in Vietnam was thieu lam, or Chinese-originated Vietnamese kung fu.

I met thieu lam master Hai—a lot of people are named Hai in Vietnam—at the huge martial arts school in the Chinatown district. Every inch of floor space was used every day, all day, to teach the martial art. Mr. Hai taught thieu lam in the foyer of a large martial arts training area in the early afternoon.

During this trip, I only trained in thieu lam for a few days. My first lesson was at Mr. Hai's house, but he wouldn't let me film it.

Then I trained with him at this sports center. A few years later, I would produce a *Martial Arts Odyssey* episode about thieu lam. A Vietnamese American viewer would write in to explain that "thieu lam" was just the Vietnamese pronunciation for the Chinese word "Shaolin." I felt like an idiot for not figuring out that on my own, but it did explain a lot.

Studying thieu lam was a lot like studying Shaolin kung fu. The entire art seemed to be nothing but forms, more forms, and more forms. There were unarmed forms and forms with various weapons. Thieu lam is great for people who like forms. I, as it happens, hate doing forms.

Mr. Hai had practiced thieu lam his entire life and still taught several group classes as well as private lessons a day. If you were casting a kung fu master in a movie, Mr. Hai would have been your first pick. He would move with the perfection of a warrior. Whether drawing swords and bows, dropping into low stances, fighting imaginary opponents, or wielding the fan as a delicate weapon, Mr. Hai had nearly half a century of experience. His favorite form, which he demonstrates to foreign visitors, is called "*lao ho thuong son.*" It encompasses 58 movements and takes nearly four minutes to complete, months to learn, and years to master.

Thieu lam can trace its origins to China. The art was developed as a hybrid—a mix of *choy gar* and *hung gar* kung fu that was originally taught in Guangdong province. Later, wing chun was added to the mix. It was brought to Vietnam by Luu Phu, who was born near Canton in 1909 and died in Ho Chi Minh City in 1971. Phu trained with his master in China until 1937, and left when Japan invaded. Because of this influence, many Chinese live in Vietnam. At the beginning, they lived in tight-knit communities, divided by dialects. At that time, kung fu wasn't taught to outsiders, so thieu lam remained a purely Chinese art. After 1975, Vietnamese soldiers learned the art and it became a national martial art. Today, thieu lam is divided into two major schools. Mr. Hai belongs to a sect in one.

Training a Chinese art in Vietnam is a unique experience. It is always fascinating to see which aspects of Chinese culture managed to stay in the art. For example, in watching and learning thieu lam, I could see the influence of the Northern Chinese styles clearly. At times, the southern influence became apparent, such as when we used pigeon toe stance. Sometimes, we'd also drop into a half-twisted low stance that is characteristic in wing chun. In fact, several of the Vietnamese students referred to their martial art as Vietnamese kung fu, the same way people in China use it as a general word for martial arts, even though vovinam is still viewed by far as the quintessential Vietnamese martial art.

"Everything we do is based on circles," Mr. Hai explained. He pointed to a yin yang symbol over his door. "We use circles both up and down for blocking. We also have animal styles such as monkey and dragon.

"Concentrate where you hit," he said once. "In China they hit in the liver. In Vietnam we hit in the heart."

As with many traditional martial arts, there was no sparring. They practiced fighting in patterns in which both parties knew the script. It was in these drills that I noticed some muay Thai and muay boran creep in. Whether this was intentional on the part of thieu lam originators, I don't know, but it goes to show how the martial arts in Asia have influenced and continue to influence each other.

For example, if I threw a kick, Mr. Hai would hit me with his knee and then kick my thigh with the ball of his foot. The most telling example to me was when Mr. Hai blocked a strike and stepped in with an elbow strike to the head. He then did a forearm smash to my elbow, trapped my hand and moved to hyperextend the elbow joint.

Because of things like this, I noticed thieu lam had a good number of elbow and knee strikes, which it must have picked up from its geographic neighbors.

The thing I really liked about practicing with Mr. Hai was doing the warm-up. A kung fu warm-up is a sensible exercise. Not only does it prepare your muscles for training, but it also strengthens your muscles and creates flexibility. It moves through all those stances and techniques in a way that is much more interesting than if you were in front of a mirror at the gym doing sets and reps. As with other traditional martial arts, I find these kinds of exercises good for your overall health. So, coupled with the training I did with the boxing team, I believed I had a well-rounded routine.

The thing that some students find boring when studying any kind of kung fu is the lack of practical application. It was true here—Mr. Hai's students never tried out techniques on opponents and only ever practiced forms. As I've mentioned, I try to do traditional martial arts every now and then but always quit because I prefer fighting arts. Kung fu is the one exception because kung fu never claims to be a fighting art. Kung fu demonstrates a deeper commitment to art than fighting.

Because I enjoy fighting arts like Khmer boxing or muay Thai more, I generally stick around in the countries where they are most popular to train. This is one reason why I only stayed for two weeks in Vietnam. However, I would later return to learn the language and study up more about the martial arts. But this is one reason why this time I packed my bags, my gloves and my cameras back into my backpack and left.

Antonio practices *thieu lam* with Mr. Hai.

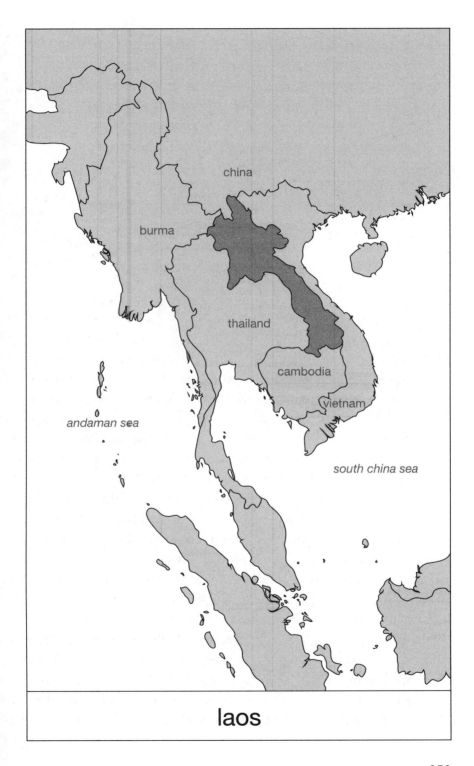

china

burma

thailand

cambodia

vietnam

andaman sea

south china sea

laos

chapter 11

FOR YEARS, I HAD BEEN WRITING about the Burmese refugees living in northern Thailand who belonged to the Shan ethnic group that the Burmese military junta was wiping out. My first introduction to the war in Burma (officially known as the Union of Myanmar) and to the Shan group specifically was when I was living with Pra Kru Ba. Many of the young monks at his monastery were Shan boys whose parents had been killed by the Burmese government.

No one knows how many minorities have been killed during the 60-plus years of conflict although at least two million have become refugees. A further 2.5 million people have found a path to legal residence in Thailand and are no longer considered refugees. There are probably millions of migrant workers and temporary illegal aliens who have fled government attacks on their villages, and the international press has not reported it.

In late September 2006, a Swedish Army special-forces officer who hung around Chiang Mai helped me make contact with the Shan State Army rebels inside of Burma. The Shan people live in Shan State in Burma, but they are fighting to form an independent country, called Shanland. The Shan agreed to smuggle me into the war zone so I could document human rights abuses. I originally thought I'd go to Shanland for a few days but it wasn't long before I realized it would be my full-time job for a few months. Until the end of the year, I made frequent trips over the Burmese-Thai border.

I can't divulge in this book, or anywhere else, how we actually entered Burma because it could jeopardize the trans-shipment of humanitarian aid and supplies. Let's just say it was a long, long, roundabout way through the jungle accompanied by two rebel soldiers while ducking patrols from hostile military forces.

I was completely on my own with no major support from U.S. or foreign media. Every time I went into Burma I needed to take a few hundred dollars with me to pay for transport, to give tips to soldiers, to buy food for myself and my assistants and bodyguards. It was expensive. Then I would come back to Chiang Mai and need to rent a hotel. In Chiang Mai, I would spend hours and hours online at an Internet cafe, sending videos and articles to Burma and pro-democracy groups.

After one 14-hour day of being online, I was careless and lost my digital audio recorder and then my USB device. I had no money to replace the lost equipment. In addition to that, I was stressed that Thai police or Burmese junta spies were following me.

Two days or so before Christmas, I was invited to a fancy party in Bangkok that was being given for a lot of big-name media channels. I took a bus from Chiang Mai and slept at a friend's apartment the night before. At the party, I ate like a horse because I was so low on money and because I had been in a war zone in Burma where accommodations aren't exactly five star. A lot of media representatives talked to me from major news networks. They wanted me to send them videos and photographs, which I did. Some even wanted me to take their crews to Burma. By the end of the evening, I had a lot of cards-but in the end, not one of those media people followed through.

I was working full-time, risking my life, but I wasn't earning any money at all. By the end of November, I had spent the last of the money I had earned from the Cambodian television show. By Christmas, I was absolutely and completely broke. I had no idea how to proceed with my writing and dreaming. My visa was about to expire in Thailand.

Originally, I had wanted to go back to Vietnam so I could write about vovinam and sell a story. But I needed photos and I didn't even have money for a visa or a ticket.

Fortunately, I stumbled across 4,000 baht while repacking my laundry. By the time I had finished closing my accounts, I had 1,500 baht left. The clock was ticking. I had two days left on my Thai visa after which time I would have to pay 500 baht per day of overstay.

The cheapest country to reach from Thailand is Cambodia. You can get there on the train for about 100 baht. But the border crossing at Poi Pet is extremely dangerous, and I was burned out on Cambodia.

My second choice was Laos. I bought a bus ticket for 1,200 baht, bought a visa at the border, arrived in the capital of Vientiane just after midnight on the final day of my Thai visa, paid for one night at a hotel, ate breakfast and had less than $3 USD left.

I sent out panicked e-mails to friends and family, explaining my situation and begging for financial assistance. Because of my work with the Shan, I had acquired a number of sponsors from around the world who kept me going while I was in Burma. For example, I was one of only a handful of journalists inside of Burma during the monk protest and aftermath in Yangon in September 2007. Though I was in the Shan State, I was able to do a few call-in radio shows to the United States to report on the situation.

By using rebel satellite and cell phones, I was able to send information out to small-circulation magazines and newspapers; the bigger networks remained uninterested. I also sent out video footage during my brief returns to Thailand. As a result, a lot of people were interested in what I was doing, and I survived with their financial support. Among the people helping were a number of deposed Shan princesses who missed their homeland.

One of the first people to respond was one of my sponsors who sent me 800 EU, which is a huge amount of money, via Western Union. I was extremely grateful but, unfortunately, I couldn't touch it. Because she had sent the money to Western Union in Bangkok, I would only be able to pick it up if I were in Bangkok. Another friend, unaware of my dire straits, sent me a link to a TV show I had helped write an episode for. It added insult to injury to see the two American hosts, who were younger and probably less culturally aware than I was, on screen. I thought about how they must be back in the United States with family and friends watching the new show.

I continued sending out frantic e-mails, explaining my situation. I was in double trouble because it was currently 11:30 a.m. on a national Laotian holiday. Banks would be closing in half an hour and wouldn't reopen for another four days. The hotel had to be paid daily. If I didn't get some money soon, I would be screwed.

The only solution was for someone to deposit money directly into my Thai account so I could access it directly here in Laos before the banks closed. I had 30 baht left on my phone credit. I called a Western television producer who I knew was loaded. I was desperate, and he knew how poor I was.

"Can't you use a credit card?" he asked when I rang him. I told him I didn't have a credit card.

"Is there someone you could call?" he asked next. He proceeded to get less helpful; he insisted he didn't have any money to spare and that the banks were closed already. I decided not to fight and let it go.

It's times like these that make life hard. Often, people write to me saying, "Wow! You are really living the life" or "I wish I could do what you're doing." The truth is that it's difficult to live from hand to mouth. I never have enough money and I often depend on the kindness of friends and strangers to survive. The adventures are great! But there are costs to living your dreams.

Then I called one of my friends in Chiang Mai, Mr. Bo. Before I even finished telling him my story he said, "I am brushing my teeth. Let me rinse, and I will run down and put 5,000 baht in your account."

The money was available a few minutes later. Mr. Bo had saved my life. A few other friends saw my e-mails and sent me enough money so I could stay in Laos and film and write for a week before going back to Thailand, then Burma. I needed that week. I had been in and out of a war zone, dodging military patrols and police, and I was exhausted and probably a little shell-shocked, too.

❂

Once I had money, I was able to appreciate Laos. The population is less than six million and nearly all the development is in Vientiane, which is one of the smallest capital cities in the world and is filled with some of the kindest and most polite people in the universe. Unlike Phnom Penh, Vientiane is relatively clean and possesses a French colonial charm.

There are clean sidewalks and boulevards. You can walk everywhere without risking your life, and there is even a mall where you can buy pirated movies for about $2 USD. The currency in Laos is kip, but they accept Thai baht and U.S. dollars. It was common to pay in one or two currencies and get back all three as change. All in all, Vientiane is a pleasant city if you have enough money to eat and sleep indoors.

Apart from the docile feeling of the city, Vientiane is surprisingly good for training. There was a weight-lifting gym and a national sports stadium where I did strength training for a small donation of 50 cents a day.

I had read on the Internet that there was an ancient martial art in Laos called ling lom (monkey wind) but I couldn't find it. My fellow bokator brother Derek had also come to Laos looking for ling lom but hadn't managed to find anything but a rumor. Generally, the main Laotian martial arts are muay Lao and *silat*. Muay Lao is the Laotian kickboxing art and is similar to muay Thai. It is also the national sport. Silat is a martial art practiced in Malaysia, Indonesia and the Philippines. There are countless styles of silat, including *pentjak* silat. Because pentjak silat was adopted into the Southeast Asian Games, nearly every Southeast Asian country now has a silat team. I didn't get to practice silat while in Laos because I was only there for a week.

What travel guides I had read were all wrong about where to find muay Lao training. Instead of at the national sports stadium in Vientiane where all sports teams trained, it was actually held outside the city at its own indoor stadium. The muay Lao stadium boasts a full size ring, a row of kick bags, and a row of uppercut bags mounted on the wall. The coaches were excellent in the ring when they worked on the pads with students. There were probably 10 fighters training at the stadium for professional fights.

While muay Lao is the national sport, it isn't as popular as muay Thai. The main reason is that Laos is a small country that only has one professional team of 30 to 40 fighters and one stadium. Professional fights are held twice a month in the national stadium. In fact, many Laotian fighters train and fight professionally in Thailand.

Unlike the Khmer, the Laotians are able to admit a few other things, too. For example, when I asked Adjarn Ngern, the head coach of the team, what the difference was between muay Laos and muay Thai, he readily said they were the same.

"But the Cambodians are angry about the name muay Thai," I said. "They feel they invented kickboxing and that it should be called by the Cambodian name bradal serey. What do you think of that?"

"Muay Thai was invented in Cambodia," the Adjarn told me. "But Thailand has the money and got it famous." I found these kinds of answers refreshingly sanguine, but at the same time, it was interesting to see how the Laotians accepted Thai-culture dominance in their small country.

During my week in Laos, I trained with the Adjarn every day. He gave me private lessons but would occasionally call over one of the muay Lao fighters to train with me, spar or do a demonstration of a technique. While very few people in Laos speak English, the citizens of Vientiane generally speak excellent Thai. So I communicated to the Adjarn in Thai.

I would arrive at 4:00 and do a warm-up. I also completed a very comprehensive stretching routine that covered all parts of the body, especially the neck and shoulders.

At first, I confused the Adjarn during the shadowboxing part of my warm-up routine because I didn't kick. As a boxer, I tend to hesitate over kicks and need to warm-up before I start kicking. This is why I shadowbox for at least 10 minutes with just my hands before I add in any kicks. I guess you can take the boy out of Brooklyn but you can't take Brooklyn out of the boy. The Adjarn made sure those kicks came. He just needed to be patient.

After warm-up, my lessons began. To help with my kicks, the Adjarn readjusted my stance. He didn't want me to hold my hands next to my face, like I do in boxing. Instead, he wanted the lead hand out in front and a bit lower because you can see over your hands better. In the classic English boxing stance, you have a lot of blind spots. He also didn't want my hands to touch my face because I might accidentally hit myself with my own hands if I were punched or kicked.

In taekwondo and other kicking arts, the right hand comes down when you kick. This is the moment when a good boxer should step in and punch the kicker in the face. Adjarn Ngern was the first person ever to show me the cross-arm defense, basically wrapping your free arm across your face to cover up when you kick. This gives you safety and power.

We also worked combinations on the uppercut bags. One. Two. One. Two. I'd switch off hands. The Adjarn was excellent about correcting my form while I trained. He made me turn out my back foot on straight punches and go up on my toes at impact. On the uppercut, he also had me up on my toes to make me turn my heel in.

We transitioned to kicks on the bag. The important point, which he kept stressing, was to get up on the toes of your base foot and rotate the foot with the kick. Next, you must be careful to twist your hip and butt into the kick. The leg must travel parallel to the ground and strike at an almost 90-degree angle, kicking in and not up, like in taekwondo. Conversely, muay Lao, like muay Thai, executes roundhouse kicks to the shin.

To help me get up on my toes and swing my hips, the coach and one of the fighters stood behind me, twisting my legs and hips and trying to get my position right. It was a lot to remember, and there was nothing natural about having two men twisting and prodding my body while I practiced. It was like a dance lesson gone wrong.

Other combinations we worked on required me to kick off the front leg. Generally, kickboxing instructors teach students to quickly switch legs so the front leg becomes the back leg; when kicking with the rear leg you get more power. However, Adjarn Ngern didn't want me to do this. Instead, he wanted me to slide my front leg back slightly and then kick off of it. My rear leg wouldn't move at all. It felt awkward at first, but it was a good technique. It was faster and less exhausting than the more common hop and shuffle. It just took a lot of practice for me to get it. To save even more time, he showed me that when you hit with your left leg, just bring it straight down instead of back to your original position. Now you're closer to your opponent and can immediately throw an overhand elbow strike with your right arm.

For the most part, I was impressed with Adjarn Ngern and how modern his training and thinking was. He was one of the few coaches I had worked with in Asia who could really analyze and discuss the sport of fighting. Sometimes though, his old-school training would suddenly appear. Once, he showed me how he could lift a heavy bucket of cement using his neck and rope, which he held in his mouth. He invited me to try, but the saliva on the rope caused me to refrain from taking part.

Instead, we opted to move on to the grappling.

In muay Lao, as in muay Thai, the fighters often lock up. They grab each other behind the back of the neck and struggle to get dominance over the opponent. It is amazing how many throws a good fighter can do from this position. A significant component in learning muay Lao is practicing grappling from the neck.

The goal in muay Lao grappling is to achieve the dominant position, which means getting your two hands on the inside. When two opponents lock up, each has his hands grasped behind the other's head or neck. You want your hands to be on the inside of your opponent's hands. He does, too. This is why there is a struggle to get your hands in the dominant position. When fighters practice, they start with one hand on the inside of the clinch and one out, then they compete to get both hands inside. Once you have both hands inside, you can plant your elbows in your opponent's chest, leverage his head and take him down. Grabbing the back of the neck is a good way to control an opponent because you are pulling against a bendable muscle and not a rigid bone.

Grabbing higher on the head gives you extended leverage, multiplying your power. The Adjarn showed me how you could grab the back of the head with one hand and slide your other hand down under the elbow for leverage. Then in one quick, jerking motion, you pull down on the head and push up on the opponent's elbows to throw him.

Another grappling exercise we worked on: One fighter would hold his hands behind his back while the other tried to throw him. It was a simple technique—step out on the right, throw on the left; or step out on the left, throw on the right.

In the end, muay Lao was pretty much exactly like muay Thai but now I knew that for a fact. I thought that studying muay Lao was essential to completing my study of the kickboxing arts of the region. Even though I thought Laos was a wonderful place and I would go back to visit, I don't think I would live there. There just weren't that many martial arts to explore.

My Laotian friend and translator, Santiphap (right), receives a New Year's blessing at the temple.

○

After my brief excursion in Laos, I returned to Chiang Mai in Thailand. Along the way, I stopped off in Bangkok and found that the free sublet I had on my friend's apartment was over. I now had nowhere to live. Fortunately, I was able to collect the 800 EU that the donor had sent me. I went to Chiang Mai and checked into a hotel for a few days, then headed back into Shanland in Burma.

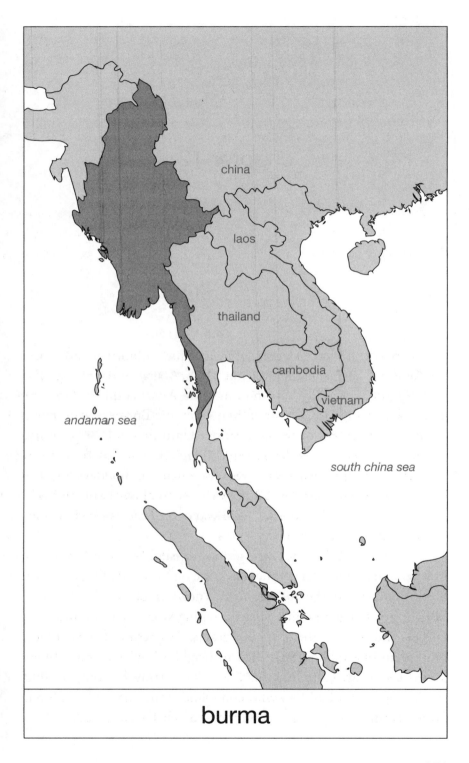

china

laos

thailand

cambodia

vietnam

andaman sea

south china sea

burma

chapter 12

BURMA IS A COUNTRY COMPOSED of many ethnic minorities and tribes, such as the Shan, Karen, Wa, Kachin, Chin, Arakan and Chinese. The military junta, officially known as the State Peace and Development Council, is comprised almost entirely of ethnic Burmese, who make up about 40 percent of the population. Until the mid-20th century, Burma was a colony under Great Britain. After it was freed from colonial rule, repressive laws were passed banning holidays and the speaking of tribal languages. Minorities were no longer able to freely move within the country. They were also denied access to education, medical care and decent jobs.

The Karen were the first group to start fighting for their independence, and that conflict has gone on for nearly 60 years. The Shan's conflict with the military junta is nearly as old and began when SPDC forces began raiding villages, raping women, and murdering farmers and burying them in mass graves. As a result of the conflict, more than one million Shan fled to neighboring Thailand. Others joined the army. Currently, the Shan State Army has only 10,000 soldiers against the SPDC who command nearly half of a million. Other ethnic groups who attempted to rebel were smashed into submission by the SPDC in the 1980s and 1990s. Today, only the Karen National Liberation Army and the SSA remain. The United Wa State Army is still armed, but it works by proxy for the SPDC in exchange for a cut of the opium trade. The opium trade is what fuels Burma's wars. (The KNLA was also the army featured in *Rambo IV* [2008].)

This conflict is very complicated, and we've only just touched the surface. The SSA continues to fight to form the independent state known as Shanland.

On my first trip in December 2006, I traveled alone, but on subsequent trips until February 2007, I often brought other journalists or foreigners with me. As always, I trained in martial arts while writing and interviewing Shan victims and soldiers. During these times in Burma, I taught martial arts.

✪

"This isn't Hollywood," a Shan lieutenant said. "When people get blown up here, they die for real."

Only the armies of the State Peace and Development Council and God knew how many other hostile armed factions were encamped on the hilltops surrounding the Shan State army headquarters at Loi Tailang, a base inside of Burma. As the home of soldiers and refugees, Loi Tailang feels like a village because it has restaurants and convenience stores. It is also surprisingly up-to-date with what's happening in the outside world because of radios, Internet and satellite phones. However, Loi Tailang also feels like a barracks because it is surrounded by barbed wire and mine fields. There is always the danger of being attacked by the United Wa State Army or the SPDC at any time. In fact, there are UWSA and SPDC outposts on opposing hilltops and visible to the naked eye from Loi Tailang. Beyond the wires, mines and war, there is a lot of jungle.

On my first visit to Loi Tailang, the SSA slaughtered a goat in honor of four journalists and myself. We were invited to dine with the commander and chief of the SSA, Colonel Yawd Serk. I sat next to him, and the Colonel kept grabbing my biceps to comment on how strong I was.

"Can you get Rambo to come here?" the Colonel asked me. "If my men could see him for just one day, it would encourage them, and they would fight like lions."

I promised to do what I could about contacting Sly. (If Sylvester Stallone ever reads this, I hope he does contact me. Any word of encouragement from him would mean a lot to the Shan.) In the meantime, the soldiers had already started calling me Rambo II. (The official languages of the Shan are Shan, Thai and English. Mainly, we spoke in Thai. Only a handful of people in Loi Tailang spoke English.)

"Rambo pretended to come to Burma, but you came for real," one of the soldiers said.

Col. Yawd Serk told me he had been in over 200 battles.

"Have you been in combat?" the Colonel asked. I felt shy to admit that I hadn't.

"How many fights have you had?"

"Counting professional fights, challenge matches, and fights in rice fields and gyms all over Asia, probably more than 150," I said

He smiled, approvingly, and asked me to teach martial arts to the men.

The next morning, I held my first class out on the parade grounds. The sergeants got the men to sit at attention and clear a place for me to train. Looking at the thousand or so green-uniformed and AK-47-holding Shan men in front of me, I wondered what I was doing here. In the face of so many modern weapons, what could I bring to the table as a martial arts instructor?

In teaching soldiers, I had to keep in mind that first of all, they weren't athletes with years to prepare. The techniques had to be simple to learn and to apply. Second, they had to be effective. Third, the techniques would have to deal with situation that might actually arise in the context of a military scenario.

Although some people question whether hand-to-hand fighting is applicable on the modern battlefield, there are some very practical reasons to teach unarmed combat. One obvious practical application is in the case of capture. A prisoner or hostage may be able to use hand-to-hand combat to overcome his guards and free himself. In a commando-raid-type scenario, soldiers could use unarmed techniques to silently subdue the sentries on watch, before infiltrating an enemy position. Finally, there is a huge psychological component to barehanded fighting that allows soldiers to release a natural instinct for violence. In sparring, they can understand how to apply that instinct. In training, you can't know how soldiers will perform under fire because they can't use weapons on each other.

Growing up as a young martial arts student and military enthusiast, my earliest heroes were William E. Fairbairn and Eric A. Sykes, who were both members of the elite British Special Air Service that wrote and set the standard for hand-to-hand combat in the World-War-II era. Their unarmed style was later adopted officially by the British military and law enforcement and was later taught to the special-forces units of countries around the world.

Their system is a hybrid art that draws on existing martial traditions like Brazilian jiu-jitsu, traditional Chinese martial arts and Western boxing and wrestling. Arguably, this was the first modern military art or possibly even the first organized system of unarmed combat developed for soldiers on a battlefield.

After WWII, armies moved away from hand-to-hand combat because of the mechanized nature of modern warfare. But in the 1990s and 2000s, militaries have sought to reintroduce such techniques with the combatives system. Combatives is another hybrid system. This one employs techniques from Western wrestling and boxing, judo, Brazilian jiu-jitsu, muay Thai and Philippine martial arts like escrima and kali.

Unfortunately, I was in the military during the period when hand-to-hand combat wasn't as valued. I remember receiving eight hours of instruction on techniques similar to the ones John Wayne taught his men in the film *The Sands of Iwo Jima* (1949). In fact, I think part of our eight hour course included watching that film. Obviously, I received a lot of martial arts instruction before and since then, but the main difference between my training and the training needed by the SSA was that theirs had to be lethal.

The training program I developed for the soldiers involved three phases: unarmed combat, rifle technique and finally knife fighting. I taught these phases over time, during several of my visits to Loi Tailang. In regard to knife fighting, I knew that the precision stabbing advocated by Fairbairn wouldn't work for the Shan. They weren't armed with slim, delicate double-edged stiletto blades, known as the Fairbairn-Sykes fighting knife. Instead, they had huge bolo knives, similar to machetes and used by farmers; or the heavy all-purpose combat Ka-Bar knife issued to U.S. Marines. I would need to offer them techniques that were about hacking and slashing instead. I also liked teaching types of techniques that could be used as nonlethal methods of subduing an armed attacker and could be done with a club, a stick or bare hands.

An interesting point that came up in training was cultural taboos. In Southeast Asia, wrestling is pretty much nonexistent. This makes sense because Southeast Asia is also predominantly Theravada Buddhist, which teaches that the head is sacred; you are never to touch someone on the head. Also, the feet are considered filthy, so the absolute worst and most insulting thing you can do is touch someone's head with your feet. Lastly, the floor is considered untouchable because the feet walk all over it. Even among the tough rebel soldiers who lived in the jungle, I found it hard to get them on the ground to teach them grappling moves.

In between training sessions, I conducted video interviews with soldiers and refugees. The stories were bleak. For instance, the SPDC would often go into villages and sequester the population to work as forced labor, to build roads, for instance. The laborers were rarely fed and often beaten. Many of the victims told me they saw people collapse or even die from overwork. One man I interviewed was kept as a forced laborer for several years before he finally escaped.

According to many of the Shan victims, SPDC soldiers would often punish laborers by slapping their ears with cupped hands. The laborer would have to stand at attention and wait for the SPDC soldier to bring down his cupped palms on his ears—an action likely to blow out the eardrums. Several of my interviewees had lost their hearing to such abuse.

I also interviewed a number of men with missing limbs who had been used, at gunpoint, as human mine detectors. They were forced to march ahead of soldiers into a minefield. When a villager was blown up, the SPDC soldiers would simply replace him with another at the front of the line.

One of the most draining interviews I conducted was with a 14-year-old girl whom SPDC soldiers gang-raped when she was 12. They dragged her out of her home in the middle of the night before setting the house on fire. She said she could hear her parents screaming in the blaze while 30 or more soldiers raped her, repeatedly. When I interviewed her, she was living in an orphan dormitory, which was home to 250 children whose parents had been murdered by the SPDC.

There were probably 350 or more families who also lived on the base. They were there because their villages had been burned to the ground by government forces. From statistics, I'd learned that as many as 200 tribal people were killed each week while 2,000 were made homeless.

After interviews, I'd sometimes go back to my bunk and just stare up at the ceiling. I couldn't look at or talk about anything else. I didn't want to know one more terrible story. At times, I was angry. I wished that I lived in a movie in which I was the hero who could run in from the jungle and hack up the SPDC soldiers with my knife. But it wasn't a movie. Because of difficult terrain, it would have taken several days of hard trekking to even reach the visible SPDC positions. All I was able to do was make my video documentaries and teach martial arts classes. In teaching the soldiers to harm their oppressors, I felt that my classes also helped me recuperate mentally to face the next day and more interviews.

During my trips in and out of Burma, I met incredible, brave volunteers from the United States, the United Kingdom and Australia. They were often from faith-based organizations and they risked their lives to provide free medical care, food and classes to Shan civilians and orphans. There was the dentist who kept a portable dental drill in his backpack. When he'd arrive in Shan villages, he'd set up a chair and treat everyone for free. Sometimes he'd see 40 to 60 patients in a day. There was the engineer who was so brilliant that he could make water flow uphill. He installed pipes in Loi Tailang so that the people wouldn't have to walk for hours to get drinking water.

There was the California sculptor who I brought back with me once. He wanted to cast life-size sculptures of the Shan to sell at fancy art auctions in order to raise awareness about the war in Burma, especially among people who could afford $80,000 USD artwork. One of the subjects in this project was a pregnant woman who had had to abandon her first two children. She was 10 months pregnant and the baby still hadn't come. I wondered if the baby just didn't want to be born into the horrors of everyday living here.

Two orphan boys were the subjects in another project. They had witnessed the murders of their parents in separate incidents in Shanland. On their first meeting in Loi Tailang, they had become inseparable, each adopting the other as his brother. They were always together, walking about and hanging on to each other. When we photographed them for the series, the sculptor said that they clung so closely together, he would make them into a single piece.

Two Shan boys pose as models for a sculpture.

Antonio conducts training sessions with Shan soldiers.

Aid workers told me that if you ignored the politics, morality and drug trafficking and instead focused solely on the suffering, you could render aid to people without getting tangled up in the complicated Burmese socioeconomic political sphere. It made a lot of sense to me, and these people definitely needed help.

In the past, the Shan people migrated to Burma from Yunnan, and I'd heard rumors that the Shan had their own brand of kung fu known as *lai tai*. "Lai" means "fighting" in the Shan language, and "tai" refers to their ethnic group in Chinese. Because the military junta keeps Burma locked away from the outside world, I believe that my articles and film footage might be the first ever documentation of lai tai. So you shouldn't be surprised if you've never heard of the art before.

In this abnormal war situation, I went about learning lai tai normally. I asked soldiers if they studied lai tai in their villages. From them, I learned that nearly every Shan boy becomes a novice monk at some time in his life, and in the temples of the Shan State, monk lai tai masters teach students to fight with their bare hands, a long stick and two short swords.

Because of this method of teaching, the soldiers I asked were able to show me some unarmed forms. From their demonstrations, I gathered that lai tai was very much like Chinese kung fu. I even recognized one of the forms as being something I learned at the Shaolin Temple.

Then, several soldiers demonstrated some armed forms with the long stick. They used a heavy staff, as opposed to the thin and flexible ones at the Shaolin Temple. I assumed that lai tai stick fighting was more akin to Thai stick fighting. But while the Shan weapon was more durable and practical than the Shaolin one, I once again noticed how the forms were similar to the Shaolin ones.

In watching these demonstrations, I felt that they illustrated how the Shan are actually a gentle people. Don't get me wrong; the soldiers in Loi Tailang were prepared to kill and be killed. The entire army was prepared to fight down to the last man for their independence. I just felt that the Shan were predisposed to be farmers and fathers with families rather than warriors. Whereas the Burmese, Khmer and Thai practice kickboxing with the idea of producing pain, the Shan practiced lai tai, which, like the kung fu at Shaolin, was clearly designed for demonstration purposes rather than combat. To me, this showed how the Shan were peace-loving people pushed to violence by a repressive government. Consider the old English idiom: "Even a worm will turn."

Kawn Wan, one of my best friends in Shanland, is the main lai tai teacher for the orphans living on base at Loi Tailang. He took me to meet his master who had just come back from the battlefront. Kawn Wan's story is like so many of the Shan people. He trained as a novice monk in a temple before the SPDC army attacked his village and killed nearly everyone. He then hiked through the jungle alone to reach the safety of Loi Tailang, where he learned to read and write his mother tongue for the first time. Kong Ja Li became his new master and hero.

Kawn Wan absolutely loved lai tai and he loved teaching me his Shan art.

"To get control of a big man, you can grab his skin or clothing," he told me during one of our training sessions. He demonstrated by throwing a punch at my face and intentionally missing.

"Now he thinks I can't hurt him," he said, then grabbed my collar to pull me into a punch. He also showed me how to control an opponent by grabbing the flesh of his forearm, armpit, shoulder, bicep, tricep, back or waist. Like Kong Ja Li's, Kawn Wan's fingers were very powerful and these holds were unbelievably painful, but they gave you great control over an adversary.

At the same time, Kawn Wan did some very subtle techniques, like walking past someone and throwing a small kick to the back of his leg to knock him down. Lai tai practitioners also use low, low kicks that can't be seen or blocked.

"You don't want to show that you are about to do something," he said, meaning that you don't want to telegraph your moves. "So keep your face even and calm. Meditate. Relax. Look polite. Smile. Look humble. Then when the enemy doesn't expect it, strike!"

Lai tai tends to look for vulnerable body points, and because of this, lai tai practitioners punch with wedge-shaped hands to strike between knuckles, joints and muscles. To get to these areas, all strikes need to be done at close range, and when done correctly, they tend to disable an opponent.

They use the hard part of the knuckle in these wedge-shaped punches to aim for what the Shan call "the dangerous places." To show me the "dangerous places," Kawn Wan said that I start with the knuckles and measure up the body from there. So the first dangerous place refers to the knuckles. Next comes the wrist. Then comes the forearm, then the elbow joint. The next dangerous place is the area between the bicep and tricep and then between the shoulder bones. Following that comes the clavicle, scapula, deltoid, neck, throat, solar plexus, floating ribs, groin and so on. Each dangerous place is a hand's distance away from the last.

Kawn Wan also showed me lots of weapon defenses. First, we did knife defenses, which were primarily simple block-and-strike techniques. Second, we did long-stick defenses. Like with other lai tai techniques, I saw similarities to Shaolin kung fu, but Kawn Wan wielded his staff like Robin Hood. He even was able to use it like a two-handed sword. When it came to sword defense, the base in Loi Tailang only had one sword to practice with. Kawn Wan showed me how to do the two-sword techniques with the sword in one hand and a wooden scabbard in the other. The sword was the same as a Thai sword, about 30 inches long, sharp on one side and designed for thrusting, slashing, hacking and blocking. I also noticed similarities to krabi krabong. For example, one sword strikes high while the other strikes low. At other times, they moved independently from each other; Kawn Wan would bring the deadly weapon around his body, close up against his head like an arnis stick. One principle I noticed throughout all these weapon techniques was the constant changing of height. One moment, Kawn Wan was in high stance, next he dropped into low, stabbing, locking, blocking and thrusting.

After training, Kawn Wan and I would sometimes sit in his hut. Once, he read me a poem by fire light called, "The Sound of a Gun Took My Family Away." An aid organization from the United States had asked a number of young Shan who spoke English to write poems for a book titled, *Letters from Shan State*. After spending so much time with the Shan, the book was incredibly painful for me to read. The voices in the book were no longer nameless to me. The poets had become my friends, and nearly all of them had witnessed the murders of their families.

Living through such traumatic events understandably bred resentment. For example, a young soldier who was also my translator had written a poem for the book. One night, he had told me how he couldn't remember his mother's face. During an interview with him, he also expressed his anger. He said he had come to Loi Tailang specifically for "revenge." Because he hadn't finished high school, the 21-year-old wasn't allowed to join the SSA yet; he was only in grade six because the SPDC had closed his village school before murdering his family. I had never met a young man more impatient to graduate high school for the express purpose of joining the army to go to war.

Kawn Wan, while sad about what had happened to him, seemed more at peace than others. He loved his martial art. I loved the fact that he loved it. Could practicing martial arts heal psychological

Kawn Wan and Antonio in Shanland.

scars? Could it mend a shattered heart? Kawn Wan taught the art to as many of the orphans as he could. Somehow, I think it helped keep them stay grounded.

When I met Kawn Wan's master, Kong Ja Li, he was 51 years old, incredibly slim and covered in religious tattoos and the scars of 25 years of war. His teeth were stained black because of betel nut. During his first demonstration, I was able to see his tattoos up close because he removed his uniform top to perform lai tai techniques. (Kong Ja Li was an SSA captain.) While standing in front of the only tree left in front of the barracks following a 45-day artillery onslaught, we talked about his tattoos.

"We believe the tiger is strong," he said, "so we [the Shan] take many tattoos, covering ourselves in black and white like the tiger." The tiger is also the symbol of the Shan army's struggle against the Burmese government forces.

The tattoos were Buddhist scripture and images that a monk had blessed in order to endow them with magical powers and protect the wearer from harm.

"The tattoos make my skin strong so even a sword will not

cut it," Kong Ja Li said. (Kawn Wan also was covered in tattoos for protection.)

Kong Ja Li also wore two religious amulets around his neck. One was to show respect to the last Shan King, and the other was to pay tribute to His Majesty Rama IX, the current King of Thailand. An image of Naresaun, the last Shan king, adorns most homes in Shanland, especially lai tai practitioners. Naresaun is always depicted wearing two crossed swords on his back with the handles sticking up behind his head where he can easily grab them. These are the same swords employed in lai tai. In regards to the latter, the Shan identify closely with the Thai people and hold the Thai king in great respect because they have a similar language, culture and religion and because they have a shared history of fighting against the Burmese. In fact, the only reason Kong Ja Li was free to demonstrate lai tai on this day was because the army was given a holiday in honor of the Rama IX's 80th birthday. Not only had the army received the day off, but no one was allowed to kill anything for a whole week to honor the Thai king. Loi Tailang also had candlelight services held at the temple each night to pray for the health of the King.

Kong Ja Li was a legend among the Shan soldiers because he often went into combat armed only with his swords. When I asked him about that, he explained that the Shan actually invented kung fu over 2,000 years ago, although I'm not sure if historians would agree.

"We invented lai tai because we don't need guns when we go to battle," he told me. "I only survived battles because of my kung fu."

In his demonstrations, I could see why Kong Ja Li could make such a statement with confidence. In one demonstration against an opponent, he leaned back slightly to avoid a punch and then executed a straight kick to the opponent's shin with the bottom of his foot. At the same time, he struck the opponent's abdomen with his fingers pointed out straight (spear hand). When his opponent launched another attack, Kong Ja Li ducked and grabbed the flesh of the opponent's armpit to control him. He dropped low and pulled the man over him before head-butting the opponent in the face. Kong Ja Li released the opponent, who swung at him again. Kawn Wan's master ducked again, blocked the strike and grabbed the opponent in a choke, lifting him off the ground by the throat. The opponent tried to strike Kong Ja Li in the head, but the lai tai master blocked it and grabbed the opponent's groin. Because of his years of harsh conditioning, Kong Ja Li's fingers are like steel. They seem to tear through the flesh, probably greatly reducing the opponent's chance to procreate. I was the opponent, by the way.

The meanest series of movements Kong Ja Li executed was a stomp kick with the knife edge of his foot to mine. If done at full speed, it would've shattered my bones. Instead, he pinned my foot with his, and then Kong Ja Li slammed his entire body into my chest, knocking me backwards. Again, if done at full speed, he would have cracked my ribs and ripped all the tendons in my ankle. It looked like what I would have seen in street fighting, but it was actually lai tai. Also, the way that Kong Ja Li practiced his lai Tai was different than the demonstrations I had seen on my first day. There was no doubt that this art was designed for practical and painful self-defense.

During our time together, Kong Ja Li demonstrated many lai tai forms. Again, I noticed the strong relationship they shared with Chinese Shaolin kung fu. He would begin every form by bowing, with his hands in a prayer position before his chest. They he would drop into a horse stance similar to the southern Shaolin style, but without his feet positioned pigeon-toed. After a brief pause to gather his internal energy or chi, he launched into his technique.

When I watched him do forms against an imaginary opponent, I saw how Kong Ja Li always tended to step out at an angle, moving his body in a circular pattern. He would go through his forms at lightning speed. He'd shift through a stork stance (one foot raised), then throw a simple kick like in southern-style kung fu. He used a lot of grabbing techniques. I clearly saw tiger claw several times as he sank, completing the form to sink his "claws" into an opponent's chest or neck. Because Kong Ja Li had just returned from several weeks of combat, our time ended for the day. Kawn Wan then took me to his hut next to the orphan's dormitory.

When I got to meet with Kong Ja Li again, he taught me how to change my stance from high to low, like Kawn Wan had told me. In many techniques, Kong Ja Li would block, grab one of my hands and then drop his body into a low stance to pull me off-balance.

In the end, this was all that Jong Ka Li was really willing to give away to me.

"If you want to learn lai tai, you must first build a relationship with the master," he said.

From my experience with martial arts, I honestly believe that a kickboxer or boxer could probably best a lai tai guy. It's just the difference between traditional martial arts and combat sports. So, I could argue that compared to other martial arts I have studied, lai tai isn't the most effective.

However, if we talk about the truest and most spiritually deep of martial artists, Kawn Wan was the winner. No other martial artist I met in all of my years in Asia had suffered as he had suffered. None had used the martial arts to heal on the scale that he had. Pra Kru Ba was probably a close second, with Kru Pedro third, while San Kim Sean was the only martial artist who had probably witnessed murder on a greater scale than Kawn Wan. Those two work to preserve their arts for reasons that I find no other martial artist has.

I often fantasized about getting Kawn Wan, Pra Kru Ba, Kru Pedro and San Kim Sean into a room together to talk. I would translate for them. I knew that Kru Pedro and Pra Kru Ba would recognize Kawn Wan's special qualities. Finally, doing this would be a way to get one of my many Shan friends out of Burma as quickly as possible.

✪

When I returned to Chiang Mai from one of my trips to Shanland, I went to see Kru Pedro to seek some healing for myself. I was on edge because I was afraid the SPDC or Thai police would get me. My film editor and friend had even received a threat from the UWSA. I missed my Shan friends. I cried a lot and felt a tremendous amount of survivor's guilt. Every single story I wrote in Burma—on rape, torture, murder—weighed heavily on me. I told Kru Pedro about it all.

"I knew you were some place dangerous," he said, which I understood to mean that his spirit teachers had told him.

Some time before, Kru Pedro and I had mutually decided that I wasn't suited to be his full-time student and live in his camp. The movies, the videos, the writing … these all took away from my focus and commitment to the art itself. Kru Pedro was concerned that I would disturb the spiritual energy of his place. But in telling him about my time in Burma, he let me know that he believed I had found something more important to serve. He encouraged me to continue with my work. He believed that I was helping people, even though I often felt powerless. He told me that I was walking my path and it was the right path that no one but me could walk. Kru Pedro's approval meant a lot to me.

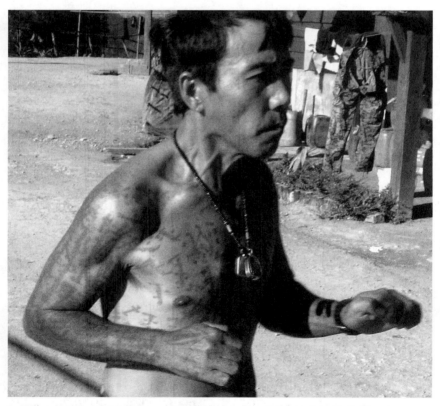

Lai tai master Jong Ka Li has many tattoos because of Shan cultural beliefs.

epilogue

I SPENT CHRISTMAS IN BANGKOK and New Year's in Laos. Shortly after, I returned to Chiang Mai to collect some foreign journalists who had asked me to take them into Burma. I had taken people with me to Shanland before, and the Colonel was always happy to see me bring media. The danger of bringing journalists and aid workers in and out of a war zone should be obvious. So I made them hire my Shan friends as translators and camera assistants. If I could have done so, I would have limited the journalists to people with military experience. However, I was rarely in a position to turn anyone down.

On a subsequent visit to Shanland with another American journalist in tow, we had a motorcycle accident with a tribal farmer on a small dirt road and within sight of three armies. The SPDC army would have killed us. The Thai army would have arrested us. And the SSA would have helped us. While I rendered first aid to those involved in the accident, I prayed the first soldiers on the scene would be the SSA. Instead, a low-ranking Thai officer appeared first. I knew I had to get myself and my colleague out of there before someone with authority showed up. I double-talked the officer and flagged down a motorcycle to take the journalist to a hospital. Then I got a pickup truck full of migrant workers to take me to the hospital.

At the small, local hospital on the border, a Thai police officer showed up looking for us. They treated the incident as a minor traffic accident and just said they wanted to know on which side of the border the accident had occurred. I honestly didn't know because the border was so porous. Fortunately, the police officer didn't do anything. He stated that he must continue his investigation and left. I was worried that he would come back to us, so I managed to convince the hospital to take my friend via ambulance to the foreign hospital in Chiang Mai. They agreed and took us. On the off-chance that authorities were waiting for us in the emergency ward, I jumped out of the ambulance in Chiang Mai at a traffic light. After all that, I still had a head injury to see to, so I checked back in to my hotel in Chiang Mai to rest.

When I was sufficiently recovered, I decided that I wanted to train as a combat paramedic. My main thought was this: When inside Burma, I would be able to render medical aid to people who had been abandoned by the international community. In the scheme of things, my motorcycle accident was minor, and my colleague and I could just as easily have been hurt by a landmine or stray bullet. What if we had had the accident deep inside Burma where evacuation would have been impossible? I wanted to have the skills to save people if they needed my help.

As my funds were never greater than the day's meals, going back to the United States for schooling was out of the question. Instead, I got in touch with Master Frank in Manila. Since he was a former military paramedic, he found me a school in Manila where I could study and be licensed to work as a paramedic anywhere in the world but the United States.

I graduated from paramedic school and hung around the Philippines, volunteering as a medic. I had every intention to go back to Shanland, but I had run completely out of money (again). A friend offered me a teaching position in Taiwan, which I took. I still get emotional over my experience in Burma. I get e-mails from Shan friends wondering where I am. If I can somehow go back,

I will. After that, who knows?

When I was a boy, my grandmother bought me a book in which every time the main character came to a crossroads, you could choose which way he should go. The story was different every time. As a child, I could never get enough of that book. I always wondered what would have happened if I had chosen to go to the ghost house instead of trying to find pirate treasure.

I've come to consider how life is like that book—the choices we make and the paths we choose determine the ends we reach. In my case, my decisions have led me through quite a labyrinth of paths and possibilities. Too often, people only imagine what it would be like to do what they hear others talk about. I've learned to make the choice to just go and do it.

If my grandmother hadn't taught me writing and languages … .

If H. David Collins hadn't taught me kung fu … .

Maybe I would have never left Brooklyn and traveled to many countries and learned about many languages. Nor would I have gotten to know about such wonderful cultures and people while sitting at their tables, studying their martial arts and sharing their friendships. Nor would I have used my writing to share these stories with people back in the Western world, with jobs, homes and families, who may not feel as if they are able to go and see the world themselves.

This book comes, hopefully, somewhere in the middle of my martial arts odyssey. From writing it, I've learned that people need to find their odyssey. It doesn't have to be about martial arts. It doesn't have to involve travel, but find that thing that excites you. That thing that can absorb all your passion. Cherish it. Live it.

A life without passion is not worth living.

Learn to live loud.

about the author

ANTONIO GRACEFFO, BORN IN NEW YORK in 1967, is a writer for *Kung Fu Magazine* and monthly travel columnist for *Black Belt*. Additionally, he is the author of six books, all of which have a connection to the martial arts. His most well-known work is *The Monk From Brooklyn*. For the last decade, he has been traveling

Antonio Graceffo (right) with his Shan translator, Hsai Lern (left), in Shanland, Burma.

through and living in Asia while studying with various martial arts masters and writing about his adventures.

Graceffo is a frequent call-in guest on regional radio talk shows in the United States. He has also worked as a martial arts consultant for both The History Channel and the Discovery Channel. He has appeared on The History Channel TV shows *Human Weapon* and *Digging for the Truth*, as well as The Travel Channel's *Samantha Brown*. He also produces a Web-TV series called *Martial Arts Odyssey*. His Web site is http://speakingadventure.com.

acknowledgments

I give special thanks to my teachers Pra Kru Ba, grandmaster San Kim Sean, Paddy Carson and grandmaster Frank Aycocho. They dedicated their lives to setting people on the warrior's path of martial arts. I also would like to give a huge thank you to all of my field translators—Hsai Lern, Sameth, Santiphap "Lee," Seiha and Tun Yee. They studied hard to learn their languages, then put up with me, my temper, my moods and my crazy requests while in the field. They worked diligently and accurately. They even risked their lives for me. I could never be more grateful. And finally, God bless the Shan people. May they someday find peace and freedom soon.

More books from Black Belt

Bruce Lee
Wisdom for the Way
Book Code 491

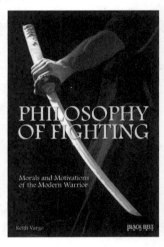

Philosophy
of Fighting
Book Code 500

Shotokan's Secret
Expanded Edition
Book Code 512

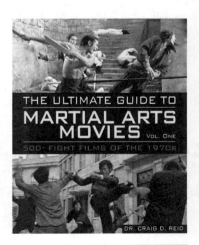

The Ultimate Guide
to Martial Arts Movies
Book Code 497

Subscribe to Black Belt
and read more from Antonio Graceffo.

To subscribe visit blackbeltmag.com